MARYLAND
One-Day Trip Book

To my very best friend,
 Patricia Vinsant Richards,
  with love, respect and gratitude.
   Thanks for always being there for me.

MARYLAND
One-Day Trip Book

*200
Day-Long
Excursions
through
America in
Miniature*

JANE OCKERSHAUSEN

EPM Publications
An imprint of HOWELL PRESS

Publisher's Cataloging-in-Publication
(Provided by Quality Books, Inc.)

Ockershausen, Jane.
    The Maryland one-day trip book : 200
day-long excursions through America in
miniature / Jane Ockershausen. -- 2nd ed.
        p. cm.
    Includes index.
    ISBN 1-57427-089-3

    1. Maryland -- Guidebooks.   I. Title.
    F179.3.O35   1999   917.52'0443
                                 QBI99-218

08 07 06 05 04 03 02 01 00 99   10 9 8 7 6 5 3 2 1

EPM Publications is an imprint of Howell Press, Inc.,
    1713-2D Allied Lane, Charlottesville, VA 22903
    http://www.howellpress.com

Cover and book design by Tom Huestis
Page layout by Scott Edie, E Graphics
Cover photograph courtesy of Maryland Office of Tourism

Grateful acknowledgment is made to the Office of Tourist Development, Maryland
Department of Economic & Community Development, for the use of its photographs.
Photos from other sources are individually credited.

Contents

THE MARYLAND ONE-DAY TRIP BOOK

CENTRAL MARYLAND

BALTIMORE COUNTY

BALTIMORE CITY

HOWARD COUNTY

ANNE ARUNDEL COUNTY AND ANNAPOLIS

EASTERN SHORE

WORCESTER COUNTY AND OCEAN CITY

SOUTHERN MARYLAND

CHARLES COUNTY

CALVERT COUNTY

ST. MARY'S COUNTY

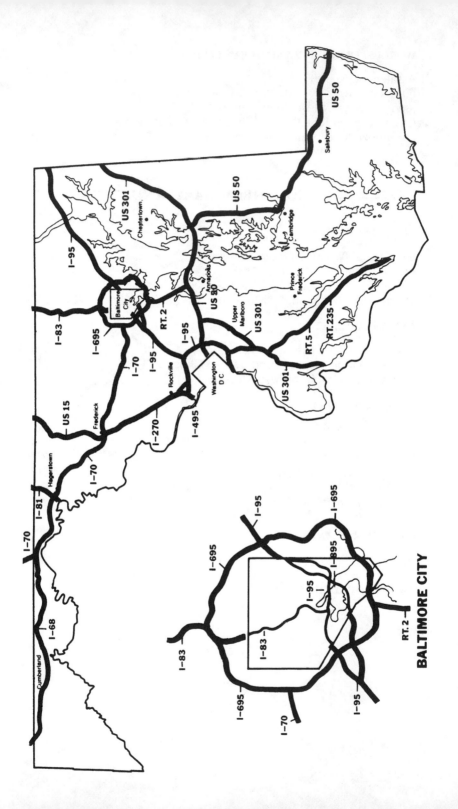

BALTIMORE CITY

Maryland Welcome Centers

Youghiogheny Overlook Welcome Center
(301) 746-5979
I-68 East, mile marker #6
P.O. Box 297
Friendsville, MD 21531

I-70 West Welcome Center
(301) 293-4161
I-70 West, mile marker #39
General Delivery
Myersville, MD 21773

I-70 East Welcome Center
(301) 293-2526
I-70 East, mile marker #39
P.O. Box 419
Myersville, MD 21773

U.S. 15 Welcome Center
(301) 447-2553
U.S. 15, 1 mile south of PA
P.O. Box 695
Emmitsburg, MD 21727

I-95 South Welcome Center
(301) 490-2444
I-95 South, mile marker #37
P.O. Box 288
Savage, MD 20763

I-95 North Welcome Center
(301) 490-1333
I-95 North, mile marker #37
P.O. Box 1058
Savage, MD 20763

Chesapeake House Welcome Center
(410) 287-2313
I-95 North/South, mile marker #97
P.O. Box 785
Perryville, MD 21903

State House Visitors Center
(410) 974-3400
State Circle
Annapolis, MD 21401

U.S. 13 Welcome Center
(410) 957-2484
U.S. 13 North, 144 Ocean
    Highway
Pocomoke City, MD 21851

Crain Memorial Welcome Center
(301) 259-2500
U.S. 301 North, 12480 Crain
    Highway
P.O. Box 158
Newburg, MD 20664

Bay Country Welcome Center
(410) 758-6803
U.S. 301 North/South
1000 Welcome Center Drive
Centreville, MD 21617

Acknowledgments

A special thanks to Mindy Scheeberger Bianca with Maryland's Office of Tourism Development for her help in revising and updating the new edition of my Maryland book.

Maryland Tourism Contacts

Allegany Co. Convention & Visitors Bureau
Western Maryland Station Center
13 Canal Street,
Cumberland, MD 21502
(301) 777-5905, (800) 50-VISIT,
Fax: (301) 777-5893

Annapolis & Anne Arundel Co. Conference & Visitors Bureau
26 West St., Annapolis, MD 21401
(410) 280-0445,
Fax: (410) 263-9591

Baltimore Area Convention & Visitors Association
Legg Mason Tower, 12th Floor
100 Light Street,
Baltimore, MD 21202
(410) 659-7300, (800) 282-6632, Fax: (410) 727-2308

Baltimore Co. Convention & Visitors Bureau
435 York Road, Towson, MD 21204
(410) 583-7313, (800) 570-2836, Fax: (410) 583-7327

Department of Economic Development
175 Main St., Calvert Co. Courthouse, Prince Frederick, MD 20678
(410) 535-4583, (301) 855-1880, (800) 331-9771, Fax: (410) 535-4385

Caroline Co. Commissioners
218 Market Street,
Denton, MD 21629
(410) 479-0660,
Fax: (410) 479-4060

Carroll Co. Office of Tourism
224 North Center Street, Room 100, Westminster, MD 21157
(410) 857-2983, (800) 272-1933, Fax: (410) 410-1560

Cecil Co. Tourism
Room 324, 129 E. Main Street,
Elkton, MD 21921
(410) 996-5303, (800) CECIL-95,
Fax: (410) 996-5305

Charles Co. Tourism
PO Box B, LaPlata, MD 20646
(301) 645-0558,
(301) 870-3000, (800) 766-3386, Fax: (301) 645-0560

Dorchester Co. Tourism
203 Sunburst Highway,
Cambridge, MD 21613
(800) 522-TOUR, (410) 228-1000, Fax: (410) 228-6848

Tourism Council of Frederick Co., Inc.
19 East Church Street,
Frederick, MD 21701
(301) 663-8687, (800) 999-3613, Fax: (301) 663-0039

Garrett Co. Chamber of Commerce, Inc.—The Home of Deep Creek Lake
200 South Third Street,
Oakland, MD 21550-1581
(301) 334-1948,
Fax: (301) 334-1919

Discover Harford Co. Tourism Council, Inc.
224 N. Washington Street, Suite 8
Havre de Grace, MD 21078
(410) 939-3336, (410) 575-7278, (800) 597-2649, Fax:
(410) 272-0830

Howard Co. Tourism Council
PO Box 9, Ellicott City, MD 21041
(410) 313-1900, (800) 288-TRIP,
Fax: (410) 313-1902

Kent Co. Tourism
400 S. Cross Street, Suite 1,
Chestertown, MD 21620
(410) 778-0416,
Fax: (410) 778-2746

Conference and Visitor Bureau of Montgomery Co., Inc.
12900 Middlebrook Rd., Ste. 1400
Germantown, MD 20874-2616
(301) 428-9702, (800) 925-0880,
Fax: (301) 428-9705

Prince George's Co., Maryland Conference & Visitors Bureau, Inc.
9200 Basil Court, Suite 101,
Largo, MD 20774
(301) 925-8300,
Fax: (301) 925-2053

Queen Anne's Co. Office of Tourism
425 Piney Narrows Road, Suite 3,
Chester, MD 21619
(410) 604-2100,
Fax: (410) 604-2101

St. Mary's Co. Division of Travel and Tourism
PO Box 653, Governmental Center
Washington Street, 2nd Floor,
Leonardtown, MD 20650
(301) 475-4411, (800) 327-9023, Fax: (301) 475-4414

Somerset Co. Tourism
PO Box 243,
Princess Anne, MD 21853
(410) 651-2968, (800) 521-9189, Fax: (410) 651-3917

Talbot Co. Conference and Visitors Bureau
Chamber Building
210 Marlboro Avenue, Suite 3,
Easton, MD 21601-1366
(410) 822-4606, 888-BAY-STAY,
Fax: (410) 822-7922

Hagerstown/Washington Co. Convention and Visitors Bureau
Elizabeth Hager Center
16 Public Square,
Hagerstown, MD 21740
(301) 791-3246, (800) 228-STAY,
Fax: (301) 791-2601

Wicomico Convention and Visitors Bureau
8480 Ocean Highway,
Delmar, MD 21875
(410) 548-4914, (800) 332-TOUR, Fax: (410) 341-4996

Worcester Co. Tourism
105 Pearl Street,
Snow Hill, MD 21863
(800) 852-0335, (410) 632-3617, Fax: (410) 632-3158

Ocean City Convention and Visitors Bureau
4001 Coastal Highway,
Ocean City, MD 21842
(410) 289-8181,
Fax: (410) 289-0058

Town of Ocean City, Tourism Division
PO Box 158,
Ocean City, MD 21842
(410) 289-2800,
Fax: (410) 289-0058

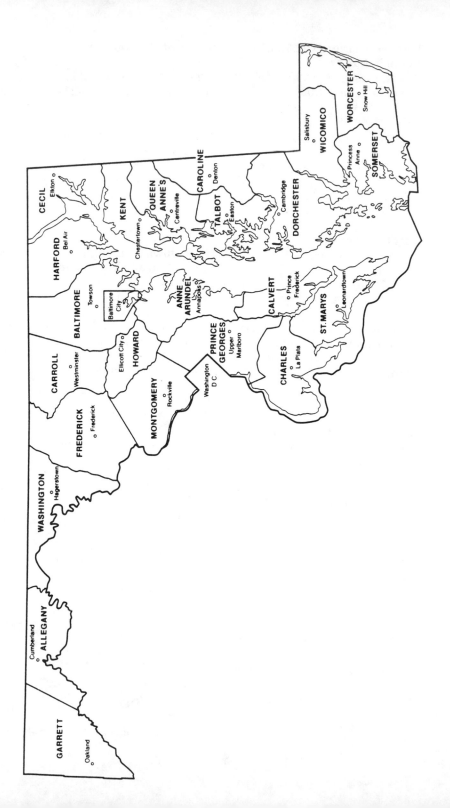

Maryland
My Maryland

I grew up, was educated, taught school and reared a family in Maryland. It was a labor of love when, more than 15 years ago, I explored my home state for the first edition of this guidebook. Returning to update the book, I again traveled from its western mountains to its eastern waters, and I discovered that it is as true today as it was then: Maryland is aptly called "America in Miniature."

Maryland offers an amazing diversity of hidden pleasures and treasures both urban and rural. There is, without doubt, something for everyone. *The Maryland One-Day Trip Book* is organized according to the state's five travel regions, grouping almost 200 sites by county. It covers all 23 counties in the state, as well as the major cities. This edition updates old favorites and adds new destinations to explore.

In revisiting personal favorites throughout Maryland, I've found that many attractions have made changes. Museums such as the one at the Maryland Historical Society's headquarters have expanded. New programs and new information have changed the historical thrust of such sites as Historic St. Mary's City and the National Colonial Farm. I encourage you to visit spots you toured years ago; even if the sites remain the same, your experience of them changes because you see them from a different perspective.

Over two decades of travel in Maryland has taken me to hundreds of historic homes, museums, parks and wildlife sanctuaries. I find that at each spot you can see or learn something new. Day trips take only a few hours, so you can pursue new challenges, revive old hobbies, or just concentrate on and expand your current interests.

The geographic focus of this book encourages you to plan a one-day outing that includes several nearby sites. I suggest you read all the selections in the city or geographic region you're planning to visit. Keep in mind the total distance you'll be traveling—a day trip from one end of the state to another may not be practical, especially with small children. Nearly every site described in the book lies within a day's drive—out and back—from Baltimore. That is why all directions to the sites are given from there. Readers in other areas of the state will have to consult their maps to gauge distances and dri-

15

ving time from wherever they are located. I urge you to consult the book's calendar of events as well; it will help you choose the attractions best suited to the time of year and to your personal interests.

Where to go and what to see are important considerations, but you also need to know when to go. The calendar of events alerts you to festivals and celebrations throughout Maryland. There are travelers who enjoy the excitement of these special days; others prefer quieter times. Timing is especially important at many nature and garden sites. Spring transforms the slopes of the London Town Publik House and Gardens along the South River into a blooming treat—first with bright yellow banks of daffodils and then the pastel hues of azaleas. Summer is the time to meander along the poolside paths at Lilypons Water Gardens, and Woodend trails are a delight when autumn tints the leaves. You can escape the chill of winter weather with a visit to the Brookside Gardens Conservatory. Birds, too, follow a natural calendar. Wildlife sanctuaries are best visited during the birds' annual spring and fall migrations.

Read through each selection when you develop your day's itinerary to be sure sites are open when you plan to visit. It is advisable to call ahead and double-check on hours as they can change. This is particularly true if you are scheduling your trip to coincide with a specific event, because event times and dates may change from year to year.

When I wrote the first of my ten *One-Day Trip* books in 1975, most families limited their exploring to an annual two-week holiday. Nowadays families have discovered that one-day vacations can provide escapes all year long. These short trips can broaden your horizons, introduce you to new ideas and interests and delight your senses. Many of these gardens, parks, wildlife sanctuaries, artists' communities and even museums do not charge admission, so you can enjoy them with very little financial strain.

I invite you to explore what I will always consider my state. Maryland, my Maryland, God did shed His grace on thee!

J.O.

Western Maryland
Introduction

It was through Western Maryland, once the country's frontier, that Indian trails established routes that later would be followed by settlers. These paths led through the Appalachian Mountains to the Ohio Valley and points west. Tales of mountain men who lived in this wilderness are told at Garrett County Historical Museum.

During turbulent times, troops would march through the region, stopping at Fort Frederick, the only surviving stone fortification from the French and Indian War. It was a supply base for the British during that conflict and a prison camp for the British and Hessian captives during the American Revolution. A small skirmish was fought near the fort during the Civil War, but it did not match the ferocity and length of the September 17, 1862 confrontation at Antietam, later called the bloodiest day of the Civil War. In this region you'll also discover the War Correspondent's Arch, one of the very few monuments honoring this profession, built on the grounds of the South Mountain estate of George Alfred Townsend, the youngest reporter to cover the Civil War. The region also boasts the first monument erected in honor of George Washington, whose French and Indian War headquarters can be visited in Cumberland.

It seemed people were always traveling through the region, and remnants of various modes of transportation can still be observed. The National Road was begun in 1811, but the first stretch proceeded so slowly and so expensively that Congress decided to let the states maintain it. The states built toll houses to collect money for the road's upkeep. La Vale Toll Gate House in Maryland is the only one surviving in this state. Casselman Bridge, the largest single arch stone bridge of its type in the country, was built over the Casselman River in 1813 as part of the National Road. Onlookers watching the removal of the giant timbers supporting the 80-foot span expected the bridge to collapse, but it still stands and is the scenic focus of one of the region's state parks. The canal was another major link to this region, and the C&O Canal terminus, the westernmost point the 184.5-mile canal reached, is part of the C&O Canal National Historical Park. You can see the last three locks, a canal boat replica and the Paw Paw Tunnel, an engineering triumph that cut through 3,128 feet of solid rock.

The transportation genius Henry Ford and his friends Thomas Edison and Harvey Firestone camped at a site overlooking the sparkling cascades of Swallow Falls. They, like so many earlier and later visitors, recognized the unparalleled beauty of this rugged mountain region. In the mid-1800s, because of the towering peaks, including the 3,360-foot Backbone Mountain in southwestern Garrett County, this part of Maryland was called the "Switzerland of America." In the vast wooded areas of Savage River State Forest, Deep Creek Lake, Swallow Falls, Herrington Manor, New Germany and other state parks, fishermen now ply the streams, eagerly casting for fish raised at Bear Creek Trout Rearing Station and the Albert Powell Trout Hatchery. In addition to fishing, the region offers myriad recreational opportunities, including white water rafting, boating, hiking, horseback riding, skiing and swimming.

GARRETT COUNTY

Bear Creek Trout Rearing Station

Small Fry Fascination

And now here's more of the story ... roughly 180,000 of the rainbow fingerlings hatched at the Albert Powell facility in Washington County (see selection) are shipped to the **Bear Creek Trout Rearing Station** in Accident.

The two- to three-inch fingerlings stay in 13 holding ponds until fully grown. The adult trout are then used to stock the streams, rivers, ponds and lakes of Allegany and Garrett Counties. One of the 13 rearing ponds holds trout weighing 1½ to 2 pounds, which during stocking are mixed with the younger fish in a ratio of 15 big trout to 1,000 smaller.

Nearby Bear Creek is stocked by this hatchery five or six times a year, starting around the first of March. There is no season for trout, but fishing is best in Maryland's freshwaters from late March to mid-November. Anglers need both a fishing license and a trout stamp to go after the brook, brown and rainbow trout. Fishing regulations restrict the catch to five trout per fisherman; there is no minimum size per fish.

Bear Creek Trout Rearing Station does not provide a guided tour, nor is there a brochure for the low-key operation. Visitors are welcome to wander around this tree-shaded glade anytime from 9:00 A.M. to 4:00 P.M. daily. If there are young children along, be sure to walk down to the lower holding pond and watch the fingerlings try to leap upstream against the water spilling from a large pipe. The hatchery staff had to add a wooden barrier to keep the young fish in the pond. The fish continually throw themselves against this barrier, instinctive behavior that's fascinating to watch. Children also like watching the staff feed the fish, but there is no set schedule for the three daily feedings.

Directions: Bear Creek Trout Rearing Station is approximately 165 miles west of Baltimore. From Baltimore take 1-70 west to Hancock. At Hancock take Route 40 west to Cumberland. At Cumberland take Route 40/48 west to Exit 14 at Keysers Ridge. Proceed south on Route 219 to Accident. Turn right on Accident-Bear Creek Road and then take the next right on Fish Hatchery Road for the well-marked facility.

Casselman Bridge State Park and Grantsville

Little Crossing Links National Road

In 1775 Colonel George Washington, aide-de-camp to British General Edward Braddock during the French and Indian War, blazed a trail along the old Nemacolin Indian path. The trail Washington marked led the British into Pennsylvania, where it crossed the Casselman River which he had named Little Crossing.

When the French empire in North America ended after the fall of Quebec in 1759, British settlers moved into western territory formerly controlled by the French and their Indian allies. One of the areas that attracted the British was Little Crossing. In the early 1760s Joseph Tomlison built an inn just a few miles east of Little Crossing. A ford and road followed, and this became a major thoroughfare for westward travelers.

In 1813 a single arch stone bridge, the largest of its type in the country, was built over the river as part of the National Road linking Cumberland with Wheeling, West Virginia. When the workmen removed the timbers supporting the 80-foot span, onlookers expected the bridge to fall. It stands to this day. In 1933 a new steel bridge on Route 40 replaced the stone arch, but the bridge remains a scenic focus at **Casselman Bridge State Park.**

One of the stagecoach inns built in 1818 beside the river crossing has been remodeled. It's now **Penn Alps Restaurant and Craft Shops**. Four dining rooms serve Pennsylvania Dutch specialties, and the gift shop is filled with handcrafted creations. Across the parking lot is an

Casselman Hotel, built in 1824 for travelers on the National Road (US 40), still provides accommodations and country cooking, as well as baked goods made in a bakery you may visit.

artisan's village with studios for potters, weavers, sculptors, stained-glass workers and a world-renowned bird carver, Gary Yoder. One of these log cabin studios dates back to Revolutionary days, another was built in 1820 and a third in the middle of the 1800s. Just foot-steps away is **Stanton's Mill**, the county's oldest operating mill. The original grinding stones from the 1797 mill are on display.

Yet another old hostelry, the **Casselman Hotel**, is still operating in **Grantsville.** Built in 1824 for travelers on the National Road, it has nine bedrooms, each furnished with Early American pieces (as are the rooms in the adjacent motor court). All the rooms on the first and second floors of the old inn have fireplaces. The restaurant serves wholesome country cooking using favorite Amish recipes. The Casselman makes all its own breads, cakes and pies in a downstairs bakery you may visit. There is a gift shop next to the bakery.

You'll also find bakery departments at two Grantsville markets that sell country produce and homemade wares. The **Hill Top Fruit Market** on U.S. Route 40, three miles east of Grantsville, has a mouth-watering selection of 50 kinds of candy in addition to fresh produce.

Just past Grantsville on Route 669 is **Yoders Country Market**, which, in addition to fresh baked goods, offers all kinds of meats: smoked, fresh, processed and canned. Homemade jams, jellies, applesauce, honey and maple syrup are only some of the made-at-home products. There is also a wide selection of candy, nuts and dried fruits. The Amish-Mennonite community of Grantsville is right off Route 40/68.

Directions: From Baltimore take Route 70 west about 90 miles to Hancock, then continue west on Route 68 to Exit 22 (Route 219 north). Turn left on Route 40 for Grantsville.

Cranesville Sub-Arctic Swamp

Ice Age Bog

Maryland has two swamps to explore: Battle Creek Cypress Swamp Sanctuary (see selection) and the Nature Conservancy's Cranesville Sub-Arctic Swamp. This may sound like a shallow boast, but each offers an unusual natural environment for nature lovers to explore.

The **Cranesville Sub-Arctic Swamp,** a 500-acre National Historic Landmark, straddles the boundary between Western Maryland and West Virginia. In fact, the boardwalk lies in West Virginia. The area was once called the Great Pine Swamp because of the abundant giant pine trees, but now it's named for the West Virginia community on its northern edge.

This sub-arctic swamp was formed during the Ice Age, between 7,500 and 10,000 B.C. The ice fields halted 100 miles north of this part of Maryland. But the "taiga," or boreal forest, that extended out from the ice formations moved into this area, taking over what was once a deciduous forest. In most regions overrun by the boreal forest, the forest retreated when the ice melted. Today, the boreal forest is found almost exclusively in northern border states and Canada.

But there are exceptions, and one of the exceptions is the Cranesville Sub-Arctic Swamp, where you can still see rare species of flora normally found only in arctic regions. There are complex reasons why this unique area survived. Of major importance is the 2,500-foot altitude, which keeps the climate cool and the growing season short. The location of the swamp also contributes to its survival. The swamp sits in a bowl-shaped valley that is a natural frost pocket.

All of this means the interested visitor has the opportunity to see a very different terrain at Cranesville. Most who venture out on the wooden boardwalk, however, will not be fortunate enough to spot the swamp's most elusive and rarest inhabitant: the northern water shrew. This pennyweight, mouse-like mammal is light enough to run across the top of the watery bog, yet it will attack animals far larger than itself in its constant quest for food. It does not go after two-footed quarry.

The bog mat you'll see is composed of spongy moss and peat. Wild cranberries, reindeer moss, blueberries, black chokeberries, St. John's wort and mountain laurel compose the low groundcover. Trees include red spruce, hemlock, red maple, eastern larch and mountain ash. This is not a "wow" sight, but rather an unusual and different environment that provides a new world for nature lovers to enjoy.

Directions: From Baltimore, take I-70 west about 90 miles to Hancock, then continue west on Route 40 another 65 miles to Cumberland; take Route 40/48 west to Keysers Ridge, Exit 14. Head south on Route 219 to Oakland; at second light, Green Street, turn right; continue through next light, which becomes Liberty Street, and then becomes Herrington Manor Road. Follow approximately six miles to Cranesville Road; turn left and proceed four miles. Just past "Bell Ringer Originals in Wood" sign, turn left onto a dirt road at a sign marked "Cranesville Swamp Nature Preserve;" proceed ½ mile and bear right onto another dirt road; in less than ½ mile, look for electric utility poles and a large marker on the right that indicates the footpath to the boardwalk.

Deep Creek Lake

A Superior Lake

Garrett County, which calls itself Maryland's Four-Season Vacation area, is rapidly being discovered through its Deep Creek Lake. The word is out—and spreading—that the lake is an absolute vacation delight!

The man-made 3,900-acre lake has 65 miles of shoreline, most of it privately held. One of the public areas is the 800-foot beach in **Deep Creek Lake State Park.** An ideal spot for a hot summer day, the beach has a wooded picnic area behind it where non-swimmers can relax in the shade and watch the fun.

Many families camp at this state park. Its five nature trails are especially appealing in the spring when the wildflowers bloom and in the fall when the leaves turn. When snow comes to Western Maryland, **Meadow Mountain Trail** is used by snowmobilers.

The Deep Creek Lake area is Maryland's largest downhill ski area. At **Wisp**, the elevation is 3,080 and there are vertical drops of 610 feet. Deep Creek Lake, Herrington Manor and New Germany State Parks offer miles of groomed cross-country ski trails.

Because 96 percent of the lake's shoreline is privately owned, the best way to explore is by boat. The park has a boat ramp for those with their own boats. If you want to rent a powerboat, rowboat or

Deep Creek Lake, a 3,900-acre magnet, draws so many swimmers, sportsmen and skiers that it is endangering Garrett County's claim of being Maryland's Best-Kept Secret.

canoe, there are a number of marinas in the area: Bill's Marine Service, (301) 387-5536; Blue Anchor Boat Rental, (301) 387-5677; Crystal Waters Boat Rentals, (301) 387-5515; Echo Marina, Inc., (301) 387-2628; Deep Creek Outfitters, (301) 387-6977. Several places, including The Aquatic Center (301) 387-8233, rent jet skis and personal watercraft.

Another popular recreation around Deep Creek Lake is horseback riding. Small Oaks, (301) 334-4991, and Western Trails Riding Stables, (301) 387-6155, offer a variety of experiences, from ½-hour rides to overnight horse trail rides. They also offer hayrides, camping and winter sleigh rides.

The lake is very popular with fishermen. Garrett County keeps track of the big fish that don't get away. From May through September the county awards weekly and seasonal prizes for the biggest fish caught. Fish must be registered at Johnny's Bait House on Route 219 near McHenry. Prizes were given in one recent year for a 1-pound, 11-inch bluegill; 5-pound, 14-ounce, 25-inch brown trout; 3-pound, 10-ounce, 25½-inch chain pickerel; 1-pound, 12-ounce, 15¼-inch crappie; 6-pound, 10-ounce, 23-inch largemouth bass; 16-pound, 10-ounce, 40-inch northern pike; 3-pound, 8-ounce, 20¼-inch smallmouth bass; 9-pound, 9-ounce, 31-inch walleye and 1-pound, 6-ounce 15-inch yellow perch. Not even cold weather stops the eager anglers; ice fishing attracts many during January and February. Bring your axe, fishing gear and plenty of warm clothes.

Directions: From Baltimore take 1-70 west 90 miles to Hancock, then continue west on I-68 to Keysers Ridge (Exit 14) and head south on Route 219. Turn left on Glendale Road for Deep Creek Lake State Park.

Garrett County Historical Museum and Oakland

Oakland Cluster

As you travel around Western Maryland, you'll hear stories about Meshach Browning. You'll learn all about this legendary pioneer hunter at the **Garrett County Historical Museum** in Oakland. He lived along Sang Run, named for the area's wild ginseng plants, the roots of which are worth about $100 a pound. A model of Browning's Sang Run cabin is displayed at the museum. He is credited with killing hundreds of deer, black bears, wildcats and lesser game. Though he lacked formal education, Browning wrote *Forty-Four Years in the Life of a Hunter*, still a hunter's classic 100 years later.

The Garrett County Historical Society and Museum, at 107 South

24

Second Street in downtown Oakland, is in the former Garrett National Bank, which later became known as the Professional Building. Within the museum's 12 rooms are special displays. One room features exhibits on the early hotels in this area, another features military displays. There is also a Victorian bedroom and a Meshach Browning room. Museum hours are 10:00 A.M. to 4:00 P.M. in June, July, August, September and October. During the winter, the museum is open during those hours on Thursday, Friday and Saturday.

After your stop at the museum, you may want to drive around **Mountain Lake Park**, just east of Oakland off Route 135. This was where wealthy vacationers built summer homes. It was a Chautauqua-type resort from 1882 to 1942. Many of the fine old Victorian homes have been restored.

In the early years vacationers often arrived at the Baltimore & Ohio Railroad station. John W. Garrett, in whose honor the county was named and who contributed the acreage for Garrett State Forest, was president of the B&O line. The handsome Queen Anne station, now unoccupied, is one of the oldest in the country and an often-mentioned candidate for conversion to a tourist attraction.

Off Old Deer Park Road, now known as Memorial Drive, you'll find the **Cornish Manor**, an excellent place for a midday break. The house was built in 1868 and serves excellent country meals.

Broadford Recreation Area is just outside Oakland. It's one of the four public swimming beaches in the county. Broadford has a 138-acre lake with 600 feet of sandy beach. There are a bathhouse, snack shop and picnic grounds, as well as paddleboats and rowboats to rent. The lake is popular with both swimmers and fishermen. The beach is open 9:00 A.M. to 8:00 P.M., and the park 9:00 A.M. to dusk. A nominal admission is charged per car.

Directions: From Baltimore take 1-70 west 90 miles to Hancock. From Hancock take I-68 to Keysers Ridge. Take Route 219 south to Oakland. Make a right turn on Green Street and go one block, then turn left. The museum is on your right.

Savage River State Forest

Wilderness and Whitewater

Garrett County has nearly 75,000 acres of wild timberland within three state forests: Potomac State Forest along Backbone Mountain near the headwaters of the Potomac River, Garrett State Forest (see Swallow Falls selection) and **Savage River State Forest.**

Savage River is the largest, with roughly 53,000 acres. Elevations within its boundaries range from 1,488 to 3,075 feet, and the two rivers that originate here, the Savage and the Casselman, flow in opposite directions to the Atlantic Ocean and Gulf of Mexico, respectively. In 1951, the Savage River Dam was finished, creating a reservoir of water for Western Maryland communities. Also, when water is released downstream a narrow and difficult 5½-mile white-water course is created. This challenging course hosts world-class paddling competitions, such as the 1972 U.S. Olympic Trials and the 1989 Whitewater World Championship Races.

Within the Savage River State Forest are two state parks: **New Germany** and **Big Run.** In New Germany the Swauger's Mill Dam contributes to the park's recreational options by creating a 13-acre lake. Visitors can rent rowboats, fish the well-stocked waters and swim. Picnic tables, fireplaces and a pavilion are located near the lake.

New Germany is one of five state parks that have rental cabins (the others are Herrington Manor, Elk Neck, Martinak and Janes Island; see selections). There are also campgrounds. Camping is also permit-ted along the 17-mile Big Savage Hiking Trail, recommended for experienced hikers only.

The best way to enjoy the wildlife and wildflowers of this forested park is by taking one of New Germany's nine trails, which are charted and ranked by degree of difficulty on an available park trail map. In winter cross-country skiers enjoy many of these same trails and the park's recreation hall is converted to a warming hut. Limited snowmobile trails have been created on Meadow Mountain near New Germany State Park. A permit, available at the Savage River Headquarters, is required to use them.

There are also trails and unimproved campgrounds in Big Run State Park. Primitive camping is available in the State Forest.

Directions: From Baltimore take I-70 west for 90 miles to Hancock, then continue west on I-68 to Exit 22 (Chestnut Ridge Road) for the park.

Swallow Falls and Herrington Manor State Parks

The Big Muddy

In western Maryland in 1918, Emmanuel Metheny, an Allegheny Mountain man, stopped to help a Packard mired in the mud. Metheny used his old Model T to pull the Packard free. He refused payment for his help but did tell the Packard's passengers they should get a car suitable for the roads; he went on to claim that the Ford Model T was the best car made. This unsolicited testimonial had an unexpected reward. One of the passengers in the Packard was Henry

Swallow Falls State Park has four falls. It was near this one in 1918 that Henry Ford, Thomas Edison and Harvey Firestone got stuck in a Packard car and were pulled out by a Model T.

Ford, who later sent his loyal customer a new Ford automobile.

Ford, along with his companions, Thomas Edison and Harvey Firestone, had come to camp on the bank of the Muddy Creek, overlooking **Swallow Falls**. These titans of American industry returned for another camping visit in 1921, joined by naturalist John Burroughs.

The campsite these influential men chose was in the first state-owned forest in the country. Nearly 2,000 acres of forestland were given to Maryland in 1906 by John and Robert Garrett for the protection of wildlife and the advancement of forestry. The original grant was expanded to 9,248 acres and became the Garrett State Forest. Within this tract is both **Swallow Falls State Park** and **Herrington Manor State Park.**

There are actually four different falls within Swallow Falls State Park: Muddy Creek Falls (Maryland's tallest), Swallow Falls, the Lower Falls and Tolliver Falls. Canyon Trail, leading from Muddy Creek to Swallow Falls, is one of the state's most scenic hiking trails. Shaded by high cliffs, it winds along the Youghiogheny River. In the spring wildflowers bloom along the river banks, and even on sweltering summer days it seems cool here. In autumn the foliage brings new color to the trail, while in winter the frozen falls create an icy wonderland.

There are 6.5 miles of trails in the park. One of the more popular is the Swinging Bridge Trail, which provides an excellent point for viewing the 54-foot Muddy Creek Falls. Muddy Creek gets its name from the brackish water found in the Cranesville Swamp where it originated (see selection). The creek meets the Youghiogheny just below Muddy Creek Falls.

You can hike, fish, picnic, camp and cross-country ski in Swallow Falls Park. At nearby Herrington Manor State Park you can swim at one of Garrett County's four public beaches. (The other beaches, described in other selections, are at Deep Creek Lake State Park, New Germany State Park and the Broadford Recreation Area.)

At Herrington Manor beach, on a 53-acre lake, paddleboats and rowboats can be rented. The lake is stocked periodically for fishing. The ten miles of hiking trails can be explored on foot during good weather and on skis after a snowfall. Twenty cabins are available within the park.

Directions: From Baltimore take 1-70 west 90 miles to Hancock, follow I-68 west to Keysers Ridge. Take Exit 14 at Keysers Ridge and go south on Route 219. Turn right on Mayhew Inn Road, then left on Sang Run Road. Make a right on Swallow Falls Road, which takes you to Swallow Falls State Park. For Herrington Manor State Park continue on Swallow Falls Road; it becomes Herrington Manor Road.

Whitewater Rafting

Wild Water

For many visitors Western Maryland's primary appeal is its scenic beauty. The Allegheny Mountains offer waterfalls, tumbling streams, mountaintop lakes and virgin forests. One marvelous way to experience this natural world is by taking a whitewater rafting trip along the Upper Youghiogheny River. The "Yock" flows north into Pennsylvania. You can also cross the West Virginia border and experience the thrills of the Cheat River.

The only problem with the Upper Yock's 11 miles of rapids is that not a one is for beginners; there are no Class I rapids, the easiest level of navigability. It has Class V rapids, considered extraordinarily difficult, with a series of long and violent sections. There are also some Class VI rapids; sometimes described as "deadly", these are strictly for the pros.

From Western Maryland you can branch out into nearby states for less hazardous whitewater rafting. The Youghiogheny River rafting trips that begin in Ohiopyle, Pennsylvania, accept paddlers aged 12 and over for normal water, and 14 and older for high water. Here the trip is eight miles with a drop of 40 feet during the first mile. The trip boasts eight major rapids separated by small rapids and even a few calm pools.

About 20 miles beyond Maryland's westernmost boundary is Albright, West Virginia, where the Cheat River trips begin. This eleven-mile rafting adventure runs through the Cheat River Canyon and includes 20 rapids with names like Big Nasty, Even Nastier and Devil's Trip. Sounds fun, doesn't it?

Don't come, the experts caution, unless you're prepared. You will get wet, so bring a bathing suit and sneakers on hot days. On cool, cloudy days in summer, or in spring or fall, wear a water-resistant jacket or even wool clothes to retain your body's warmth. Be sure to bring a change of clothes. Trips run rain or shine. The only time rafting trips are canceled is when the river is dangerously high. Most rafts hold four to eight passengers.

There are a number of companies running these exciting whitewater trips. Write or call:

White Water Adventures, P.O. Box 31, Ohiopyle, PA 15470, (800) WVA-RAFT

Mountain Stream & Trail Outfitters, Box 106, Ohiopyle, PA 15470, (800) 723-8669

Precision Rafting, P.O. Box 185, Friendship, MD 21531, (800) 477-3723

Laurel Highlands River Tours, P.O. Box 107, Ohiopyle, PA 15470, (800) 472-3846

ALLEGANY COUNTY

C&O Canal National Historical Park (Upper)

Barge Right In

The B&O Railroad and the C&O Canal once vied for travelers and trade. Now they are merely reminders of the early years of westward expansion. It is a rueful footnote to this rivalry that the **C&O Canal National Historical Park** Visitor Center is located in Cumberland's Western Maryland Station Center on Canal Street.

This impressive and commanding station reflected the railroad's success. It was built in 1913, at the height of the railroad era. Inside the station, both railroad and canal memorabilia are on display. Old photographs recall these alternate means of transportation. The C&O Canal National Historical Park Visitor Center is open Tuesday through Saturday from 9:00 A.M. to 5:00 P.M. during the winter. During the summer it is also open on Sunday from 9:00 A.M. to 5:00 P.M.

A path leads from the station to the C&O Canal terminus. From this point it was 184.5 miles along the canal to Georgetown in the District of Columbia. On July 4, 1828, President John Quincy Adams turned the first shovel of earth to begin construction of the canal. On that same day Declaration of Independence signer Charles Carroll laid the first stone in Baltimore for the B&O Railroad. It was to be a race to the west!

The canal did not reach Cumberland until 1850. That was eight years after the B&O Railroad got there. By the time the canal was fully operational it was practically obsolete. The last three locks of the canal, numbers 73, 74 and 75, were finished in 1840. Stop at North Branch and see these locks, as well as a canal boat replica. The boat has a re-created captain's cabin, hay house and on-board mule stable. The canal boats almost always had two teams, so that one team rested while the other worked. Canal traffic was seasonal from the very beginning, because the barges couldn't maneuver once there was heavy freezing. Tours are given of the canal boat on weekends from 1:00 to 5:00 P.M. June through August.

One last canal site you might enjoy is the **Paw Paw Tunnel**, 30 miles below Cumberland. This was one of the most astonishing engineering achievements of the entire canal project. It was also completed late, 12 years behind schedule. The tunnel, through 3,118 feet of solid rock, was built to eliminate a six-mile set of bends in the Potomac River.

Today you can walk through the tunnel. Wear comfortable shoes and be sure to bring a flashlight. Imagine the tunnel in operation,

1850 to 1924. Talk about a traffic jam! Only one boat could negoti-ate the tunnel at a time, so there was often a one-mile backup at each end of the tunnel.

It takes approximately 20 minutes to walk through the tunnel; as you get near the middle the light dwindles and the sense of being beneath an enormous rocky mountain grows. It's easy to empathize with the workers who hacked and blasted their way through this rock. Violence between the immigrant work crews, cholera epi-demics and frequent accidents added to the ordeal.

If time permits after you explore the tunnel, you may want to hike along the Tunnel Hill Trail that leads up and over the ridge above. This is a strenuous walk that takes about an hour.

Directions: From Baltimore take 1-70 west 90 miles to Hancock, then go south on Route 522 to Berkeley Springs, West Virginia. Turn right on Route 9 and continue for 28 miles to Paw Paw. Head over the Potomac River bridge back into Maryland and follow signs for the Paw Paw Tunnel on your right. For Cumberland and the C&O Canal National Historical Park Visitor Center take I-68 west from Hancock to Cumberland, Exit 43C. Turn left off the ramp onto Harrison Street, follow Harrison Street to and thru the first stoplight into the Western Maryland Station Center parking lot. For North Branch locks take Exit 43B, Route 51 south from Cumberland. Turn right five miles south at the sign which reads "C&O Canal Lockhouse 75 Area." This is the PPG Road, follow it to Lock 75 parking area about ½ mile.

George Washington's Headquarters and Fort Cumberland Tunnels

Time Tunnel

In a one-room cabin at Fort Cumberland, George Washington stud-ied military strategy and planned his first campaign. Having surveyed in the Cumberland Valley for Lord Fairfax in 1748, Washington, five years later at the age of 21, was given a commission by Virginia Governor Dinwiddie to carry a warning to the French on the Ohio River not to remain in British-claimed territory. He carried out this fruitless mission, on two occasions nearly at the cost of his life. He was ambushed and fired upon by hostile Indians, and he fell into the icy Allegheny River.

A year later, in 1754, when the French still had not heeded the warning, Fort Mount Pleasant was built on the bank of Wills Creek. It was from here that Lt. Colonel Washington led a small force north to a spot just over the Pennsylvania state line (Fort Necessity National Battlefield Park) and fought his first battle. Washington built a small temporary fort "of necessity" but had to surrender when he was attacked by a far superior force.

In 1755 a large fort was built on the Maryland hill overlooking Wills Creek. Fort Cumberland, as it was called, was the biggest fort in the colony at that time, measuring 400 feet long and 160 feet wide. The dimensions of the fort are marked out on the streets of Cumberland, also the original location of Washington's headquarters.

General Braddock rode a chariot into Fort Cumberland in May 1755. George Washington, as his aide-de-camp, marched with him on the ill-fated attack on Fort Duquesne. The British lost the battle and their general, but the colonies gained their greatest hero (Washington's heroism would contribute to his appointment as commander of the American revolutionary forces). Though he had three horses shot from under him and his uniform was riddled with bullet holes, Washington helped two other officers carry the mortally wounded General Braddock from the battlefield. Then he returned to battle, riding all night to lead the men and wagons to safety.

As president, Washington came again to Fort Cumberland in 1794 to review the troops marching north to suppress the Whiskey Rebellion in Pennsylvania. Despite its historic significance, the fort fell into disrepair. When the land was sold to private developers, timbers from the one-room cabin that had been **George Washington's Headquarters** were saved and eventually moved to the banks of Wills Creek near the site of the old fort (now Riverside Park), where it has been restored. When you peer through the windows of the cabin, you see a mannequin dressed in a British uniform resembling a youthful Washington. A message on audiotape provides background on Washington's involvement in the French and Indian War and on Fort Cumberland.

If you plan ahead you can arrange through the pastoral offices of Emmanuel Episcopal Church (301) 777-3364 to explore the **Tunnels of Fort Cumberland.** The church is built on the site of the fort and some of the network of trenches that crisscrossed and surrounded Fort Cumberland are still visible amid the foundations of the church.

These stone-lined trenches are the only surviving earthworks from the French and Indian War. One section is identified as a possible powder magazine. Walking along these winding tunnels, you can get quite a thrill realizing that Washington may well have found his way along the very same route.

On your way to the tunnels, be sure to stop for a look at this Gothic church. Two of the windows were done by Tiffany himself, a third by his studio. The windows reveal such depth of color that they seem to glow with an internal fire. *The Adoration of the Shepherd* by Bongereau over the altar is not to be missed. The church is at 16 Washington Street in Cumberland's historic district (see History House selection).

Directions: From Baltimore, take I-70 west to Hancock (about 90 miles). From Hancock, continue west on I-68 to Cumberland. Take

George Washington, at the age of 21, planned his first military campaign in this one-room cabin at Fort Cumberland in Allegany County.

Ron Lytle

Exit 43A, right onto Lee St. Continue to traffic light, turn right onto Greene St. Proceed two blocks to where Greene St. turns left. Headquarters cabin is on the right. One block ahead on Greene St., turn left onto Washington St.; Emmanuel Church is on the left.

History House

Up the Stairs, Back in Time

Cumberland's tree-shaded Washington Street has a wealth of historic homes from the last half of the 19th century. Architectural styles range from Federal through Georgian Revival, but the clear favorite is Victorian. Most of the families who built in this section of Cumberland made their money between 1860 and 1920, when both the railroad and the canal were vying for the westward traffic that passed through Cumberland.

In 1867 the president of the C&O Canal, Josiah Gordon, built his home at 218 Washington Street. The most striking exterior feature of his Second Empire design is the mansard roof. The house has 18 rooms, plus servants' quarters. Today it is the headquarters of the Allegany County Historical Society, which has overseen the remarkably thorough restoration and decoration of **History House.**

When you enter the house, notice the entranceway ceiling light; this was one of Cumberland's first gas lamps. The first room you'll see is the great room with a square grand Knabe piano, a chandelier made of Tiffany-type glass and cloisonne and a changing exhibit of period collections.

The Victorian parlor where the Gordons entertained has an 1839 square grand piano plus a charming "courting couch." In the music room there is a reed parlor organ. The Edison Standard Phonograph and music box reflect popular tastes of the period. The large windows in the dining room make it bright and cheerful and draw visitors' attention to the wallpaper border on the ceiling.

The kitchen, which is in the basement, adjoins the oldest original room in the house: the pantry. Its crude horsehair plaster and original gas jets can still be seen. The kitchen boasts utensils such as a pig scraper and sausage stuffer, and old pots and cauldrons hang in the large, open stone fireplace.

On the second floor, you'll find two 19th-century bedrooms with heavy Victorian pieces, a boudoir, as well as a 1918 bathroom with its commodious footed tub. The Costume Room has changing exhibits of clothing from the late 1800s through the 1920s and fashion accessories to match. Toys, dolls, a dollhouse and books fill the day nursery and the night nursery.

The third floor has still more to explore. Dental-phobes might feel squeamish when they see the foot-operated tooth driller in the Medical Room. The metal hot water bottle doesn't look pleasant, either. There's an early x-ray machine and other old-fashioned instruments.

The dunce cap in the Schoolroom was never a popular piece of headgear. The Military Room has a model of Fort Cumberland, a frontier outpost built by the British during the French and Indian War (see Fort Cumberland Tunnels selection). The military exhibits include artifacts from the Civil War and both World War I and II. There's also a Research Room for visitors tracing their family roots.

History House is open year round. From June through October times are Tuesday through Saturday from 11:00 A.M. to 4:00 P.M. and Sunday 1:30 to 4:00 P.M. Costumed docents guide house tours and offer a Museum Explorer tour for children. The remainder of the year it is closed on Sunday. Special events throughout the year include a Victorian Christmas celebration and Children's Teas. Admission is charged.

Directions: From Baltimore take 1-70 90 miles west to Hancock, then follow Route 68 west to Cumberland. Take Exit 43A and stay right through exit. After the traffic light proceed to Washington Street, then turn right. The museum is at 218 Washington Street.

La Vale Toll Gate House

Pay As You Go

Have you ever become hopelessly confused trying to navigate a road with multiple names? Such confusion is as old as one of the country's earliest links between the Eastern Seaboard and the West: the National Road or Cumberland Road.

This link, now U.S. 40, was called the **National Road** because it was the first and only road built and maintained by the federal government. George Washington had wanted to build a road as well as a canal linking East and West ever since he had surveyed as a young man in western Maryland.

When Congress began debate on the road's construction, the legislators called it the **Cumberland Road** in honor of the city. The contract for the first stretch from Cumberland to Eckhart was granted on May 8, 1811, but work was not completed until 1818. At a cost of $21.25 each 24¾ cubic feet of road, the building proceeded slowly and expensively. By 1830 it was decided that the states could assume the costs of any additional building as well as maintenance.

Ohio and then Maryland took over their portions of the National Road and built toll houses to collect money to pay for them. The **La Vale Toll Gate** was the first toll house built along the Maryland section of the National Road and is now the only surviving toll gate house in the state.

The toll house has a two-story, seven-sided main section flanked by two one-story sections. The main part looks like a stunted lighthouse. From the windows in the upstairs bedroom the gatekeeper could see clearly in both directions. He was paid in the first year of operation $200, or 12 percent of the gross receipts. The Report of the Superintendent of the National Road for the following year, 1837, noted that 20,000 travelers had used this section of the National Road and recommended raising the gatekeeper's salary to $300.

The toll rates posted on the gate house windows reveal that a horseback rider was charged four cents, and a four-wheel carriage with two horses, 12 cents. It would also cost 12 cents if you were driving a score of cattle, but only six cents for a score of sheep or hogs. There was no toll for vehicles with wheels eight or more inches wide, nor for mail carriers, soldiers or for anyone going to church or a funeral.

When the railroad reached Cumberland in 1842, traffic along the National Road diminished. In 1878 the toll gate house became the property of Allegany County, which collected tolls until around 1900. Later it was sold to a private owner for use as a residence. The Maryland Historical Trust assumed ownership in 1969 and began its restoration. For many years the M.F.W.C. (Maryland Federation of Women's Clubs) La Vale Century Club maintained the restored and furnished toll gate house. Allegany County assumed ownership of the house in 1989, adding a picnic pavilion and benches on the land-scaped grounds as well as public restrooms. From mid-May through late October, it can be toured on Saturday and Sunday from 1:30-4:30 P.M. A nominal donation is requested.

Just five minutes from the Toll Gate House you'll find one of Maryland's best dining bargains at **Fred Warner's German Restaurant**. It's worth the approximately three-hour drive from cen-tral Baltimore to dine on Fred's Wiener Schnitzel (the most tender, delicate veal) served with wafer-thin potato pancakes. Housed in an old stone building that is decorated with needlework, coats of arms, beer mugs, painted plates and hanging grapes, the restaurant offers inexpensive lunch platters, including homemade breads and your pick of a well-stocked salad bar. Fred Warner's puts on special festi-vals four times a year during the first part of May, August, October and December.

The restaurant is open year round Tuesday through Sunday for lunch and dinner, except during July when it is closed on Sundays and Mondays. Call (301)729-2361.

Directions: From Baltimore go west 90 miles on I-70 to Hancock. Continue west on I-68 to Cumberland. Stay on I-68 to La Vale, Exit 39, which is Route 40 Alternate. The Toll Gate House is on the left ¼ mile after you exit. To get to Fred's German Restaurant go east on Route 40 Alternate for a short distance and just before the first traffic light bear right on Route 53. Turn left on Route 220, which takes you to Cresaptown and Fred Warner's (on your right).

WASHINGTON COUNTY

Albert Powell Trout Hatchery

Hatching 600,000 Fish Stories

If you have never seen a fish hatchery but are curious about how one operates, visit the **Albert Powell Trout Hatchery** just off I-70 east of Hagerstown. Although there is no visitor center or display area, you can stop at the hatchery office to ask questions and stroll a central walkway between a series of raceways brimming with fingerlings and adult trout.

Before young trout are released into the outdoor raceways they are incubated and hatched indoors. This Washington County facility receives 600,000 trout eggs each year from a Washington State commercial hatchery. From hatching trays the newborns are transferred to troughs where they are held for approximately three months.

The fingerling trout are transferred to the outside raceways when space becomes available during the spring stocking season. Approximately 250,000 year-old trout 11 to 12 inches long are stocked in Maryland waters by this hatchery annually; another 40,000 are kept to grow an additional year. At the end of the second year they are roughly 16 inches long. Some of these larger trout are included in every truckload of fish that leaves the hatchery each spring. Powell Hatchery also supplies fingerlings to the Bear Creek Rearing Station (see selection) in Garrett County. This facility rears approximately 200,000 fingerling trout to adult size. Powell Hatchery supplies adult trout from Washington County eastward, while the Bear Creek Rearing Station stocks its trout in Garrett and Allegany Counties.

You can visit the Albert Powell Trout Hatchery from 9:00 A.M. to 4:00 P.M. There is no charge.

If you are in the area on Sunday afternoon you might want to head south on Route 66 to Beaver Creek Road and visit the **Beaver Creek Country School.** This turn-of-the-century one-room school is filled with curios. The old wooden desks are lined up in front of the teacher's desk. Slate tablets and pencils, an old chalkboard, wallcharts, books and mannequins complete the picture. The mannequins, dressed in period outfits, represent both teacher and students.

A museum room across the hall, divided into sections, brings back an old-time millinery shop, a cobbler's shop, part of a Victorian parlor, even old-time kitchen utensils.

The Beaver Creek Country School is open Sunday afternoons June 1 through October 1 from 2:00 to 5:00 P.M. A nominal admission is charged.

Directions: From Baltimore take 1-70 about 60 miles to Exit 35 (Route 66). You'll see the fish hatchery on the left as soon as you get onto Route 66 north. From the fish hatchery go south on Route 66 to Beaver Creek Road, where you make a right. Proceed up Beaver Creek Road and take a right on Beaver Creek Church Road for the Country School.

Antietam National Battlefield

Where Have All the Young Men Gone...

The fields and hillsides around Antietam Creek are empty now; the air is clean and all is quiet. But the modern exhibits help today's visitors imagine a landscape of fallen soldiers, the air choked with smoke and the sound of constant gunfire.

Soldiers' quotes give a poignant perspective to what is called the bloodiest day of the Civil War, September 17, 1862. Confederate Lieutenant Pendleton commented, "Such a storm of balls I never conceived it possible for men to live through. Shot and shell shrieking and crashing, canister and bullets whistling and hissing most fiendlike through the air until you could almost see them. In that mile's ride I never expected to come back alive." Similar reactions were expressed by Lieutenant Graham with the 9th Regiment, New York Volunteers. He wrote, "I was lying on my back, supported on my elbows, watching the shells explode overhead and speculating as to how long I could hold up my finger before it would be shot off, for the air seemed full of bullets. When the order to get up was given I turned over quickly to look at Col. Kimball, who had given the order, thinking he had become suddenly insane."

At the **Antietam National Battlefield** Visitor Center there are visual reminders of the battle—four large paintings done by Captain James Hope from sketches he had made on the battlefield. An audio-visual program helps put the events at Antietam in perspective. A 26-minute film, *Antietam Visit,* shown on the hour, focuses on President Lincoln's visit with Commander-of-the-Army George B. McClellan after the battle. Lincoln reviewed the troops, visited the numerous wounded and urged McClellan to pursue the Confederates into the South. Special interpretive programs are given by park rangers and volunteers on a scheduled basis.

After this introduction you're ready to tour the battlefield. There were three phases to this one-day battle that left more than 23,000 casualties. Your tour begins with the morning action, which took place from 6:00 to 9:00 A.M. Much of the early fighting took place in the northern part of the field around a cornfield and the Dunker Church. The church you'll see was reconstructed in 1961-62. The original was destroyed not in battle but during a storm in May 1921. Additional information is available at the Visitor Center explaining the history of the Dunkers.

A bitterly contested area during the morning hours was the cornfield. Union General Joseph Hooker reported, "In the time that I am writing every stalk of corn in the northern and greater part of the field was cut as closely as could have been done with a knife and the slain lay in rows precisely as they had stood in their ranks a few moments before. It was never my fortune to witness a more bloody, dismal battlefield."

Antietam, the one-day battle that left more than 23,000 casulties, is known as the bloodiest one-day battle of the Civil War. Along "Bloody Lane" (above), 4,000 men fell in four hours.

Bad as the morning action was, it solved nothing; neither side conclusively won their ground. There was worse to come. For nearly four hours, 9:30 A.M. to 1:00 P.M., the opposing forces fought along a sunken country lane that came to be known—after 4,000 casualties— as Bloody Lane. The tower you'll see overlooking this section was built in 1896 and used by visitors and military organizations as a vantage point from which to study the battle strategy.

The third and final afternoon phase, 1:00 to 5:30 P.M., centered around the Lower Bridge, now called Burnside Bridge. Four Union divisions under General Burnside had been attempting to cross the bridge since 10:30 A.M. Holding them off were approximately 450 Georgia riflemen. Burnside and his men finally crossed the bridge around 1:00 P.M., but then spent two hours reforming their line before driving the Confederate troops toward Sharpsburg. This delay, too, proved disastrous. It gave A.P. Hill time to arrive from Harpers Ferry with his Confederate division and drive Burnside back. Hill's action helped the Confederate army avoid destruction.

At the conclusion of your battlefield tour, take the footpath to the Hawkins Zouave Monument. It marks the spot where the battle ended at 5:30 P.M. You can look out over the entire battlefield and reflect on the tragic loss of so many young men from both North and South.

Of the 12,410 Federal casualties, 4,776 are buried at Antietam National Cemetery. Most Confederate dead are buried in a cemetery in nearby Hagerstown. Despite such heavy losses, this was not a decisive victory for either side. Lee's failure to successfully carry the fighting into the North caused Great Britain to delay recognition of the Confederate government. Five days after the Battle of Antietam, Lincoln issued the preliminary Emancipation Proclamation. He had hoped to do it at a moment of Union strength, not on the heels of a Federal debacle. The proclamation freed all the slaves in the rebellious states, providing a dual northern purpose for the war: the preservation of the Union and the abolition of slavery.

Civil War enthusiasts will want to take advantage of the unique opportunity to stay overnight on the battlefield in the historic **Piper House**, the headquarters of Confederate General James Longstreet. After the battle the farm house served briefly as a field hospital. There are four bedrooms, each with a bath, in the 19th-century log and frame house. Period antiques fill the rooms and a sense of history fills the house. Rooms at this battlefield bed and breakfast should be reserved at least a month in advance. Call (301)797-1862.

Another bed and breakfast, **The Inn at Antietam** overlooking Antietam National Cemetery, is an attractively furnished turn-of-the century Victorian house. Its southern breakfast reflects more of gracious hospitality than continental caution; it's a repast to be remembered. Call (301) 432-6601 for reservations.

Antietam National Battlefield Visitor Center is open daily except Thanksgiving, Christmas and New Year's Day. Hours are 8:30 A.M. to 5:00 P.M. September through May and 8:30 A.M. to 6:00 P.M. June through August. A nominal admission fee is charged. Cassette tapes can be rented ($5.00) with details of the major points of interest along the battlefield tour, which takes about 1½ hours.

Directions: From Baltimore take I-70 west past Frederick to exit for Alt. Route 40. Take Alt. 40 west to Boonsboro where it intersects with Route 34. Take Route 34 south to Sharpsburg. The Visitor Center is north of Sharpsburg on Route 65.

Boonsboro Museum of History and Crystal Grottoes Caverns

Caverns and Curios

Just a few miles apart, the **Boonsboro Museum of History** and Crystal Grottoes Caverns offer treasures both natural and unnatural (that is, man-made). Although speaking of the unnatural, the museum does have a display of supernatural oddities associated with the magic of Wizard Zittle, a faith healer who lived near Boonsboro in 1845. Superstition and witchcraft are among the many topics investigated at this remarkably thorough museum. Many of the Civil War artifacts were found on nearby Antietam, South Mountain and Harpers Ferry battlefields. You'll rarely find such a comprehensive collection of carved "mini balls," the name given to lead bullets that soldiers shaped into poker chips, checkers, mustache combs, chessmen, tops, bottle stoppers, initials and decorative shapes.

Mementos of Confederate Officer Henry Kyd Douglas fill an entire case. This young soldier grew up at nearby Blackford Plantation, which now serves as the C&O Canal National Historical Park Headquarters. Look for the letter Douglas wrote to his father on Union stationery with the federal emblem crossed out. Henry is the author of the now famous *I Rode with Stonewall*. A copy of the original text, which was first called *The Stonewall Papers*, is displayed. So is the diary Douglas kept during the war and an original order signed by Stonewall Jackson.

Weapons appear to be everywhere, from prehistoric Indian arrowheads to handmade "shanks" confiscated from a local prison. Not all the weapons were used on this side of the Atlantic. There is a matador's sword, a Japanese sword from World War II and a set of an African witch doctor's knives.

One of the most horrifying items on display is the hand-wrought slave punishment collar, lined with long, iron spikes. One wonders how a person could possibly endure wearing it and yet some slaves, we are told, were made to wear these collars night and day.

A more poignant memento is a piece of wooden fence from the Antietam battlefield. Young Sergeant Wright rushed the fence and was shot in both legs. He received the Congressional Medal of Honor for his valor and later returned to the battlefield to claim a piece of the fence. To this piece of fence, he affixed a small plaque that reads, "I volunteered to help pull this down. September 17, 1862."

Other collections include a large selection of Chinese ceramics including Tang tomb figures, Sung celadon, and Ming blue and white pieces. There is also a religious display that includes Ethiopian silver crosses, Russian icons and tabernacles, a Byzantine reliquary and a Jewish silver Torah printer. You'll even see sunken treasure from a downed Spanish vessel.

The museum has a 19th-century general store fully stocked with items that run the gamut from hand-wrought items of 1795 to mass-produced products of 1875. The glassware display is quite extensive. Though you are given a printed guide, the owner-director Doug Bast, who has been called a historical packrat, is on hand to tell about the many unusual items he has single-handedly amassed. The museum is open May through September on Sunday from 1:00 to 5:00 P.M. and

41

other times by appointment. Call (301) 432-6969. A nominal admission is charged.

Heading out of Boonsboro on Route 34 you'll quickly spot the **Crystal Grottoes Caverns,** Maryland's only commercial underground caverns. The caves were discovered in 1920 when the state was building Route 34. The road crew was quarrying limestone when the drill bit fell into the as yet undiscovered cave. They dynamited the drill holes, crawled into the opening and saw for the first time what came to be known as Crystal Grottoes. The caverns opened to the public on April 2, 1922, and have stayed in their natural state. No colored lights or fancy signs mar the natural beauty of the limestone formations. There are some large chambers, and many of the formations sparkle with their crystalline covering. It takes about 30 minutes to explore them all.

The caverns are open daily from 9:00 A.M. to 6:00 P.M. with the last tour starting at 5:00 P.M. There is an admission charge, roughly comparable to an evening movie admission.

Directions: From Baltimore take 1-70 west past Frederick to exit for Alt. Route 40. Take Alt. 40 west to Boonsboro. The museum is at 113 North Main Street. Go south on Route 34 to the caverns just out of town on the left.

Fort Frederick

Frontier Defense

Once there was a chain of forts protecting Maryland's western frontier; of these only **Fort Frederick** remains. The frontier settlers wanted to stay out of the conflict between the English on the coast and the French who were firmly entrenched in Canada. Neither nation was of much concern to the people struggling to carve homesteads out of the wilderness. But the French prompted their Indian allies to attack the homes along the Maryland frontier. In 1756, following General Braddock's defeat by the French at Fort Duquesne, the Governor of Maryland insisted that the Maryland Assembly appropriate money to build a fort.

Governor Horatio Sharpe took a personal interest in the North (now Fairview) Mountain fort. After supervising much of the work, he named it Fort Frederick in honor of Maryland's Lord Proprietor, Frederick Calvert, Sixth Lord Baltimore. The flag you'll see flying over the fort shows the Union Jack, indicating the colony's allegiance to England, plus the black and gold colors of the Calvert family.

Fort Frederick was a more formidable fort than was traditionally built along the frontier. It was both larger and more durable. Unlike other forts in the chain, it had stockade walls of stone instead of wood or earth.

There is another reason why the fort still stands: It was never attacked. Perhaps the imposing walls deterred assault, even though the fort was important as a supply base for the English during the French and Indian War. In the American Revolution it was reactivated as a prison camp for British and Hessian prisoners and remained unmolested. A small skirmish was fought at Fort Frederick on Christmas Day, 1861, with Union troops holding the fort against Confederate raiders.

To fill in the historical details about Fort Frederick, stop first at the Visitor Center and watch the 17-minute movie; it will make the self-guided walking tour more meaningful. The tour map (available at the Visitor Center) will direct you up the path to the fort. On your right you'll see the garrison garden. Eating salted meat (with occasional fresh game), dry beans and bread could get monotonous, so the troops garrisoned here planted vegetables outside the stone walls to supplement their diet. Food was so scarce during the American Revolution that fort commandant Colonel Rawlings permitted local farmers to hire his British and German prisoners, who were fed in return for their labor.

Just outside the fort walls you'll see a cannon resembling the four that guarded the diamond-shaped corner bastions. A cannon this size was capable of firing six-pound iron balls. As you pass through the gateway you'll see two barracks within the 1½-acre fort compound. Guides dressed in uniforms of the French and Indian War period are on hand to answer questions about the fort and about military life from 1756 to 1763. The barracks' rooms have been furnished to represent enlisted men and noncommissioned officers' quarters of the late 1750s. You're invited to step into the public room and get a feel of 18th-century barrack life. Don't try to bounce on the beds though; they're made of bare wooden planks.

Across the parade ground are the west barracks. These two barracks were planned to hold about 4,000 enlisted men. The fort was rarely garrisoned up to strength, however, so the rooms were used for other purposes. In the west barracks you'll see a storage room, laundry and dining area. The second floor has been converted into a museum depicting the history of the fort.

The location of the governor's house, which served as fort headquarters, is now indicated by stone foundations at one end of the parade ground. Also marked are the officers' quarters and a storehouse. For lack of sufficient documentation, these structures could not be rebuilt. Much of what restoring could be done was done by the Civilian Conservation Corps during the Depression in the 1930s.

The barracks and Visitor Center are open May through September . The hours are Monday through Friday from 8:00 A.M. to 4:00 P.M. and from 9:00 A.M. to 5:00 P.M. on Saturday and Sunday. There is a nominal charge. Each May the reactivated Maryland Forces present "Fort

Frederick Rendezvous" depicting life during the French and Indian War, frontier skills and ranger tactics. In late July "Military Field Day" is held here with roughly 450 uniformed men representing all three conflicts in which Fort Frederick played a role. In late September there are competitive matches during the "Governor's Invitational Firelock Match." The schedule ends with an evening ghost walk on the Friday closest to Halloween.

You can picnic at Fort Frederick, and **Captain Wort's Sutler Shop** sells snacks, soft drinks and crafts. Two nature trails provide more diversion if you have a day to spend at Fort Frederick. And there is a primitive family campground on the bank of the Potomac River. You can fish in the Potomac and in the 92-acre Big Pool Lake. Rental boats are available.

Directions: From Baltimore take 1-70 west about 80 miles to Exit 12. Take Route 56 south toward Big Pool. Fort Frederick will be on your right.

Gathland State Park

A Monument "Quite Odd"

Gathland State Park, just outside Burkittsville, encompasses the ruins of **Gapland**, the South Mountain home of George Alfred Townsend, the youngest reporter to cover the Civil War. It is also the site of Townsend's commemorative arch honoring all correspondents of the war. Townsend went on to become a noted journalist and author during the Reconstruction Period. He used Gath as one of his pen names. The first three letters were his initials; the added h was inspired by the biblical passage, "Tell it not in Gath, publish it not in the streets of Askalon" (II Samuel 1:20).

Townsend eventually used Askalon for the name of the third of nine major buildings he erected on this 100-acre tract. Planning, designing and building were a diversion for Townsend, a change of pace from his hectic writing schedule.

A walking tour of Gathland State Park (to which there is a self-guiding tour map) starts at **Gapland Hall**. This was once a substantial fieldstone summer and weekend home. A stone tablet embedded when the house was built in 1885, but long since lost, explained the derivation of the name: "I sought for a man that would stand in the gap before me in the land" (Ezekiel 22:30). The main wing of the house has been restored but lacks the original ornamentation, grillwork and porch. The path continues down to Gapland Lodge, which was also built in 1885 and served as servants' quarters, kitchen and summer dining room. It is now one of the park's two museums.

The next stop is eye arresting. The **War Correspondent's Arch** is the most unusual structure Townsend designed. Ruthanne Hindes, a journalist, described it this way in her biography of Townsend: "In appearance the monument is quite odd. It is fifty feet high and forty feet broad. Above a Moorish arch sixteen feet high built of Hummelstown purple stone are super-imposed three Roman arches. These are flanked on one side with a square crenellated tower, producing a bizarre and picturesque effect." The arches are said to represent Description, Depiction and Photography. The arch cost $5,000 to build and donations were made to the building fund by Thomas Edison, Joseph Pulitzer and many others.

Stop four on your walking tour is the previously mentioned Askalon, the third of Townsend's original buildings. He built a large wooden frame house, using it first as a stable, then as servants' quarters. Continuing on, you come to the barn ruins. The next stop, Mt. Gath, is a private residence and can only be noted, not visited. Mt. Gath was a guest house added by Townsend in 1892. Moving up the trail, you'll come to the ruins of the library where Townsend had his living quarters.

Finally, you'll see the mausoleum where Townsend hoped to be buried. He was actually buried in Philadelphia. Over the empty tomb the inscription, signed Gath, reads: "Good Night."

If this short hike is not enough, you can pick up the Appalachian Trail, which passes through the park. A six-mile hike will take you to the Weverton Cliffs. You can also pick up a map of an auto tour of the **South Mountain Battlefield**, which covers 12 miles and takes about 30 to 45 minutes.

Gathland sits in Crampton's Gap, the southernmost gap that was fought over during the Battle of South Mountain, fought on September 14, 1862. Here, William B. Franklin's VI Corps pushed a much smaller Confederate force from behind a stone wall near the town of Burkittsville, through the gap and into the valley on the west side of the mountain. Franklin's failure to follow up on the advantage he had gained on the 15th allowed Lee's army to divide in two and slip away. Had Franklin used his chances, it might have brought an early end to the war. Instead, Lee regrouped his forces along the banks of Antietam Creek, where the Battle of Antietam (see selection) was fought on September 17th.

Two museums at Gathland State Park are open weekends, April through October, from NOON to 5:00 P.M. Admission is free.

Directions: From Baltimore take 1-70 west past Frederick to Exit 49, Alternate Route 40. Take Alternate Route 40 west to Middletown, then follow Route 17 south to Burkittsville. From Burkittsville go west one mile on Gapland Road to the top of South Mountain for Gathland State Park.

Hager House and Washington County Museum of Fine Arts

A Window on Maryland Frontier Life

Jonathan Hager, a 22-year-old German, emigrated to America on the *Harle*, a Dutch ship, arriving in Philadelphia on September 1, 1736. For the next three years he explored the wildernesses of Virginia, Maryland and Pennsylvania. On June 5, 1739, he purchased 200 acres he called Hager's Fancy. The land he bought already had "3 acres of corn field fenced in and two sorry [poorly built] houses."

Hager built a two-and-a-half-story stone house on part of the foundation of one of the earlier dwellings. His stone house rested over two springs, giving him a protected water supply in the event of Indian attack. Its 22-inch walls could serve as a frontier fort if necessary. (You'll notice the windows on the lower floor are wider on the inside than on the outside, making it easier to defend the house.)

Hager met Elizabeth Kershner, who was a neighbor on this western Maryland frontier. They were married a year after he settled in present day Hagerstown. When Hager formed the town, he named it Elizabeth Town, but everyone else called it Hager's Town.

Because it was a frontier home, this place is quite different from the coastal colonial plantations. You can still see the mud and straw insulation. The house is original but the furnishings are not; they do, however, represent life on the frontier in the 18th century. You'll notice Hager's front room also served as a trading post. A variety of hides on the table indicate what kind of game was found in the region in the 1740s: rabbit, deer, beaver, bear and even buffalo.

From the front room you'll move to the kitchen, the center of family life. The dishes and utensils there today are far more numerous than they would have been in a typical frontier home, but the simplicity of the pottery and pewter is representative. Pewter dishes contained lead, which was responsible for some of the ill health and early deaths of this period. The old brick fireplace is surrounded by cooking pots and dried herbs.

At **Hager House** you get to explore both upstairs and downstairs. In the master bedroom upstairs there is a four-poster canopy bed. It was customary during the 18th century to use the bedroom as a social center, so you'll also see table and chairs as well as a 1735 clavichord.

Next you'll see the basement where the two springs still flow. The large fireplace was used for cooking during the summer and by Hager for minor forging jobs.

In six years his family had outgrown their place and he sold it at four times its initial per-acre cost to Jacob Rohrer, in whose family the property remained until the 20th century. Hager purchased a 1,780-

Hager House was built in 1739 by the founder of Hagerstown. Its 22-inch walls could serve as a fort, and the two springs on which it rested gave Hager a protected water supply.

acre tract two miles away. He called his second home Hager's Delight, but nothing remains of this house. On November 6, 1775, Hager was accidentally killed when a log hit him in the chest while he was supervising the building of the German Reformed Church on land he had donated to the town. Hager has been called the Father of Washington County. The Hager House is open Tuesday through Saturday 10:00 A.M. to 4:00 P.M. and Sunday 2:00 to 5:00 P.M. It is closed Mondays. Admission is charged.

While in the City Park area, take time to explore the nearby **Washington County Museum of Fine Arts,** open at no charge Tuesday through Saturday 10:00 A.M. to 5:00 P.M. and Sunday 1:00 to 5:00 P.M. The museum's major emphasis is on American art. The collection contains portraits by Thomas Sully and the Peales; landscapes by George Inness, Frederic Church, Thomas Moran and Albert Bierstadt; still lifes by Severin Roesen and John LaFarge. Maryland artists are also well represented: John Beale Bordley, Hugh Bolton Jones and Grace Hartigan. Old Masters are included in the museum's permanent collection. The 11 galleries offer a wide spectrum of special exhibitions.

The Washington County Museum of Fine Arts was given to the county by William Henry Singer, Jr., an American Post-Impressionist, in honor of his wife Anna Brugh Singer. Some of his paintings now hang in the Singer Gallery within the museum.

Directions: From Baltimore take I-70 west to Exit 32 (Route 40) into Hagerstown. Route 40 becomes Franklin Street. Turn left at Prospect Street for City Park, where you will find both the Hager House and the Washington County Museum of Fine Arts.

Maryland Heights and Kennedy Farm

Staging a Raid on Harpers Ferry

The historic town of Harpers Ferry is in West Virginia. But a sizable portion of Harpers Ferry National Historical Park is in Maryland, as is the **Kennedy Farm**, which served as the staging area for the historic 1859 raid by John Brown and his band of abolitionists.

Behind St. Peter's Catholic Church in the town of Harpers Ferry you'll find the stone steps that lead up to Jefferson Rock and the famous view therefrom, which Thomas Jefferson described as "worth a voyage across the Atlantic." (At that time Jefferson had not yet crossed the Atlantic.) Across the Potomac River on **Maryland Heights** another overlook provides a vantage point for viewing the town nestled on the mountain side. Two trails traverse Maryland Heights: Overlook Trail and Stone Fort Trail. The latter leads to the remains of a Civil War fortification. On the West Virginia side of the river the

Loudoun Heights Trail connects with the Appalachian Trail.

To trace the events that put Harpers Ferry on the map, start at the Kennedy Farm, known locally as the John Brown Farm. Here Brown and his followers hid while planning their raid on the Harpers Ferry arsenal. The community was curious about the newcomers, particularly because it was known that they included blacks. John Brown kept all his band inside, however, and refused to admit any visitors into the Widow Kennedy's farm house. A month after the raid, *Frank Leslie's Illustrated Newspapers* printed a sketch of the farm. Newly restored, it looks much today as it did in that sketch.

In the steps of Brown and his committed band, you make your way from the farm to the Harpers Ferry arsenal. As you travel, think back to October 16, 1859, when the raiders attacked the Federal arsenal hoping to obtain arms for the slaves they anticipated would flock to their banner. They gained neither recruits nor arms. Indeed, helping to defeat them were two soldiers who went on to lead Southern troops: Lt. Col. Robert E. Lee and Lt. J.E.B. Stuart. Ten of the raiders were killed when the Federal troops stormed the armory fire engine house (now called John Brown's Fort). Four raiders escaped, but Brown and another four conspirators were captured. As the ringleader, Brown was tried and convicted. He was hanged on December 2, 1859, less than two months after his unsuccessful raid—swift justice even in those days!

At the Harpers Ferry Visitors Center you can watch a seven-minute film encapsulating these dramatic events. A longer 30-minute film is shown at the John Brown Museum just down the street. Throughout the day the National Park Service offers special tours that are well worth catching. Authentically clad mid-19th century "residents" introduce you to the community and the gun factory that employed many of the townsfolk. The armory was defended by the North and seized by the South. You'll miss a lot of local color if you explore on your own, but there is a helpful guide for those who just want to amble around.

Most of Harpers Ferry sites can be enjoyed without charge. If you bring a picnic to enjoy along the river, you can have a very inexpensive but pleasant family outing. For those who feel no outing is complete without shopping, the town does offer a number of quaint shops and boutiques.

The Kennedy Farm is open weekends May through October from 9:00 A.M. to 1:00 P.M. For additional information call (301)791-3130. The Harpers Ferry National Historical Park Visitors Center and exhibits are open daily 8:00 A.M. to 5:00 P.M. During the summer the special tours are given from 10:00 A.M. to 4:00 P.M. Entrance fee is $5.00 per vehicle or $3.00 per person for cyclists and walk-ins. For more information call (304)535-6029.

Directions: From Baltimore take I-70 west to Frederick. At Frederick take Route 340 west toward Harpers Ferry. Before crossing

The Miller House gives visitors a look at life within a townhouse in Hagerstown between 1820 and 1850. Its graceful hanging staircase is an architectural gem.

the Potomac River into Virginia, take the Harpers Ferry Road north to Samples Manor and then go north on Chestnut Grove Road to Kennedy Farm. For Harpers Ferry, continue west on Route 340 and follow signs.

Miller House

From Hanging Staircase to Patent Medicines

What you'll see today on a tour of the **Miller House** in Hagerstown is a typical townhouse of the 1820s and an eclectic collection of clocks, dolls, carriages, pottery and country-store commodities. The house's graceful hanging staircase is one of its most outstanding architectural features. The tour starts in the front drawing room, which was the formal room for receiving visitors in the mid-1800s. Both formal and informal evenings were enjoyed here; the family played games, read aloud and sang. You'll see a "tea caddy," customarily locked to protect the expensive green and black tea from servant pilfering. The gilded valances over the window represent the 1850s, but the other furnishings are from 1818 to 1825.

A curious architectural feature, a gib door, actually a window that doubled as a door, can be seen in the back drawing room. The hallway off this room leads to the older wing of the house, built in the flounder style, so called because it was flat and narrow with windows on only one side.

The back wing of the house was built in Hagerstown in 1818 by a local potter, Peter Bell. He had originally bought half of Lot 91 in Jonathan Hager's plan of Elizabeth Town in 1802 and erected a log cabin on it. His second building on the other half of the lot was used as a pottery by his son, Peter Bell, Jr. and grandson, John Bell. Examples of their work can be viewed today in one of the dependencies of the main house.

The main section of the house was built for William Price, who, though he served as a Maryland legislator and a U.S. District Court judge, is known today for having been the grandfather of Emily Post, the etiquette expert. The house passed to the Neill family in 1844. They owned it until 1911, when it was purchased by the Miller family. Dr. Victor D. Miller, Jr. built a one-bay addition in 1915. It was his descendants who gave their family home to the Washington County Historical Society, which headquarters here now.

The house has an early 19th-century kitchen with utensils and a large fireplace for cooking. In the basement you'll find a turn-of-the-century country post office complete with a mannequin postmistress. There is also a country store with fully stocked shelves. The patent medicines include Dr. Fahrney's Teething Syrup, concocted from alcohol, morphine and chloroform. Equally potent was Dr. Tenney's Pleasant Syrup, a compound of alcohol and belladonna believed to get rid of round worms. The store has an extensive collection of kitchen utensils, other household tools and farm equipment.

Back upstairs are the music room, the Civil War room and the canal exhibit. The old clock collection and the doll display are quite impressive. You'll discover that the tall clocks, or tall case clocks like the ten in the Miller exhibit, began to be called grandfather clocks in 1898 after a popular song, "My Grandfather's Clock." At the end of the tour you visit the dependencies and see the pottery and carriage collections.

The Miller House is open Wednesday through Friday 1:00 to 4:00 P.M. and Saturday and Sunday 2:00 to 5:00 P.M. It is closed January, February and March. Admission is charged.

Directions: From Baltimore take 1-70 west to Hagerstown. At Exit 32 take Route 40 west into the city to Prospect Street. Turn left, then left again onto Washington Street. The Miller House is on your right.

Washington Monument State Park

You Too Can Salute Washington from Tent, Mountain Top or Stagecoach Inn

The first county named for George Washington also boasts the first monument built in his honor. The townsfolk of Boonsboro in Washington County didn't want to raise money for the monument; they wanted to build it with their own hands as a labor of love. On July 4, 1827, at 7:00 A.M., most of the 500 residents of Boonsboro met at the public square and marched behind the Stars and Stripes to the summit of South Mountain to build their monument.

The mountain had an abundance of "blue rocks" to use for the stone tower. They were carefully cut and laid without mortar to form a dry circular wall. By the end of the day the townsfolk had completed 15 feet of the monument, half of the plan. After that hard work the Declaration of Independence was read, and three veterans of the American Revolution climbed the newly built steps and fired a three-round salute.

They agreed to complete the monument at the end of "the busy season." And, true to their word, once the crops were harvested, they gathered again and added the last 15 feet. Their speedy work gained for Boonsboro the distinction of erecting the first monument dedicated to George Washington. The citizens of Baltimore had raised $178,000 by lottery and started their monument in Washington's honor 12 years earlier, but theirs was still not finished by 1827.

It has been said, "As monuments go, none was ever built with purer or more reverent patriotism." Had it been built with mortar as well, it might have withstood the weather and vandalism that reduced it to rubble within 55 years. In 1882 the Odd Fellows Lodge of Boonsboro rebuilt the monument and added a canopy over the top and a road up the Mountainside. A crack appeared within a decade, and the monument crumbled into ruins once again.

The tower you see today was rebuilt between 1934 and 1936 by the Civilian Conservation Corps. The original cornerstone was reset, and a facsimile of the dedication tablet was added: "Erected in Memory of Washington July 4, 1827 by the citizens of Boonsboro."

If the weather is clear it's worth the climb up the 34 steps to take in the three-state panorama. You will be rewarded by an appealing vista of the Potomac River winding through the rolling countryside. **Washington Monument State Park** now encompasses 108 acres and remains open year-round. There is a circular hiking trail and the Appalachian Trail passes through the park. The Cumberland Valley is a flyway for migratory birds and each year ornithologists gather here for a count of passing hawks and eagles. The park has 13 acres set aside for family tenting.

A small museum in the park can be opened on request. Displays inside the museum include information on George Washington's life, geology of the area and data on the Battle of South Mountain. This important battle of the Civil War occurred on September 14, 1862 and was part of Lee's first campaign into Northern territory (see Gathland State Park). It is also the site of the first major battle fought in Maryland, occurring three days before the Battle of Antietam. Here, Confederate forces under the overall command of General D.H. Hill held off the Army of the Potomac commanded by General George B. McClellan, for an entire day, allowing Lee the chance to regroup his divided forces along the banks of the Antietam Creek. The Battle of South Mountain was the turning point of Lee's first campaign into the North. After being forced from the gaps on the mountain, Lee was actually beginning his withdrawal back to Virginia when the Battle of Antietam (see selection) occurred on September 17th.

General D.H. Hill made his headquarters in a house now known as **Old South Mountain Inn Restaurant**. You can dine at this historic inn among ghosts that date back to around 1750. When the National Road was built outside the inn's door, the stagecoach brought many a distinguished traveler, including Henry Clay and Daniel Webster, who stayed often. In 1876 the inn became the summer residence of Madeleine Vinto Dahlgren, widow of Admiral Dahlgren. She called it her Sky Farm. The inn is open Tuesday through Friday 5:00 to 9:00 P.M.; Saturday, NOON to 10:00 P.M. and Sunday, NOON to 8:00 P.M. Sunday brunch is served 10:30 A.M. to 2:00 P.M. For reservations call (301)371-5400.

Directions: From Baltimore take 1-70 west past Frederick to Exit 49, Alt. Route 40. Take Alt. Route 40 west five miles beyond Middletown to the top of South Mountain (Turners Gap). At Turners Gap, Old South Mountain Inn is on your left and the entrance to Washington State Park is on your right.

Capital Region
Introduction

Montgomery, Prince George's and even Frederick County are now considered part of the suburbs of Washington, D.C. Thousands of their residents commute daily into the city and others spend their leisure hours enjoying the historical and cultural attractions of the Nation's Capital. But they also enjoy the many attractions to be found at home within Maryland's Capital Region.

The tumultuous Great Falls of the Potomac River take first place among the state's many scenic spots. There are spectacular views from the falls' overlook, and there are more serene vistas along the Chesapeake and Ohio Canal, which winds along beside the river from Georgetown to Cumberland. For an understanding of early-day life along the canal, take a ride on the Canal Clipper and experience the locking maneuver that raised the canal boats from one level of the canal to another. When you reflect that there were 74 locks, you'll realize that travel to and from Washington has never been without slow-downs. The canals and the railroads vied to connect the country, and the winner is now celebrated in the Brunswick Railroad Museum.

Another form of transportation in D.C. were trolleys—from the horse-pulled cars of the Lincoln era to the electric cars of the Kennedy years. The National Capital Trolley Museum, located in Wheaton, provides an opportunity to ride a trolley and learn about streetcars from around the world. The place to go to learn about the Wright brothers and aviation firsts is the College Park Aviation Museum. NASA's Goddard Visitor Center and Museum concentrate on space age technology, and at the Paul E. Garber Facility airplane restoration has become a fine art.

Maryland's Capital Region is historically significant, from Fort Washington, built to defend the new country, to sites associated with the Civil War. In addition to the Monocacy National Battlefield, one can visit the homes of three women remembered for their connection to the Civil War. Barbara Fritchie's legendary encounter with Stonewall Jackson was immortalized in John Greenleaf Whittier's classic poem. Mary Surratt was hanged for her involvement with John Wilkes Booth and the assassination of Lincoln. Clara Barton, founder of the American Red Cross, was called the Angel of the Battlefield because of her courageous nursing of the Civil War wounded.

Although Washington's urban megalopolis embraces it, Maryland's Capital Region still has rural connections and scenic oases. The

National Colonial Farm and Oxon Hill Farm recall the rural roots, and the Beltsville Agricultural Research Center develops modern farming techniques—even futuristic ones. Sugarloaf Mountain and Catoctin Mountains both offer hiking or fishing escapes in a wooded setting with panoramic vistas. Wildlife is prevalent at Patuxent River Park, Merkle Wildlife Sanctuary and Woodend. For a close-to-town getaway, it's hard to beat Brookside Gardens with its conservatories, specialty gardens, nature center, innovative playground and miniature railroad.

FREDERICK COUNTY

Barbara Fritchie House and The Home of Roger Brooke Taney

Dramatic Duo

Some students of history may dispute the facts, but if the details are questionable the sentiment and character are true—Barbara Fritchie was a stalwart Union supporter during the Civil War who proudly flew the Stars and Stripes from her upstairs window in Frederick. The story passed down by Frederick townsfolk is that a youngster was sent to warn 96-year-old "Auntie" Barbara that Confederates were going to be marching through town. Fritchie, who also kept a small silk U.S. flag in her Bible, misunderstood the message. Believing it was Federal troops coming, she went out with her small flag and waved it to the passing soldiers. The resulting confrontation was immortalized by the abolitionist poet John Greenleaf Whittier:

> Up rose old Barbara Fritchie then,
> Bowed with her four score years and ten,
> Bravest of all in Frederick-town,
> She took up the flag the men hauled down;
> In her attic-window the staff she set,
> To show that one heart was loyal yet.
> Up the street came the rebel tread,
> Stonewall Jackson riding ahead.

Under his slouched hat left and right
He glanced; the old flag met his sight.
"Halt"—the dust-brown ranks stood fast,
"Fire"—out blazed the rifle-blast.
It shivered the window, pane and sash;
It rent the banner with seam and gash.
Quick, as it fell, from the broken staff
Dame Barbara snatched the silken scarf,
She leaned far out on the window-sill,
And shook it forth with a royal will.
"Shoot, if you must, this old gray head,
But spare your country's flag," she said.
A shade of sadness, a blush of shame,
Over the face of the leader came;
The nobler nature within him stirred
To life at that woman's deeds and word;
"Who touches a hair on yon gray head
Dies like a dog! March on!" he said.

Thus, Barbara Fritchie's name became enshrined among the heroines of American history. Doubt may exist about the details of this Civil War confrontation, but this feisty lady did indeed make her mark on Frederick. She was 40 when she married 26-year-old John Fritchie, son of suspected Tory spy Caspar Fritchie, and the match kept local tongues busy with gossip. The story of her life is reviewed in the orientation video program you'll see before you begin your tour of the **Barbara Fritchie House.**

Rooms both upstairs and down have furnishings that belonged to Barbara and John Fritchie. Many historic heirlooms have been lost due to the repeated flooding of Carroll Creek. In the room where Barbara once entertained local townspeople and family, you'll see the desk where Federal General Jesse Reno penned a letter to his wife on his way through Frederick. He died two days later at the Battle of South Mountain. Upstairs there is the poet's corner dedicated to Whittier's tribute and the bedroom where Barbara died 13 years after her younger husband. Outside there is a triangular garden with 18th-century herbs and flowers.

The Barbara Fritchie House at 154 West Patrick Street is open Monday and Thursday through Saturday from 10:00 A.M. to 4:00 P.M. and Sunday 1:00 to 4:00 P.M. Closed on Tuesday and Wednesday.

Just up the road, at 121 South Bentz Street, is the house of Chief Justice Roger Brooke Taney, who delivered the Supreme Court opinion in the famous 1857 Dred Scott case. Among other things, the decision concluded that under the U.S. Constitution, slaves were not citizens and that freed blacks could not be citizens either—an ember that helped ignite the Civil War. Even though he had freed his own slaves years earlier, Taney felt that the compromise of the

Constitutional Convention was the only safe ground for the Court.

In his earlier years, Taney had set up a law practice in Frederick with Francis Scott Key. Key eventually moved to Baltimore, but Taney, who had married his partner's sister Anne, remained. The house on South Bentz Street was his country home, which he visited on weekends.

Today it is furnished with Taney heirlooms. You'll see the drawing room, dining room and bedroom and outside, the kitchen and slave quarters. Upstairs there is a small collection of memorabilia associated with both Taney and Key. **The Home of Roger Brook Taney** does not have regular hours, so you must arrange your visit in advance by calling The Tourism Council of Frederick County, (301) 663-8687.

Directions: From Baltimore take 1-70 west to Frederick; use the South Market Street exit. Go north on Market to Patrick Street. Turn left for the Barbara Fritchie House. To park, go past the house and turn left after the creek bridge. You can then take a short walk up to the Taney House on South Bentz.

Brunswick Railroad Museum

All Aboard!

The railroad boomtown of Brunswick had its heyday in the late 1800s. Its significance is recognized by the inclusion of 320 acres at the town's center on the National Register of Historic Places. Most of the buildings in this district have survived intact, as has the spirit of the town. It is still essentially a rail community; according to residents, it's the only one of its kind in Maryland.

Russell Baker described the town as it was in the 1920s in his book *Growing Up:* "On the outer edge of my universe lay Brunswick. I first walked in that vision of paradise hand-in-hand with my father, and those visits opened my eyes to the vastness and wonders of life's possibilities. Two miles north of Lovettsville, across the Potomac on the Maryland shore, Brunswick was as distant and romantic a place as I ever expected to see. To live there in that great smoking conurbation, rumbling with the constant thunder of locomotives, filled with the moaning of train whistles coming down the Potomac Valley, was beyond my most fevered hopes. Brunswick was a huge railway center on the B&O Main Line, which linked the Atlantic coast to Chicago and Midwestern steel centers. Approaching it was almost unbearably thrilling. You crossed an endless, rickety cantilevered bridge after pausing on the Virginia bank to pay a one-dollar toll. This was a powerful sum of money, but Brunswick was not for the pinch pennies of the earth."

The railroad arrived in Brunswick in 1850, eight years before the

C&O Canal. To fully appreciate that accomplishment, visit the model railroad layout on the top floor of the **Brunswick Railroad Museum.** This is the kind of place where you're apt to see children tugging at their fathers to get them to "come on." The HO layout is a genuine spellbinder with about 700 pieces of rolling stock—freight cars, locomotives, passenger cars and cabooses—huffing and puffing along a ⅓-mile track. The track represents the actual Chessie line from Union Station in Washington to Brunswick Yard, which is depicted in the layout as it was during the 1950s, when it was seven miles long. This is one of the most extensive model railroads you're ever likely to see. Enormous effort has been expended to depict such stops along the line as Silver Spring, Rockville, Gaithersburg, Dickerson and Point of Rocks. The two main track lines cross rivers, negotiate tunnels and chug through towns.

On the museum's two lower floors you'll discover more about railroading and about the town of Brunswick. The Victorian era is recaptured both at home and at work. Period furniture fills a turn-of-the-century parlor, kitchen and bedroom. Display cases are filled with popular fashions of the 1890s, and household utensils and photographs help complete the picture of home life. Exhibits of the working world feature an extensive collection of railroad tools. The museum itself is located in the 1904 brick Red Man's Lodge, the meeting place of a fraternal organization interested in Indian lore.

To get the feel of the town take time to walk or drive the streets of downtown Brunswick. You'll see Victorian houses and shops as well as the "company town" railroad houses that have changed very little over the years.

The Brunswick Railroad Museum, 40 W. Potomac Street, is open mid-April to January on Saturdays from 10:00 A.M. to 4:00 P.M. and Sundays 1:00 to 4:00 P.M. During the summer months the museum is open on Thursdays and Fridays from 10:00 A.M. to 4:00 P.M. Admission is charged.

Directions: From Baltimore take Route 70 west to Exit 52. At Frederick head southwest on Route 340. Then turn left on Route 17 for Brunswick and take a left on Potomac Street for the museum.

Catoctin Mountains

Where Whiskey Flowed and Water Falls

On quiet days in the mountains during the summer of '29 you'd occasionally hear the thump from the moonshiner's wooden keg; but on July 29, 1929, it was still. No noise betrayed its location.

Two men drove along Big Hunting Creek until they came to a narrow, rough road up the Mountainside draw. They parked and, toting an empty whiskey jug, started up the draw. Before they'd gone very far, they were halted by a rifle-toting still blockader (so called after the blockade runners of earlier seafaring days). They were told to "git" and git they did—but only long enough to assemble the rest of the posse. The raid on the **Blue Blazes Whiskey Still** was under way.

Stories are still told in Frederick County about the shoot-out that ensued. You can hear about this dramatic confrontation from the park rangers who oversee the Blue Blazes Whiskey Still. The present still is not nearly so large as the operation raided back in '29. The original was no fly-by-night setup. It was one of the biggest stills ever destroyed in Maryland, having produced over 25,000 gallons. Such big stills were called steamer stills and held roughly 40 barrels of moonshine. The smaller apparatus operated at **Catoctin Mountain Park** since 1970 was originally a Smoky Mountain still seized by Treasury agents, or revengers. But it wore out, so the usable parts were used to build another old-time model.

A self-guided nature trail leads from the National Park Service Visitor Center (301-663-9388) to the Blue Blazes Still. This is just one of the 16 trails that offer more than 30 miles of hiking within the Catoctin Mountain Park and **Cunningham Falls State Park,** directly across Route 77. You can also take a 14-mile scenic drive along the Catoctin Ridge; it begins at the Visitor Center on Route 77 where you can obtain a map of both parks.

The most scenic spot in these two parks is Cunningham Falls. Even armchair travelers can negotiate the easy ten-minute walk from the parking lot of the William Houck Area. The Lower Cunningham Falls Trail is also easy but the Cliff Trail, which also leads to the falls, is strenuous.

The cascading Cunningham Falls drops 78 feet and offers many photographic possibilities, so be sure to bring a camera. If you have a zoom lens or binoculars you'll be able to enjoy a closeup look at the woodland birds. On hot summer days the falls might whet your urge for a swim but remember there is absolutely no swimming in the falls itself. Head over to the 43-acre Hunting Creek Lake, and there you'll find two sandy public beaches and a bathhouse for changing. On summer weekends it's advisable to arrive by 10:00 A.M. if you want to find a parking spot. Those more interested in fishing than dipping can throw a line in the well-stocked lake or in Big Hunting Creek, a catch-and-return fly stream which has native Brook trout.

Little Hunting Creek is for fishing with artificial lures. A license is required for anyone 16 and over and a trout stamp is required for anyone possessing or fishing the special regulation areas for trout. Canoes can be rented during the summer and on some fall weekends. A fishing pier for the handicapped is accessible by wheelchair.

Other park options include camping, hunting, picnicking, cross-country skiing, horseback riding on designated trails, snowshoeing, sailing and a half-acre recycled tire playground. On the second and third weekends in March, the park hosts a Maple Syrup program. Rangers demonstrate tree tapping, sap boiling and give talks every hour from 10:00 A.M. to 3:00 P.M. A sausage and pancake breakfast is served in the concession stand.

At the southern end of the Cunningham Falls State Park off Route 15, on Route 806, you'll see the remains of the Old Catoctin Furnace, one of three furnaces operated here from 1776 to 1903. The Mountain Tract, as the surrounding land was called, was issued to Benedict Calvert and Thomas Johnson for the purpose of erecting an iron works. In the last triumphant stages of the Revolution this furnace supplied ten-inch shells for the Continental Army. The stack you see today is from the Isabella Furnace built in 1867. Signs along the self-guided trail explain just how this furnace operated. There's a new visitor center at the adjacent Manor Area.

Directions: From Baltimore take I-70 west to Frederick. Head north on Route 15 for 13 miles to Catoctin Furnace. The Manor Area of Cunningham Falls State Park is on the left, Route 806 on the right. To get to the Houck Area of Cunningham Falls State Park continue north on Route 15 to Thurmont. Take Route 77 west, which leads to both the Catoctin Mountain Park Visitor Center and the Houck Area where you can pick up the trail to Cunningham Falls.

Frederick Historic District

Old But Not Square

Florence, Italy, has its lucky bronze boar. Frederick, Maryland, has an iron dog some would say is lucky, too. This faithful pet in front of Dr. John Tyler's house was stolen in 1862 by Confederate troops marching through Frederick. They intended to melt it down for bullets, but the dog was found undamaged after the battle at Sharpsburg (see Antietam selection).

As is true for all historic cities, it is much better to take an escorted walking tour than to head out on your own with a self-guided brochure. The background stories and anecdotes the guides relate add a depth you're unlikely to uncover alone. Brochures can be obtained at the Visitor Center, 19 East Church Street (call (301)663-8687). A walking tour is available every Saturday, Sunday and most Monday holidays, April through December at 1:30 P.M. The tour departs from the Frederick Visitor Center. Approximately ten of the 20 recommended tour sites are along Church Street, where the early German and English settlers established their churches. These include the Evangelical Lutheran Church (1738-1855), Trinity Chapel (1763-1807), All Saints Episcopal Church (1855) and the Evangelical Reformed Church (1848). Natives still regale visitors with the story about Stonewall Jackson attending the Presbyterian church in Frederick. It seems Jackson slept through the impassioned sermon the Reverend Zacharis preached about the necessity of preserving the Union. When leaving the church the Confederate General, who was giving his all to severing the very ties Zacharis was trying to bind, complimented the confused minister on his wonderful sermon.

In addition to these historic old churches, the town also boasts homes of a number of figures from the pages of history. Civil War heroine Barbara Fritchie flew her flag from her Frederick house. A few doors away is the home of John Hanson, first President of the United States under the Articles of Confederation. The home of the author of *American Creed,* William Tyler Page, is around the corner from Dr. John Tyler's on Church Street. Just beyond the perimeters of the inner city walking area is the home of Supreme Court justice Roger B. Taney (see selection).

In 1993, muralist William M. Cochran initiated a community project that transformed the **Carroll Street Bridge**. Hundreds of Frederick volunteers worked on the large-scale mural that transformed the plain concrete bridge, creating the illusion of an old, ivy-covered stone bridge. Participants contributed their ideas to the *trompe l'oeil* stone carvings on the bridge mural. Be sure to get out of the car and take a close look at the carvings and medallions at the top of the bridge columns. The bridge is in downtown Frederick next to the Delaplaine Visual Arts Center on South Carroll Street.

Frederick has two shopping areas you may want to explore, plus Patrick Street's Antiques Row. Between Church Street and Second Street on East Street you'll find Shab Row. This former "shabby area" is now a series of restored log cabins and Federal-style townhouses that have been converted to craft boutiques and antique shops. In the next block, at the intersection of Patrick, Church and East Streets, is **Everedy Square**, a renovated pots and pans factory, with unusual specialty shops and a restaurant.

There are several charming spots where you can enjoy a midday break for lunch or an early dinner. On Market Street you can find saloon-like atmosphere and good food at **Bushwaller's**. The restaurant is housed in a building erected in 1840 for a group of French refugees from the slave uprising in Haiti. Although the saloon has the look of a long-time Frederick landmark, it actually opened in 1981. To enhance the old-time feeling, the walls are lined with old photos, drawings and memorabilia.

Also on Market Street you'll find a quite different but equally appealing eatery, the **Province** at 131 North Market. Colorful quilts hang on the walls and the rear dining room overlooks the restaurant's much-used herb garden.

If you want to take the good taste of Frederick home with you, stop at **McCutcheon's Apple Products** on South Wisner Street. They sell an absolutely delicious country-style apple butter, as well as their

About half of the tour sites in historic Frederick are found on Church Street. All Saints Episcopal is but one of four churches built by German and English settlers.

popular pear butter, jellies, preserves and cider—all made at this family operated business.

Directions: From the Baltimore Beltway (I-695) take I-70 west to Frederick. At Frederick, use the Patrick Street/Historic District exit and follow the signs to the Visitor Center.

Grotto of Lourdes and National Shrine of St. Elizabeth Ann Seton

Contemplative Combination

Two shrines in Emmitsburg provide inspiration for the devout of various denominations. The **Grotto of Lourdes** was the first Catholic Shrine established in the 13 original states. Father Dubois came to western Maryland and in 1805 founded St. Mary's Catholic Church. He discovered a cave with a natural spring on a mountainside near his church. Dubois placed a cross in front of the cave. Subsequently other priests added paths and a fountain. In 1875 Patrick Duffy, a seminarian at Mount St. Mary's College, decided this would be an ideal place for a replica of the famous French shrine known as Lourdes.

A kneeling statue of St. Bernadette of Lourdes reminds visitors of the French saint, but she is not the only saint remembered here. There is a replica of Our Lady of Lourdes as she appeared to St. Bernadette. The path to the shrine is flanked with azaleas and rhododendron, particularly scenic in spring when the blossoms contrast to the mountain greenery. At the base of the path there is a 120-foot campanile with 14 bells. A gilded bronze statue of Mary, Mother of God, crowns the bell tower. Over one million visitors come to the Grotto of Lourdes annually.

Near the parking lot you'll see a replica of the log cabin that Mother Seton and her followers used for six weeks when they first arrived in Emmitsburg in 1809. This cabin is an invitation for you to continue investigating the years Mother Seton spent in Emmitsburg. Your next stop should be the **National Shrine of St. Elizabeth Ann Seton,** approximately two miles away on Route 15 north.

The life and work of St. Elizabeth Ann Seton, who is credited with having founded the parochial school system in the United States, are presented at the Visitor Center of the National Shrine. A 14-minute video provides background, which lends greater significance to the pictorial story, exhibits and personal memorabilia on display. If you want to study each panel of the displays, you should plan to spend an hour or more here. Daughters of Charity are available to answer any questions you may have.

If you have time for a leisurely visit, you can follow "The Seton Way," a self-guided walking tour. The first stop is the 200-year-old

Stone House, where Mother Seton established her religious community after moving out of the log cabin. When speaking of the Stone House, Pope John XXIII said, "In a house that was very small, but with ample space for charity, she sowed a seed in America which by Divine Grace grew into a large tree."

The second stop is the White House where she began the Catholic Parochial School System in 1810. Next come the Mortuary Chapel (1846), Cemetery and Basilica which contains the Altar of the Relics of St. Elizabeth Seton.

The Spartan furnishings in the house reveal the simple life-style of Mother Seton and her followers. It is fascinating to learn that she arrived in Emmitsburg by covered wagon. Hers was virtually a frontier existence for a time.

Life improved when she and her 16 residents moved into the "White House" in February 1810. Here she finally had ample room to teach her ever-expanding enrollment drawn from all races and religions. The first floor of the White House consisted of a chapel and classroom. The second floor provided sleeping quarters for the children and students while the third floor was occupied by the sisters. The classroom has authentic furnishings from Mother Seton's tenure. There is a grandfather clock made by an Emmitsburg craftsman and flanked on the walls by samplers stitched by the school's sisters and boarders.

The chapel on the first floor retains its original altar. You can see where Mother Seton knelt to receive communion. Adjoining the chapel is the room where she died on January 4, 1821. There is a replica of her bed, which was on wheels so it could be moved to permit her to participate in the daily Mass.

The last stop on the walking tour is the cemetery. Mother Seton was originally buried beside an oak tree next to her sister-in-law, Harriet Seton. In 1846 a mortuary chapel was completed for her remains at the request of her son, William Seton. At the time of her beatification by Pope John XXIII in 1962 her remains were exhumed and placed in a small bronze casket. In 1968 they were transferred to a resting place beneath the altar of St. Elizabeth Ann in the Shrine Chapel at St. Joseph's Provincial House of the Daughters of Charity. At her canonization on September 14,1975, Pope Paul VI said, "Elizabeth Ann Seton is a Saint. She is the first daughter of the United States of America to be glorified with this incomparable attribute."

The Seton Shrine is open daily 10:00 A.M. until 4:30 P.M. except on Christmas, the last two weeks in January, Easter, Thanksgiving and on Mondays from November to April. The Eucharistic Liturgy is celebrated Saturday and Sunday at 9:00 A.M.

Directions: From Baltimore take I-695 to I-795 to Route 140 west to Emmitsburg. Make a left at the town square onto Seton Avenue and go ¼ mile to the Seton Shrine. Or take I-695 to I-70 west to Frederick, then take Route 15 north to Emmitsburg. Make a left onto S. Seton Avenue and go ½ mile to the Seton Shrine on the right.

This imposing campanile stands near Emmitsburg at the entrance to the replica of the Grotto of Lourdes, the first Catholic shrine established in the 13 original states.

Lilypons Water Gardens

Fish 'n' Fry

Lilypons can make two claims to fame: it is the largest propagator of ornamental aquatic plants in the country (perhaps in the world), and it is the smallest town in Maryland. Both distinctions were an outgrowth in a very real sense of the ripple effect.

C. Leicester Thomas, Frederick County farmer and businessman, began growing water lilies and raising goldfish on his 275-acre farm in a pond near the road. The beauty of the flowers and darting fish caught the attention of passing motorists. Before long Leicester Thomas was selling enough plants and fish to warrant expanding his hobby into a business. Thus **Lilypons Water Gardens** (originally named Three Springs Fisheries) was born.

Having founded a business that from its earliest days in 1917 sold a great deal of its merchandise by mail (now it is about 60% mail order), Thomas needed a post office. He was an enthusiastic fan of Lily Pons, a star of the New York Metropolitan Opera as well as Hollywood films. Thomas wrote the diva that if she had no objections he would like to name his business and post office in her honor. She readily assented and even attended the post office dedication on June 22, 1936. For years she regularly mailed her Christmas cards from the Lilypons Post Office. A Lily Pons Festival, celebrated the third weekend of June, marks the anniversary of her visit.

Though the setting remains much as it was, the business has become a major industry with offices on the second floor of the old farm house. There are now 100 ponds at Lilypons, a second facility in Brookshire, Texas and a third near Palm Springs, California.

The farm is open 51 weeks a year (closed Christmas week), but the best time to visit is during June, July and August when the lilies and lotus bloom. Contrary to expectation the baby goldfish are not gold in early summer but rather gray-black. The fish fry are allowed to grow to two inches, then harvested and sold.

Scavenger birds find the fish delectable. A keen-eyed osprey, attracted by the fish's bright colors, can consume as much as $300 worth of goldfish or Koi (Imperial Japanese carp) in a day. While the birds threaten profits, they delight visitors. Herons, egrets, bitterns, osprey and kingfishers and also such waterfowl as wood ducks, mallards and migratory geese might be spotted.

Only 45 miles from Baltimore and 35 miles from Washington, Lilypons Water Gardens is open Monday through Saturday from 10:00 A.M. to 5:00 P.M. and Sunday NOON to 5:00 P.M. March through October. From November through February hours are 10:00 A.M. to 3:00 P.M. Monday through Friday.

Directions: From Baltimore take 1-70 west about 40 miles to Exit 54. Turn right taking Route 85 (Buckeystown Pike) south eight miles to Lilypons Road and turn left. Proceed one mile to Lilypons Water Gardens on your left. From the Washington Beltway (I-495) take I-270 north 26 miles to Exit 26. Bear right taking Route 80 west for 1.5 miles. Turn left on Park Mills Road south for 3 miles. Turn right on Lilypons Road for 0.5 miles.

Linganore Winecellars at Berrywine Plantation

Time for Wine

Day trippers like variety in their destinations. A brief stop at a local winery offers a change of pace. There are three vineyards in Frederick County, any one of which can be combined with a visit to the region's historic and natural attractions.

You can drop in on the Aellens. They—like many families in Virginia, Pennsylvania, New York, Oregon and other grape-growing states—own and operate a vineyard and winery. In fact, the Aellens' **Linganore Winecellars at Berrywine Plantation** is the oldest in the county. Son and winemaker Anthony Aellen describes it as "a hobby that got out of hand." Anthony explains that his parents, Jack and Lucille, moved to the former 230-acre dairy farm in 1972 and began planting grapes. His grandfather gave them his hand-operated equipment when he stopped making wine for himself. By 1976 the first grapes were crushed in the old dairy barn, signaling its conversion into a winery. By 1983, the federal government designated the "Linganore" as Maryland's first Grape Growing Area.

The Aellens have planted hybrids in the Linganore and make over 30 award-winning dry and sweet wines from their grapes, as well as from berries and honey. In the winery's modern tasting room, Lucille Aellan helps visitors with the tasting, describing each wine and how it can be used in food. She has a cookbook with additional suggestions available along with the wines and other items in the gift shop.

Linganore Winecellars hosts a wide variety of indoor and outdoor events annually, including monthly festivals from May to October (excepting September) with live bands, food, guided tours and crafts. For details call (410) 795-6432 or check out their website at www.Linganore-wine.com.

Linganore is open daily from 10:00 A.M. to 6:00 P.M. except Sunday, when it opens at NOON.

Elk Run Vineyards and Winery was established in 1980 in the state's Piedmont region. This winery blends advanced technologies from California with old world viniferia grapes. You can visit for tours and tastings at this Mt. Airy area winery, operated by Fred and Carol Wilson, from Wednesday to Saturday from 10:00 A.M. to 5:00 P.M.

and Sunday from 1:00 to 5:00 P.M. For information on the winery and on its special events, call (410) 775-2513 or check out their website at www.alantech.net/elkrun.

In 1982, Bill and Lois Loew established **Loew Vineyards**. They grow both vinifera and French-American grapes at their Mt. Airy winery. You can sample their estate-bottled wines, tour the winery and purchase your favorites on Saturday from 10:00 A.M. to 5:00 P.M. and Sunday 1:00 to 5:00 P.M. For more information call (301) 831-5464.

Directions: Take I-70 west 30 miles to Exit 62 for New Market. Turn right on Route 75 north for 4.5 miles. Then turn right on Glissans Mill Road for 4 miles to the winery on the right. From Washington, take I-270 northwest for 21 miles to Exit 22 for Hyattstown. Follow Route 75 north signs for 14 miles from the end of the exit ramp. Then turn right on Glissans Mill Road and continue 4 miles to the winery on the right. For Elk Run, take I-70 to the Mt. Airy exit and turn right on Route 27. Continue for 8 miles to Taylorsville and turn left on Route 26. Elk Run is 2½ miles on the left. From Washington take I-270 to Father Hurley Highway and turn right on Route 27 and follow above directions. Loew Vineyards is also on Route 26 in Mt. Airy. It is located at 14001 Liberty Road (Route 26).

Monocacy National Battlefield and National Museum of Civil War Medicine

Defeat Saved the Day

In July 1864, two years after the heavy losses General Lee experienced while trying to carry the war into the North at the Battle of Antietam (see selection), Confederate troops fought again in the Frederick area. Although this time they won the battle, they were prevented from taking the capital. The last campaign to carry the war into the North failed.

Confederate troops under General Jubal Early marched north to the fields outside Frederick in hopes they could divert Union troops from their siege of Petersburg—the longest siege in American history. Grant had tried unsuccessfully to break through Lee's defenses in June 1864, but the Confederates had held them off. Jubal's northward raid had the desired effect. Grant sent a division under General Ricketts, then a full corps under General H.G. Wright to protect Washington.

Until these troops arrived, it was up to Major General Lew Wallace (who would later write *Ben Hur*) and his 2,300-man force, most of which had never seen battle, to stop Early's troops. They met in the fields outside Frederick on July 9, 1864. Wallace was not sure if the Confederates were heading for Baltimore or Washington, so he entrenched his men at Monocacy Junction, a site three miles southeast of Frederick where the major roads to both cities, as well as the Baltimore and Ohio Railroad, all converged. If he could hold them at this junction, he could protect both cities.

Wallace positioned his men along a six-mile stretch of the Monocacy River, thus protecting the Georgetown Pike turnpike bridge leading to Washington and the bridge on the National Road to Baltimore as well as the railroad bridge. Although his men were stretched thinly, the higher bank on the river's east side provided a natural breastwork for some of his men. Others sought protection behind farmers' fences or dug crude trenches with available farm tools. Assistance came with the arrival of the 2,500-man division under James B. Ricketts.

After Confederate General Rodes's division encountered the troops defending the National Road bridge and General Ramseur's men, the Federals on the Georgetown Pike bridge, Early decided to try a flanking operation using John McCausland's cavalry. Some of the heaviest fighting occurred when these troops attacked Wallace's left flank. The numerically superior Confederate force, numbering around 15,000, forced the Union troops to sacrifice their position. A three-pronged attack on the Federal left flank by Confederate brigades kept up a steady barrage and forced them back still farther. By late in the day, the Federal troops began retreating to Baltimore, after 1,294 of their men were either killed, wounded or captured.

Confederate losses fell between 700 and 900 killed, missing or wounded. Equally damaging to their cause was the loss of a day's time. By the time Early's men arrived at the earthworks of Fort Stevens which guarded Washington, they could see the Union troops under Wright's command marching into the fort. Early soon withdrew his troops across the Potomac River, and Washington survived its final test of the war.

In writing about the Monocacy battle, General Grant said, "...General Wallace contributed on this occasion, by the defeat of the troops under him, a greater benefit to the cause than often falls to the lot of a commander of an equal force to render by means of a victory." Wallace recognized this, as he retreated from the battlefield, he ordered the fallen men be buried on the battlefield and a monument erected reading: "These men died to save the National Capital, and they did save it."

You can take a four-mile round-trip auto tour of **Monocacy National Battlefield** that begins at the small visitor center and continues to three stops on the battlefield. At the center an electric map will orient you to the battlefield and you can pick up an auto tour map. There are five monuments on the battlefield.

Monocacy National Battlefield is open daily at no charge from 8:00 A.M. to 4:30 P.M. from Memorial Day to Labor Day. The rest of the year it is open Wednesday through Sunday.

During the four-year Civil War, the Union and Confederate armies lost hundreds of thousands of lives from battlefield wounds and disease. The battles fought in this area, Antietam and Monocacy, saw heavy losses on both sides. After the former, there were 8,000 wounded in the 29 hospitals set up in Frederick (this was at a time when the population of Frederick was also 8,000). In the heart of historic Frederick in an 1832 building that was used as an embalming station after the Battles of Antietam and South Mountain, you can visit the **National Museum of Civil War Medicine** (NMCWM). This museum is the center for the study and interpretation of the medical history of the Civil War. You will discover that this war-time medicine brought changes in surgical techniques, reconstructive surgery, women's role in medicine, hospital care, triage, sanitation and embalming.

There are self-guided tours of the museum and a docent-lead Civil War Walking Tour every weekend from April through December 1. The museum is open Monday through Saturday from 10:00 A.M. to 4:00 P.M. and Sunday 11:00 A.M. to 4:00 P.M. There is a nominal charge. You'll find educational items in the museum store.

Directions: From Baltimore take I-70 west to Frederick, then head south on Route 355, the Georgetown Pike. The visitor center is on the left, one-tenth of a mile past the Monocacy River Bridge. The NMCWM is in downtown Frederick; use the South Market Street Exit from I-70. Go north on Market to Patrick; the museum is at 48 E. Patrick Street.

New Market

To Market, To Market, To Buy...

"Everything old is new again" could well be the motto of **New Market**, the Antiques Capital of Maryland. This tiny town, virtually one long street, boasts more than 35 antique shops for visitors to explore.

Now on the National Register of Historic Places, New Market has been serving travelers since it was founded in 1793. Its location on the National Pike between Baltimore and Frederick made it an ideal spot to overnight. There were six to eight inns to accommodate the traffic, most with barns and pens for the livestock.

Today there are two charming bed and breakfast inns on Main Street. Jane Rossig's **Strawberry Inn**, (301)865-3218, is the oldest in Frederick County. Practically next door is the **National Pike Inn**, (301)865-5055, run by Tom and Terry Rimel. As befits this antique haven, the rooms in both country inns are furnished with period pieces.

71

In order to maintain the ambience of New Market, the only stores permitted by the town council are antique shops, aside from a country store and service-related businesses that cater to the community. The old-time, small-town flavor is remarkably intact and the diverse architectural styles make a stroll down Main Street worthwhile even for those with only a minimal interest in antiques.

Antique enthusiasts should plan to spend at least half a day here, leaving time for a meal at **Mealey's Inn**. The name is derived from Dick and Nellie Mealey, who, with a partner, bought the Utz Hotel, as it was then called, in 1919. The inn's oldest section is a colonial log house built the same year the town was founded. It probably served as both house and shop. Additions and changes saw Mealey's evolve into a Colonial brick, then a late Federal brick design. The main dining room was once the Pump Room, and the old pump that once furnished water for the Utz Hotel guests now rests in front of the fireplace. Today Mealey's is owned by the Jefferies, and it is more popular than ever. Reservations are a must on weekends. Call (301)865-5488.

New Market is worth visiting on any pleasant weekend, but in late September during the weekend-long New Market Days it is even more fun. The streets are lined with craftspeople demonstrating and selling their wares, and there is a festive atmosphere in the shops.

All of the shops and restaurants are open on weekends. Mondays all shops and Mealey's are closed. Mealey's opens on Tuesdays, and from Wednesday through Friday about 15 other shops are open also. When you arrive in town stop in front of the Post Office and pick up a guide to Historic New Market at the Visitors Information Bulletin Board.

Directions: From Baltimore take I-70 west. Use Exit 62 (Route 75) and proceed north one block for the left turn onto Route 144 and Main Street in New Market.

Rose Hill Manor and Schifferstadt Architectural Museum

Carriages and Crafts, Farm and Flowers

Rose Hill Manor is an historical house museum planned with children in mind. The downstairs rooms contain hands-on exhibits that give youngsters a chance to be actively involved with the 18th century.

This rural Georgian manor house was built in the early 1790s by John Grahame and his wife Anne Johnson Grahame. The house was built on land given to the couple by the bride's father Thomas Johnson, the first elected governor of Maryland. One of the most sig-

Rose Hill Manor, in a 43-acre park, invites youngsters to touch and try as many as 300 different household tools including such items as a loom, rolling pin and kraut cutter.

nificant contributions of Thomas Johnson's long and distinguished political career was his nomination of George Washington as Commander-in-Chief of the Continental Army. After Governor Johnson retired, he spent the last years of his life living at Rose Hill with his daughter and son-in-law.

Rose Hill Manor guides recall the days when Governor Johnson lived with the Grahames. The costumed interpreters invite visitors into the touch-and-see parlor, allowing time for younger guests to enjoy the 18th-century toys and dress-up clothes. The textile room gives visitors a chance to try their hand at quiltmaking or at carding wool to prepare it for spinning. A sizeable number of the 300 items included in the Rose Hill Children's museum are found in the kitchen. There youngsters can churn imaginary butter, turn the hand of a vegetable chopper or roll dough for beaten biscuits. The hands-on approach is not followed in the upstairs rooms. The bedrooms and governor's study are furnished with valuable period pieces.

The manor house is but one part of this 43-acre park. There are five additional areas to explore. On weekends when Rose Hill hosts special events, a blacksmith demonstrates old-world skills in the fully stocked work area. Speaking of old world, a log cabin has been moved onto the park grounds. The rustic home, furnished with handmade furniture and utensils, takes you back to the days of the settlers who made Frederick County their home in the early 18th century.

As you make your way from one area of the park to the next, take time to smell the flowers. The 18th-century garden is filled with such aromatic herbs as mint, lavender, oregano and basil. A vegetable patch, like the one that once served the manor's needs, is in full growth by mid-summer. Flowers were grown to grace the table. Sour cherry, apple, pear and plum trees fill the orchard beyond the gardens.

Two museums, the Farm Museum and the Carriage Museum, provide exhibits of the nitty-gritty tools of trade for farming and the conveyances of an earlier era. There are hundreds of farm implements in the bank barn and dairy barn. Exhibits depict the evolution from wooden plows to steam tractors. The Carriage Museum has more than 20 restored vehicles ranging from the buggy with the fringe on top to a Russian sleigh.

Walk-in tours of Rose Hill Manor are available Monday through Saturday from 10:00 A.M. to 4:00 P.M. and Sunday 1:00 to 4:00 P.M. April through October, and weekends in November and December. The house is closed January and February. Throughout the year colonial craft demonstrations are scheduled, highlighting such 19th-century skills as soapmaking, candle dipping, quilting, carpentry, broom making, spinning and waving. Check the Calendar of Events for specific happenings.

Just a mile from Rose Hill along Carroll Creek is **Schifferstadt Architectural Museum,** another 18th-century house, but one that is far more modest. Schifferstadt, a stone manor house was completed in 1756, making it the oldest house still standing in Frederick. It provides a window into life in the 1750s as well as early German-American construction techniques. An historically accurate 18th-century German garden completes the story of everyday farm life at the site.

The house was built by Joseph Brunner and his son, Elias. They named it after their family's birthplace near Mannheim, Germany. The Brunner family name is first mentioned in the Frederick area rent rolls in 1744, two years before Joseph Brunner purchased the land on which Schifferstadt was built. The 303 acres cost ten English pounds, or about half of a year's salary at that time.

The walls of locally quarried sandstone measure over 2½ feet thick. The stones, though uniformly laid at the front, are haphazard on the back and sides. The native oak beams are all hand-hewn. You can still see the wooden pegs that pin the braces together. The house tour gives you a chance to see the underside of the wooden roof beams in the attic, where you'll also get an unusual perspective of the huge vaulted "wishbone" chimney. This architectural tour covers the cellar as well as the attic. The cellar, also vaulted, extends beneath the northern half of the house, which was the original portion. The wing was added during the 1820s. Though thee house is not furnished, you will see the original five-plate jamb stove dated 1756. It was cast in Mannheim, Germany, and bears a German inscription, "Where your treasure is, there is your heart." The brick-wing addition has a seven-foot squirrel-tail, brick bake oven.

The wing also houses the museum shop, with an eclectic mix of gifts, many handmade, as well as books, items of local interest and specialty foods. Schifferstadt is open Tuesday through Saturday 10:00 A.M. to 4:00 P.M. and Sunday NOON to 4:00 P.M. from April to December.

Directions: From Baltimore take 1-70 west to U.S. 15 north in Frederick. For Rose Hill take Motter Avenue Exit off U.S. 15. For Schifferstadt take Rosemont Avenue Exit; the museum is at the intersection of the exit ramp.

Sugar Loaf Mountain

How Sweet It Is!

On a clear day, though you can't see forever, you can see a great deal of the picturesque Maryland countryside from 1,283-foot **Sugar Loaf Mountain.** It stands alone, a landmark for those traveling across the surrounding terrain. Reportedly first charted in 1707, the mountain was named by early settlers who felt it resembled a loaf of sugar bread.

From Sugar Loaf's summit you'll see Virginia's Bull Run to the south, the Catoctin and Blue Ridge mountains to the west, and Frederick Valley to the north. Mention of Sugar Loaf appears in many historic journals. General Braddock passed by in 1775 on his way to the disastrous Battle of Fort Duquesne. During the Civil War the mountain was used as a Union lookout post. From here a sentry spotted General Robert E. Lee leading his men across the Potomac River just before the Battle of Antietam. Afterward, wounded soldiers from both North and South were treated at log cabins still standing at the base of Sugar Loaf Mountain.

Gordon Strong discovered the charms of Sugar Loaf during a 1902 vacation. He was so impressed he purchased many acres of it and gradually acquired the entire mountain. In 1912 Strong built a Georgian colonial mansion, Stronghold, high on Sugar Loaf's slopes. One of the illustrious guests here was President Franklin Delano

Roosevelt. Roosevelt was as taken with Sugar Loaf as Strong had been, and wanted to acquire the mountainside estate as a presidential retreat. In spurning Roosevelt's overtures, Strong suggested the President turn his attention to the 10,000 acres already owned by the government outside Thurmont. At Roosevelt's direction, Shangri-La, a mountain hideaway, was built on the federal land. During the Eisenhower administration it was renamed Camp David after the President's son.

Although few visitors since Roosevelt have considered buying Sugar Loaf, many have been captivated by its scenic beauty. In fact, it is now protected as a National Natural Landmark. There are trails along Sugar Loaf's slopes, and if you have a mount you can enjoy the riding trail.

If mountain climbing, even on little mountains, is too strenuous for you, try the winding road that leads almost to the top. The road has numerous overlooks along the way. Sugar Loaf can be visited from 7:00 A.M. to sunset daily. A snack bar is open on summer weekends and holidays, and there are picnic tables and rest rooms.

Directions: From Baltimore take I-70 west about 30 miles to exit for New Market and Route 75. Go south on Route 75 to Hyattstown and turn right onto Route 109. Pass under 1-270 and go another 3.3 miles to Comus. Turn right on Route 95 and go 2.5 miles to Sugar Loaf Mountain.

MONTGOMERY COUNTY

Brookside Gardens
at Wheaton Regional Park

A Bloomin' Retreat

Once discovered, **Brookside Gardens at Wheaton Regional Park** may well become a destination you'll return to any time during the year. It is close enough to the suburbs of Baltimore and Washington to be an easy drive, and diverse enough to be consistently interesting for all ages.

From early spring through late fall the many specialty areas of the 50-acre garden complex are in flower, and in the coldest months the blossoming continues in the conservatories. Tropical plants in the glass-enclosed gardens provide a backdrop for the seasonal displays that flank a meandering path along an indoor stream. Camera buffs appreciate the wooden footbridge for pictures.

The big holiday display lasts well into January—glorious poinsettias, cyclamen, Jerusalem cherries and many other winter flowering plants. The next major exhibit is the winter/spring extravaganza of lilies, azaleas, fuchsias, hydrangeas and forced bulbs. By late March the spring bulbs begin to bloom outdoors, peaking in late April with an outstanding display of tulips. During the azalea season the paths of Brookside are lined with brilliantly colored shrubs. In June more than 87 cultivars of roses reach their peak, continuing their bloom until the first hard frost. New varieties of annuals can also be seen in the trial garden. All summer long there is a riot of colorful annuals in the gardens and a wide selection of herbs in the Fragrance Gardens.

In the autumn the outdoor garden makes a final burst with chrysan-themums, then in November the show moves indoors with the fall display. This is a real winner; multiple varieties of chrysanthemums grow in cascades, on upright columns and even as miniature trees.

One of the most charming areas at Brookside is the Japanese-style garden—worth exploring even on mild winter days. A Japanese Teahouse sits amid tranquil ponds, surrounded by attractive trees and shrubs.

There are wheelchair routes at Brookside Gardens, also a horticul-ture library and horticultural information sheets. Guided tours are given and educational classes offered. No pets, food or drinks are permitted. A generous donation by Elizabeth A. Turner resulted in a three million dollar Brookside Gardens Visitor Center which opened in 1997. The center's auditorium will be used for educational pro-grams and plant society meetings. There are also classrooms, work-shops, a library, offices and a gift shop.

The Wheaton Regional Park's **Brookside Nature Center** is only a short walk along a path from the visitor center parking lot. Here you can learn about the flora and fauna of the surrounding forest through exhibits, films and guided walks.

Families will want to stop at the park's **Adventure Playground** with slides and climbing structures for children of all ages, including those with physical challenges. Behind the playground is the well-stocked 5-acre Pine Lake, where fishermen can try their luck catching bass, bluegill, crappie and catfish.

Youngsters enjoy riding the **Wheaton Line Railroad**, a 24-gauge reproduction of an 1865 steam train. The two-mile track travels over the meadow and through the woods before arriving back at the sta-tion. The park's carousel is also a hit. Wheaton Regional Park has activities around the calendar. If it's not picnicking, hiking, riding trails and ballfields outdoors, it's tennis and ice skating indoors.

Directions: From Baltimore take 1-95 south to the Washington Beltway (1-495) and go west to Exit 31A (Georgia Avenue). Go north on Georgia Avenue to Randolph Road and turn right. Then make a right on Glenallan Avenue for Brookside Gardens and Brookside Nature Center. The playground, carousel, and train station can all be reached by turning right off Georgia Avenue onto Shorefield Road.

Brookside Gardens in Wheaton Regional Park offers floral extrava-
ganzas every day of the year except Christmas. The park has a steam
train for children and an Old MacDonald's Farm. BROOKSIDE GARDENS

Clara Barton National Historic Site and Glen Echo Park

The Angel of the Battlefield

Clara Barton gave this account of one of her experiences at Antietam: "A man lying upon the ground asked for drink. I stooped to give it and, having raised him with my right hand, was holding the cup to his lips with my left, when I felt a sudden twitch of the loose sleeve of my dress. The poor fellow sprang from my hands and fell back quivering in the agonies of death. A ball had passed between my body and the right arm which supported him, cutting through the sleeve, and passing through his chest from shoulder to shoulder." (See Antietam selection.)

Barton was working as a clerk in the Washington, D.C., patent office immediately before the Civil War. With the outbreak of hostilities she devoted her time to aiding injured soldiers. Filling wagons with needed supplies—bandages, linens, anesthetics and oil lanterns—she worked with the field surgeons at the Battles of 2nd Manassas, Antietam, Fredericksburg, the Wilderness and Spotsylvania (1861-65).

After the war the Angel of the Battlefield made it her mission to locate and identify soldiers the U.S. Army had listed as missing. Total Civil War casualties numbered 359,528, with only 172,400 identified. In four years of grueling work Barton located and identified 22,000 missing soldiers. She was instrumental in having the burial grounds of the infamous Andersonville prison in Georgia declared a national cemetery in 1865. It contained the graves of nearly 13,000 Union soldiers.

Such work took its toll and Barton suffered an emotional breakdown. She went to Europe to recover, but rather than rest she became involved in the great cause of her life, the International Red Cross. Barton's supposed convalescence included duty with the Red Cross in the Franco-Prussian War. She returned to the United States and devoted herself to establishing the American Red Cross, of which she served as president from 1881 to 1904. Barton significantly expanded the scope of Red Cross relief work by involving the organization in peacetime aid, such as the Johnstown Flood of 1889 and the Galveston Hurricane in 1900.

On a hilltop overlooking the C&O Canal and Potomac River, Edward and Edwin Baltzley built Miss Barton a house in 1891 as part of their Glen Echo development. Now a National Historic Site, this Victorian house is architecturally intriguing. From the main hallway you look up to railed galleries on the second and third floors, the latter gallery seemingly suspended over the floors below. A top floor bedroom seems to hang from the sides of the house with no visible means of support, a delightful structural oddity.

One thing this house doesn't lack is closets; the main hallway is lined with them. These storage areas were used for disaster supplies. Two rooms are re-creations of the home offices Barton used from 1897 to 1904, and the house still has some of her furniture. She spent the last 15 years of her life in this house and died at Glen Echo on April 12, 1912, at age 90. After your tour, you are apt to agree with one of Miss Barton's guests who wrote, "I often think of your nice warm house, so full of your individuality. The crime of being commonplace can never be laid to your door—and your home is just as it should be, unlike anybody's else."

Barton was not without her flaws. She was ousted from her position with the Red Cross not only because members felt she was too old but because they found her disorganized and unbusinesslike. There was even talk of a congressional investigation of her financial records before her resignation in 1904.

The heroism and the flaws of this remarkable woman are presented during a guided tour of the house. The **Clara Barton National Historic Site** is open daily at no charge. The house is shown only by

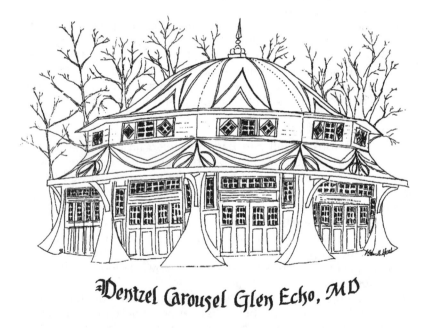

Dentzel Carousel Glen Echo, MD

Folk art specialists consider the Dentzel Carousel at Glen Echo one of the finest in the country. Hand-carved, it was built in 1922.

ALANA MAUBURY HUNTER

guided tour. These are given on the hour from 10:00 A.M. to 4:00 P.M. Closed Thanksgiving, Christmas & New Year's Day. Call (301)492-6245 for details.

Barton accepted Glen Echo for her home because she was interested in the Chautauqua self-improvement movement, which used facilities at Glen Echo. She was considerably less enthusiastic about the amusement park built here after 1899. The only reminder of the artistic Chautauqua years is Glen Echo's old stone tower, now an art gallery, which was used for Chautauqua gatherings in 1891. However, the spirit of the Chautauqua does remain; **Glen Echo Park** now offers workshops and classes in the arts. Artists create, teach, demonstrate and sell their work on the grounds.

The only working reminder of the amusement park era is the hand-carved Dentzel Carousel, which is considered by folk art specialists to be one of the finest carousels in America. There is always a rush to ride the carousel animals that go up and down while the music plays on and on. You can hop on your favorite on Wednesday, Thursday, Saturday or Sunday from May through September. In addition to carousel rides, summer activities include performances for children by the Adventure Theatre (301)320-5331 and other cultural events. For general information on Glen Echo call (301)492-6282.

Directions: From the Baltimore Beltway, take 1-95 south to the Washington Beltway (1- 495). Head west on 1-495 to Exit 40, for the Clara Barton Parkway to Glen Echo. Exit from the parkway at MacArthur Boulevard and turn left. Proceed on MacArthur Boulevard to Oxford Road, turn left; signs will indicate the parking lot for the Clara Barton National Historic Site.

Great Falls, Chesapeake & Ohio Canal (Lower) and Seneca

On the Rocks

On sunny afternoons the rocky promontories at **Great Falls** become a rookery of sunbathers. Visitors who take the trail to an overlook get a spectacular view of Great Falls. The trail is a self-guided nature walk that teaches you about the surrounding bedrock terrace forest. Visitors are forwarned that some have drowned in the Potomac while sunbathing or rock hopping (which is not only dangerous but prohibited).

The best way to experience canal life is to take a boat ride on the **Canal Clipper**, a canal boat that plies the narrow waterway from mid-April. through October. Right after you board the boat the captain blows the giant lock horn and begins the "locking through" maneuver designed to bring the boat up to a higher water level. The barge enters a lock and then a valve is opened, raising the water level eight feet in five minutes. In 1870 there were 74 of these lift-locks on the 185.5 miles of canal stretching from Georgetown to Cumberland.

Once the boat is locked through, mules are hitched up and the one-hour canal voyage begins. The boats usually covered only four miles an hour, the speed limit imposed by the Canal Company so that the wake of the boats would not erode the sides of the canal. It took about ten minutes for each locking through maneuver; with 74 locks that meant a minimum of 12 hours to pass all of the canal's locks. If a boat traveled at the maximum allowable speed of four miles per hour for ten hours a day, it could travel the distance from Cumberland to Georgetown in about six days.

On quiet evenings the boat captain, who often traveled with his entire family, would pull out his harmonica or jew's harp, and passengers and crew alike would join a sing-along. Some of the park interpreters use music in their programs and invite visitors to help recreate these songfests on the boat ride. Other interpreters tell about the history of the C&O Canal.

In the spring and fall the boat trips are Wednesday through Friday at 2:30 P.M. and on weekends at 11:00 A.M. 1:00, 2:30 and 4:00 P.M. From mid-June through mid-September boat rides leave Wednesday through Friday at 11:00 A.M., 1:00 and 2:30 P.M. with an added 4:00 P.M. trip on weekends. Boat tickets go on sale two hours before each departure. They sell out quickly on weekends. For more information and specific times, call (301) 299-3613. There is a per vehicle entrance fee for Great Falls park. Boat rides are also given at the C&O Canal in Georgetown, and tickets for them are sold at the Georgetown Visitor Center on Thomas Jefferson Street. Call (202) 653-5190 for information.

If this glimpse of life aboard the canal boats whets your appetite, you can easily extend your day and visit Riley's Lockhouse in **Seneca** at Lock #24. On weekends from 1:00 to 4:00 P.M. Girl Scouts conduct free tours of this small laches overlooking Seneca Creek and the Potomac River. Youngsters will particularly enjoy the tour led by young girls in Victorian period dresses. The four-room laches is furnished to represent the period 1870-85. John Rile tended the lock from 1892-1924, and he lived in this small house with his wife and their seven children. Different Girl Scout troops sponsor different activities at the laches. Some act out scenes of family life; others engage in demonstrations of crafts and skills. They wash clothes, pop corn, whittle, weave, sing, dance, crochet, garden, sew quilts, make cornhusk dolls, churn butter and play old-time games. These programs are not run from mid-December through February.

After your tour, if you hike a short way up the canal you'll pass the ruins of the Seneca Red Sandstone cutting mill. The Smithsonian Castle in Washington was built from these distinctive stones. You'll also see the turning basin where canal boats were maneuvered to make the return trip to Georgetown.

Directions: From Baltimore take 1-95 south to the Washington Beltway (1-495) and head west to Exit 41. Take the Clara Barton Parkway heading toward Carderock and Great Falls. At the end of the Clara Barton Parkway, turn left onto MacArthur Boulevard which leads directly into the park at Great Falls. From I-270 take Exit 5, Falls Road, heading toward Potomac. Follow Falls Road through Potomac until you come to the end where it intersects with MacArthur Boulevard. At this intersection turn right and you will enter the park.

John Poole House, White's Ferry and Seneca Schoolhouse

Medley Historic Triple

In 1793 when John Poole II built a single-room log store with an overhead sleeping loft, at the crossing of two plantation roads, he never imagined a town would grow around his modest establishment. But this enterprising 24-year-old divided part of the 15 acres given to him by his father into lots. Other merchants purchased the lots, set up stores and formed the nucleus of the town of Poolesville.

The sign over the door of Poolesville's oldest building reads "General Merchandise, John Poole, Jr." The front room of the house features items that might have been sold during the store's operation from 1793 to 1810. You'll see leather hides, leaf tobacco, slabs of bacon and old tools.

Not long after John Poole built his home and business, a lean-to kitchen and second fireplace were added. Between the two huge stone chimneys there is a pent, a rarely seen colonial storage area. Because the stone walls made this one of the only areas of the house not at risk from fires, the family stored their valuables here.

Just outside the kitchen of the **John Poole House** you get a glimpse of the Arboretum; you'll want to explore it before departing. Started in 1976, it features plants indigenous to this part of Maryland before 1850. At certain times of the year plants and herbs are sold at the John Poole Store. In the Herb Garden are annual and perennial culinary herbs, medicinal plants, a dyer's garden and a fragrance garden. An arboretum map and guide help identify and locate the various specimens.

In addition to the original section of the house, there are frame additions built in 1810 and 1866. The upstairs has an original bedroom and a museum area. In the bedroom is a poplar thistle bed with rope webbing a feather mattress, covered by a signed quilt made in 1834 by John Poole II's daughter-in-law, Evalyna W. Hyde.

The museum area has a Civil War collection, much of which was found in and around Poolesville. The town's proximity to

Washington made it a major communication link with the capital. By October 15, 1861, roughly 15,000 Union soldiers were camped in the fields around Poolesville. On sale are copies of a town map drawn by a Union soldier on December 29, 1863, to show his parents where he was living. His map shows gun placements, but they are not shown on the walking tour guide of Poolesville. The churches and many of the houses on the 1863 map still stand.

In September 1862, General Lee wanted to capitalize on the Confederate victory at the Second Battle of Bull Run by carrying the war into the north. Lee staged his first large-scale invasion of the north by crossing the Potomac River at White's Ford. After your tour of the John Poole House, open Sunday NOON to 5:00 P.M. from mid-April through November, continue down Route 107 to **White's Ferry.**

At this crossing the *Jubal A. Early*, the only ferry still operating on the Potomac River, journeys back and forth throughout the day. It runs daily year-round from 5:00 A.M. to 11:00 P.M. The fare is $5.00 round-trip, or $3.00 one-way. The ferry is named for General Jubal Early, who took command of Stonewall Jackson's 13,000-man force after Jackson's death following the Battle of Chancellorsville in May 1863. General Early led his men across the Potomac River just below the ferry landing on July 14, 1864. General Early's was the only Confederate force to come within striking distance of the capital, prompting President Lincoln to have a steamboat standing by on the Potomac in case he needed to be evacuated.

In addition to its historical significance the area around White's Ferry is popular with fishermen, canoeists, bicyclers, hikers and picnickers. You can rent boats here or use the available boat ramps. Fish found include bass, catfish, perch, crappie and carp. Live bait, tackle and licenses are available at White's Ferry Store, also canoes and bicycles to rent.

Poolesville and White's Ferry are part of the Historic Medley District, one of Maryland's early voting districts, where ballots were cast at Mr. Medley's tavern. In the same area, at 16800 River Road, is the **Seneca Schoolhouse,** the only one-room schoolhouse built of stone in Montgomery County. It is open Sundays 1:00 to 5:00 P.M. from March 15 to December 15. Upton Darby, a miller in Seneca, collected money from his neighbors in 1865 to build it, and the red stones were quarried nearby (see C&O Canal National Historical Park selection).

Inside, the old double desks are still lined up. The boys sat on one side of the room and the girls on the other. In the center stands the bench on which the youngsters sat to recite their lessons. Children 6 to 16 attended grades 1 through 7. The desks used by the older students have inkwells; those in the front rows do not. There's a pot-belly stove like the one that warmed the school, but there are no lights. On severely overcast days students were simply dismissed. Classes were taught here from 1866 until 1910 in such subjects as

84

When John Poole II built his single-room log store in 1793 he had no idea it would become the nucleus of the town of Poolesville. Nowadays craft items and plants are sold in the store.

reading, writing, grammar, geography, history, arithmetic, good behavior and orthography. Every Friday afternoon Seneca School had a spelling bee.

A small gift shop sells copies of McGuffy Readers, slates, penny candy that costs 5 cents and a charming children's novel, *Country School Boy*, by Bess Paterson Shipe. Included with the novel is a personal recollection from a former student at Seneca Schoolhouse.

Directions: From Baltimore take I-70 west. At the Route 27 exit, head south. You'll turn left on Route 355 and go a short way to Route 118 where you continue south to the intersection with Route 28 (Darnestown Road). Turn right on Route 28 and continue west. Take a left fork at Route 107 into Poolesville. Signs will indicate the John Poole House on the right at 19923 Fisher Avenue. For White's Ferry continue west on Route 107. For Seneca Schoolhouse go east on Route 107 to Partnership Road and turn right, which leads to River Road. Turn left on River Road and proceed for just a short distance to the Seneca Schoolhouse on the right at 16800 River Road.

National Capital Trolley Museum

Trolleys Hold the Line

The first trolleys in the nation's capital were horse cars that traversed the city during the tumultuous presidency of Abraham Lincoln. The last were electric streamliners that transported passengers during John F. Kennedy's administration a century later. The era of trolleys in Washington ended on January 28, 1962 but some of the streetcars are still running at the **National Capital Trolley Museum** in Wheaton, Maryland.

The man who saved the cars, transit company vice-president A.E. Savage, literally hid some of the streetcars in the Navy Yard Car House so they wouldn't be junked for scrap. Nostalgia buffs who enjoy riding old No. 766, the car that made the District's last run, can thank Mr. Savage and the volunteers who repair, maintain and operate the cars at this trolley museum.

The museum's roster of equipment includes three cars from Austria and two from Germany. The Berlin car was operated during flower festivals in Karlsruhe, Germany. The red, white and black Vienna car has wooden seats and bell-shaped lights. From the U.S. there are cars from New York and Pennsylvania and six from Washington. Long-time residents of the area may recognize car No. 1101, Washington's first PCC streamliner, which entered service in 1937 and celebrated its 50th birthday in 1987. In 1996, the museum acquired a bright red Canadian Light Rail Vehicle which was known in Toronto where it ran as a Red Rocket.

Most of the streetcars stand in the car barns and are brought out only for trolley festivals held on the third Sunday of April (or a week later if this is Easter Sunday) and September. Rides are offered on several cars during museum hours, which are 12:00 to 5:00 P.M. on weekends January through November as well as on Memorial Day, July 4 and Labor Day. During July and August the museum is also open from 11:00 A.M. to 3:00 P.M. on Wednesday. December hours are 5:00 to 9:00 P.M. for Holly Trolleyfest. Closed for Christmas Eve and Day and New Years Eve and Day.

Purchase your ride ticket, at a nominal fee, from the Visitors Center, built to resemble an old-time railroad station. Streetcars leave the station every half-hour. While waiting, check out the model trolley exhibit. The conductor rings the trolley bell, punches the tickets and reminisces about the days when a person could travel anywhere in Washington by streetcar. These gentle rides are a pleasant respite from today's gridlocked beltway scene.

The trolley museum hosts special programs, antique car exhibits and trolley parades, plus movies and lectures. For details call (301) 384-6088.

Directions: From Baltimore take I-95 to the Washington Beltway, I-

The National Capital Trolley Museum displays one of the finest collections of American and European antique trolley cars. Rides are available on some of them.

495, and proceed west to Exit 28 (New Hampshire Avenue). Take New Hampshire Avenue north for 5.4 miles and turn left on Bonifant Road. The museum is at 1313 Bonifant Road in the Northwest Branch Regional Park.

Stonestreet Museum of 19th Century Medicine, Beall-Dawson House and Strathmore Hall Arts Center

Rockville Trio

When you see the medical instruments at the **Stonestreet Museum of 19th Century Medicine** in Rockville, you'll be glad the doctor isn't in. In fact, this is one collection that certainly doesn't evoke nostalgia for the good old days.

Some of the medical tools on display here were put to gruesome uses, and look it. There are sharp blades for amputation and devices for bloodletting. The drugs certainly must have helped patients forget their problems even if they did not cure. Many of the old nostrums included a considerable amount of opiates. The human skeleton on display is a favorite with the younger set.

This museum was once the office of Dr. Edward E. Stonestreet, who practiced medicine in the Rockville area from 1852-1903. During the Civil War, Dr. Stonestreet was an Examining Surgeon for local Maryland draftees. A photograph of the doctor, his wife and their six daughters hangs in the museum. His saddlebags and boots still hang behind the door. He kept them in the office to be used on his frequent house calls. Dr. Stonestreet's office sits on the grounds of the **Beall-Dawson House.** Tours are given at both sites Tuesday through Saturday from NOON to 4:00 P.M. and on the first Sunday of the month from 2:00 to 5:00 P.M. Admission covers both sites.

Upton Beall, son of Maryland tobacco merchant Brooke Beall, built his Rockville "mansion house" around 1815. The exact date is not known, but a Beall family legend says that the lumber Upton Beall acquired for construction of his house was used instead by American troops retreating through Rockville in 1814, during the War of 1812. Tax records for 1820 valued the house Beall built at $1,500. When Beall was a 40-year-old widower he married 17-year-old Jane Neil Robb, daughter of a prominent Rockville tavern keeper. Upton and Jane Beall had five children. Three of the girls lived but none married, so this Rockville house remained their home.

After the Civil War, when death claimed two of the sisters, Margaret Beall invited her cousin, Amelia Holliday Somerville, to live with her. When Amelia married John Dawson the newlyweds made their home with Miss Margaret, a condition she demanded before giving her permission to their union. Margaret Beall died in 1901 at the age of 84. The house was inherited by the Dawsons and did not pass from the Dawson family until 1946.

This Federal-style brick house is now the headquarters of the Montgomery County Historical Society. It has been restored to its 19th-century appearance. The downstairs rooms are furnished to represent the years Upton and Jane Beall lived here, 1815 to 1847. About six pieces actually belonged to the Bealls, other pieces duplicate items listed on the inventory of Upton Beall (1827) and Jane Beall (1847). Over the parlor mantel hangs a portrait of Upton Beall. The parlor also has a pianoforte bought for Margaret Dawson in 1834. One of Amelia and John Dawson's nine children, Margaret used it when she gave dancing lessons to Rockville youngsters. Several of the upstairs rooms are used for changing exhibitions on different aspects of county history.

Many of the Society's books are in the adjacent frame library, built in the late 1940s. The library can be used by genealogical and local history researchers. Hours are the same as for the Beall-Dawson House and the Doctor's Museum. For more information call (301)762-1492 or (301)340-9853. If you are in Rockville on a Tuesday or Wednesday, plan to include afternoon high tea at the **Strathmore Hall Arts Center.** This elegant English Georgian country mansion serves as a showcase for the visual, literary and performing arts. At the weekly teas served at 1:00 P.M. September to May, there are chamber music, fashion shows and literary readings. This is a delightful addition to a day spent exploring historic Rockville or shopping at White Flint Mall. Strathmore serves its own blend of teas with scones and other light refreshments. Gallery walls display changing art exhibits. Hours at the gallery are Monday through Saturday from 10:00 A.M. to 3:00 P.M. For information on upcoming programs or reservations for the always popular teas, call (301) 530-0540.

Directions: From Baltimore take 1-95 south to the Washington Beltway (I-495) and head west to Exit 34N (Rockville Pike, Route 355). Strathmore Hall is on your right just past the Grosvenor Metro Stop at 10701 Rockville Pike. For the Beall-Dawson House continue out Rockville Pike about four miles to Middle Lane, across from the Rockville Metro Stop. Turn left on Middle Lane, go two blocks then turn left on Adams Street and right on West Montgomery Avenue. The Beall-Dawson House is at 103 West Montgomery Avenue.

Woodend

Towhees or Vireos, Anyone?

The regional Audubon Naturalist Society, which predates the National Audubon Society, was formed in 1897 to protect the country's bird population. One of its earliest and most influential members, President Theodore Roosevelt, prepared a list for the Society of all the birds he had seen in and around Washington. He also established the Forest Service, five national parks, 51 bird sanctuaries and four game reserves.

Roosevelt would have loved **Woodend**, a 40-acre wildlife sanctuary that serves as headquarters for the Society. Bordering Rock Creek Park in northwest Washington, it is home for roughly 30 species of birds, including towhees, indigo buntings, woodpeckers, red-eyed vireos and yellow throats. These species are augmented by migratory birds that use Woodend as a resting stop. A nature trail winds through fields, thickets and woods, then past a stream and pond. If you want to spot the birds and resident mammals (gray squirrels, cottontail rabbits, opossums, raccoons, woodchucks and foxes), tread quietly and slowly. Sometimes you have to stop and watch to discover the birds hidden among the foliage or the shy animals in the underbrush.

Be sure to pick up a nature trail guide that identifies the 17 numbered points of interest along the trail. Woodend is noted for its diverse native and ornamental trees. The gardens that once graced this estate are no longer maintained as such, yet you'll still see year-round blooms. In winter even you can find snowdrops and aconite, also known as wolfsbane or monkshood. In the spring, flowering trees and wildflowers join with garden favorites to tint Woodend with pastel hues. Day lilies abound in summer, but the trails are at their most colorful in the autumn when fallen leaves carpet your path.

Nature is not alone in filling the calendar at Woodend. There is a full schedule of natural history lectures, birdseed sales, nature study classes, children and family programs, free scheduled nature and bird walks, conservation forums and special events. One of the biggest annual events is the Holiday Fair, featuring juried fine crafters from all over the world. It is held on the first weekend in December. For more information, call (301)652-9188.

These events are held in the Georgian Revival mansion, built in the 1920s for Captain and Mrs. Chester Wells. Mrs. Wells wanted her home patterned after her family estate in Australia. The house was designed by John Russell Pope, architect of the National Gallery of Art and the Jefferson Memorial. Mrs. Wells bequeathed her estate to the Audubon Naturalist Society to be preserved as a wildlife sanctuary. The grounds are open daily dawn to dusk. The mansion is open Monday through Friday from 9:00 A.M. to 5:00 P.M. and in spring for Sunday open houses. It has a well-stocked bookshop that specializes in optical equipment, environmentally-themed crafts and gifts, bird-feeders and books on natural history. The bookshop is open Monday through Friday 10:00 A.M. to 5:00 P.M. and Sundays from mid-March to mid-April (except Easter) from 1:00 to 5:00 P.M.

Directions: From Baltimore take 1-95 south to the Washington Beltway (1-495) and go west to Exit 33 (Connecticut Avenue). Head south on Connecticut Avenue towards Chevy Chase for ¾-mile. Turn left on Manor Road and then make a right on Jones Bridge Road. Go left at the "T" on Jones Mill Road. Woodend entrance is at 8940 Jones Mill Road on the left.

PRINCE GEORGE'S COUNTY

Adventure World

The Thrill Park

Sports enthusiasts are accustomed to the cliff-hanging thrills emanating from the Largo skating arena, but another Largo attraction, **Adventure World**, provides 100 thrill rides, including five roller coasters. One of the coasters is in the 25-acre "Paradise Island" water park. This one-price family theme park includes rides, shows, water attractions and play activities.

ROAR is a mammoth wooden coaster that starts with a spine-chilling 50-degree plunge into a 113-degree right turn. Riders may briefly experience weightlessness in the spiraling 180-degree second drop which subjects them to nearly 3.5Gs. The highest banked turn of the ride takes place within a roofed section of the track. Added to the park in 1998, this new classic coaster has 12 drops, 6 reversals and 20 cross-overs.

The Wild One is a vintage wooden coaster that was originally located at Paragon Park in Boston. Excitement builds with a climb up a 98-foot hill, followed by a five-second drop. Riders are lifted off their seats by a series of speed bumps and then travel at 55 mph through a 90-degree spiral helix. The park's Mind Eraser was one of the world's first inverted looping coasters. Coaster fans enjoy its rollovers, dives, sidewinders, double spins and unique corkscrew sequence.

The last of the "dry" coasters is the Python, which takes riders up a steep hill, then upside down through a 65-foot-high look, then back up a steep hill followed by a repeat of the thrills—backwards!

One of the very first water thrill coasters is the Typhoon Sea Coaster, which features the world's deepest descent. The ride also has a backward descent at high speed through a "camel hump" chute. The Crocodile Cal's Outback Beach House, an interactive aquatic adventure, is a five-story treehouse that contains 14 slides and numerous other water features.

While in the park visitors can experience a free fall from a 140-foot steel tower, enjoy the flying carousel or ride in a miniature NASCAR-style stock car. For children under 54 inches, there is a special circus area with 14 rides and a big top tent with a circus band and performers.

Adventure World opens in early May. Call ahead for hours (301) 249-1500, or check the park's website at www.adventureworld.com.

Directions: From Baltimore take I-695 to I-97 south to exit 7 (Route 3/301 south) to Route 214 west. Adventure World is three miles on the right.

Belair Mansion and Belair Stables Museum

Good Bloodlines

Most fathers hope the man their daughter marries will provide an appropriate house; Benjamin Tasker made sure his did. He supervised (though he did not pay for) the construction of his daughter and son-in-law's country house, **Belair Mansion.** At least that is the legend that persists despite historians' efforts to debunk it. The union between 18-year-old Anne Tasker and 47-year-old Provincial Governor Samuel Ogle certainly bore watching. The match raised eyebrows in the high society of Annapolis; even in colonial times the disparity in ages was considered excessive.

Governor Ogle had requested that, upon his death in 1752, Belair be sold to pay for his son's education. It was not. Benjamin Tasker, Jr., brother of Anne Ogle, took over the estate. He planted the handsome avenue of tulip trees that still graces the property. Other aspects of this early concern for landscaping can be appreciated by modern visitors as well. The grounds of Belair contain a number of horticultural state champions, among them Maryland's largest cucumber magnolia tree (Magnolia acuminata). A brochure available at the estate will help you identify it and other tree specimens on the grounds.

Two early Maryland governors later owned this property and the architectural features of the house remain to impress today's guests. The house recently received a $3½ million restoration and now looks as it did in its heyday. It is furnished with period antiques portraying the life of the mansion from 1745 to 1955. Among the highlights of the collection are four paintings known to have hung in the house from 1747 to 1871. *The Seasons* were done by Philippe Mercier (1689-1760), who was the principal painter to the Prince of Wales. They are the only known Mercier paintings in the American colonies. Tours of Belair Mansion are given Sunday from 1:00 to 4:00 P.M. and on Friday from 1:00 to 4:00 P.M.

Maryland's first families are not the only ones to have roots at Belair; the blood lines of some of horse racing's most valuable horses can also be traced to Belair. The stables are called the Cradle of American Racing, and you can retrace 200 years of racing history during your free tour of them. Samuel Ogle returned from his honeymoon in England with two of the most famous horses of his day— Spark and Queen Mab. The stallion, Spark, had been given to Charles Calvert, fifth Lord Baltimore, by Frederick, Prince of Wales and father of George III. Calvert in turn gave the stallion to Ogle, who had also acquired the filly Queen Mab.

Belair's second owner, Benjamin Tasker, Jr., was also interested in acquiring horse flesh, and he imported Queen Mab and Spark from England. A later owner of Belair, William Woodward, continued the thoroughbred horse tradition.

Restoration has returned Belair Mansion to its appearance in the 1750s when Benjamin Tasker, Jr., planted the avenue of tulip trees that impresses today's visitors. More than trees flourished at Belair; the bloodlines of some of horse racing's most valuable horses can be traced to its stables.

The Woodward era, from 1898 to 1957, saw the restoration and expansion of the manor house. During the Woodward years, there were three great horses stabled at Belair: Gallant Fox, Omaha and Nashua. The first two won the Triple Crown, and Nashua collected over a million dollars in prize money, making him the greatest money winner of his day.

Belair Stables Museum exhibits the white and red silks of the Belair Stables. The colors had been used by the Marquis of Zetland in England as early as 1763. The silks are still used by descendants of William Woodward. You can explore the Belair Stables Museum, in the beautiful 1907 English-style stone stable, Sundays from 1:00 to 4:00 P.M. during May, June, September and October.

Across the street from the stable museum is the **Prince George's County Genealogical Society Library** which houses over 3,000 volumes, 300 periodicals, surname files, family group sheets, Bible records and microforms. The library at 12219 Tulip Grove Drive is open 10:00 A.M. to dusk each Wednesday, except the first of the month when it closes at 1:00 P.M. It is also open the last Saturday of the month from 1:00 to 5:00 P.M.

While in the Bowie area, if time permits, stop at scenic **Allan Pond**. A paved walkway extends along the pond edge to a hilltop gazebo. Swallows glide through the wooden gazebo while ducks and geese float serenely on the pond. In the spring and fall migratory birds frequently rest at the pond. Youngsters can fish from the pond banks, and canoes and rowboats can be rented during the summer. Children also enjoy playing on the old caboose located along the walkway.

Another spot worth visiting is the **Huntington Railroad Museum** in Old Bowie. The town, called Huntington until 1880 when it was renamed Bowie, was chartered in 1870 at the junction of the Baltimore and Potomac Railroad's two branch lines to Southern Maryland and Washington, D.C. The railroad, founded by Governor Oden Bowie, began service two years later. In 1902, the B&P merged with the Pennsylvania Railroad. Today Amtrak and MARC (the state commuter line) trains use the line. You can see three railroad station buildings from the town's railroad heyday. The switching tower was built in 1911, and the freight building and passenger waiting shed were added in 1933. The buildings have been restored to their original appearance (although they are not on their original location). The museum is open on the fourth Sunday of the month, April through October. For additional information, call (301) 262-6200.

Directions: From Baltimore take Route 3/301 south to Route 50, take Exit 11 for Bowie/Collington Road, Route 197 north. Turn at the traffic light and proceed north on Collington Road, Route 197. Once past the traffic light at Kenhill Drive, turn right on Tulip Grove Drive and the Belair Mansion will appear approximately one mile ahead on your right. For the stable museum and genealogical library continue down Tulip Grove Drive until it terminates at Belair Drive. Allan

Pond is south off Route 197 just past the Route 50 overpass. Turn right off Route 197 at Northview Drive. For the Huntington Railroad Museum continue straight on Route 197 north for four miles. Then turn left onto Route 564 into Old Bowie. Route 564 makes a right and goes over the bridge crossing the railroad, but you should continue straight on 11th Street and make a right onto Chestnut Street. The museum is at the end of the block alongside the tracks.

Beltsville Agricultural Research Center

Uncle Sam as Jolly Green Giant

Crop monitoring via satellite, cloning apple trees and developing machine-harvestable fruits are just a few of the 3,000 ongoing projects that keep employees busy at the **Beltsville Agricultural Research Center.**

You can arrange a guided tour of the 7,000-acre facility by calling (301)504-9403. This is a spot where you need a knowledgeable guide because the background imparted by the tour leaders is fascinating. For instance, it is hard to get excited about the concrete cattle feed lot until the guide begins his story about experiments on alternative livestock diets. Visitors are amazed to learn that the cattle here once ate newspapers and phone directories, but couldn't tolerate the comics or yellow pages. The dye was bad for them. This paper feed was part of a test developed to see if cattle could be fed without competing with people for scarce food crops. And why a concrete feed lot? By being crowded onto this small area the cattle are unable to exercise; thus the meat is more tender.

Then there are the pigs. Considered the smartest animals on the farm, they are also invaluable for medical research because they metabolize food as humans do. The sow (mother pig) is not to be underestimated. She will fiercely defend her young even from employees she recognizes.

If you want to see the animals at their best, plan a spring visit when lambs, calves and piglets gambol in the Beltsville fields and paddocks. This is not a petting farm, however. One of the firm rules at Beltsville is that visitors should never touch the animals; they are all under preventive quarantine. That doesn't mean they are sick—just the opposite. Animals often contract illnesses from humans. These are disease-free and the staff would like to keep them that way.

Cute newborns and longtime residents are only part of the picture at this agricultural research center, the largest such facility in the world. During the summer months, employees conduct plant research in the extensive fields. For more than 40 years they have been studying turf grasses. Horticultural collections include blueberries, strawberries, thornless blackberries and dwarf fruit trees. You'll also see fields of soybeans (some as high as eight feet), alfalfa, potatoes, tomatoes, sunflowers and day lilies. Some of the crops are genetically engineered.

Beltsville also has a large greenhouse area divided into four sections: fruits and vegetables, ornamental flowers and shrubs, major economic crops and an area devoted to testing pesticides. Precision farming, another area of interest, uses computers and satellites to reduce the use of chemicals on the ground. Anyone interested in agricultural research can use the **National Agricultural Library**, which contains more than four million items. It's the world's largest agricultural library. The research center's slogan is Agriculture Makes Tomorrow Better. At Beltsville they keep working to realize that goal.

Tours of the facility take two hours and are given at no charge between 8:00 A.M. and 4:00 P.M. Monday through Friday.

Directions: From Baltimore take I-95 south Exit 29, Powder Mill Road, Route 212. Go east on Powder Mill Road. You will enter the grounds of the Beltsville Agricultural Research Center after you cross U.S. 1, about 2.5 miles. The Visitors Center will be on your left on Log Lodge Road. The center, built by the CCC in 1937, was modeled on the lodge at Yellowstone.

College Park Aviation Museum

The Cradle of American Aviation

If you've been to the National Air and Space Museum in Washington, D.C., and long for the early days of flying, visit the **College Park Aviation Museum** at the oldest continuously operated airport in the world.

After making the first motor-driven, heavier-than-air flight on December 17, 1903, Orville and Wilbur Wright were anxious to sell their flying machine to the U.S. Army. They brought their plane to Fort Myer, Virginia, for test flights. The Wright plane was well built, but many problems still needed to be worked out. This became evident during one of the tests at Fort Myer, when the plane crashed and Orville broke his thigh. (His passenger, Lt.Thomas E. Selfridge, died, becoming the first military aviation fatality.) The Army decided to accept the Wright plane anyway and on August 2, 1909, it became Signal Corps Airplane #1, on the condition that the Wrights would instruct two officers in the art of flying.

In October of that year the Army moved its operations to a field near the Maryland Agricultural College in College Park, and Wilbur began the training of the two Army officers. From the earliest days, a succession of dramatic aviation firsts occurred at the College Park

Airfield. The first flights by Army officers and the first flight in the U.S. with a woman passenger kept College Park in the news. After Army specifications for the Wright plane had been met and the officers taught to fly, a minor accident damaged the machine. It was crated and sent to Fort Sam Houston, Texas. Money had not yet been appropriated by Congress for aviation, so Army activities at College Park's Airfield temporarily came to a halt with the departure of Signal Corps Airplane #1. Civilian aviators, however, have always kept the airfield busy, and it is now recognized as the world's oldest continuously operated airport, the "Cradle of American Aviation."

One of the civilians working at College Park was Rexford Smith, who perfected one of the earliest biplanes. A private firm, National Aviation Company, began offering instruction at College Park on Wright, Curtiss and Bleriot airplanes. With the civilian aviation market expanding, the government finally appropriated money for aviation, and in June 1911 a Signal Corps aviation school was established at College Park.

Records were again being made at the airport. It was here that the first bomb-dropping devices were tried, the first mile-high flight was flown, and the first machine guns were fired from an airplane. This "aerodrome" was also the starting point for one of the first "long cross-country flights," from College Park, Maryland, to Frederick, Maryland. The two-man craft made it to Frederick all right, but the pilots couldn't find their way back. When they landed to ask directions the plane stalled on takeoff. The red-faced pilots ended up returning by train!

The U.S. Post Office air mail flights that began in 1918 had their share of problems, too. Although official mail flights began at College Park, test flights were carried out by the Army at Potomac Park in Washington. On May 15, 1918, the first delivery was scheduled to embark from Potomac Park. President Wilson was on hand, and he watched... and watched! When the pilot started his takeoff, the plane wouldn't go. Officials paced while mechanics checked out the engine for 30 minutes. Someone finally thought to check the fuel tanks—they were empty. This was far from the only hitch; once under way the pilot, perhaps rattled by his rocky start, flew southeast instead of north to Philadelphia. He had followed the wrong railroad tracks. On landing in Waldorf, Maryland, to ask directions, he broke the propeller. The 140 pounds of air mail was eventually delivered to Philadelphia by truck.

Another series of aviation experiments began at the airport in 1920, these involving vertical aviation. The father and son team of Emile and Henry Berlin began testing a machine that could rise vertically. After several years of testing and experiments, in 1924 the machine made what many consider the first successful controlled flights by a helicopter. The Berliner helicopter is currently on exhibit here (on loan from the Smithsonian Institution).

Yet another government agency became active at College Park

between 1927 and 1935. Those were the years the Bureau of Standards ran experiments on flying "blind," or by instrument, which led to the development of the first radio navigational gear and all blind landing equipment that today is standard equipment.

The former College Park Airport Museum has a new name and a new facility designed to represent a wing of the Wright Flyer. Within are four galleries displaying photos of aviation firsts, aviation equipment, memorabilia from the earliest flying years, field aviation films and a collection of early air mail items and photographs. An exciting new addition is a replica of the 1909 hangar with an animatronic Wilbur Wright that harkens back to the field's early history. There is a nominal admission charge. The museum is open daily 10:00 A.M. to 5:00 P.M. It is closed on major holidays.

You may want to plan lunch at the adjacent **94th Aero Squadron Restaurant**, which looks like a French farm used by American forces during World War I. Adding to the atmosphere are the tables that overlook the action on the still-active runways at College Park Airport. Some tables even have hook-ups so you can listen to the cockpit conversations.

Directions: From Baltimore take Route 295, the Baltimore Washington Parkway, to Greenbelt Road. Take Greenbelt Road toward College Park, then make a left on Kenilworth Avenue. Head south on Kenilworth to the intersection with Paint Branch Parkway and make a right turn. Make another right at the first stoplight on Cpl. Frank Scott Drive for the College Park Aviation Museum. The entrance for the 94th Aero Squadron is also off Calvert Road just before the museum entrance.

Cosca Regional Park and
Cedarville State Forest

Au Naturel

A garden for butterflies, paddle boats on a quiet lake, a tram train, innovative play equipment plus hands-on science games at the nature center make the Louise F. **Cosca Regional Park** a diversified outing.

Among the discoveries is the Prince George's County butterfly garden, a quarter-acre plot filled with flowers favored by indigenous butterflies. Bright red zinnias, yellow black-eyed Susans and purple flowering butterfly bushes are among the 35 varieties that attract an almost equal number of different butterflies. According to the park naturalist, the best time to spot these colorful flutterbys is during July and August in the heat of the day, between 10:00 A.M. and 3:00 P.M.

You'll also want to explore the herb garden at the **Clearwater Nature Center**. This 48-by-15-foot garden is not ornamental but rather a collection of "edible wild plants." Like those in the nearby sensory garden, many of the herbs and wildflowers are highly aromatic. Although the plants are billed as edible, it is never advisable to taste a leaf or berry unless you are on a guided nature walk. The herb garden is right behind the nature center, which is open Tuesday through Saturday from 9:00 A.M. to 4:00 P.M. and Sunday 11:00 A.M. to 4:00 P.M. Naturalists are available to answer questions about both of the gardens. They also lead walks through the bog.

A cool-climate bog located at the southern limit of its range, the **Suitland Bog** is a rare ecosystem. Its fragile environment is now protected by a high fence and can only be observed under the watchful eyes of the naturalists. Without their help these unique carnivorous plants cannot be spotted. The best time to see the bog is in the late spring and early summer. For dates of guided walks call ahead, (301)297-4575, or stop at the Clearwater Nature Center and pick up a schedule of activities.

The Nature Center is well worth a visit, particularly for families with grade school children. The center has live specimens of fish and turtles in a large tank in the middle of the room. There is also a rabbit, several snakes and some incredibly huge cockroaches. The exhibit hall has a number of participatory activities, such as enjoying "lunch" at the woodland cafe and going underground to view a fox den. The exhibits focus on Prince George's County's natural treasures.

Science is so much fun at the Clearwater Nature Center that youngsters need no additional incentive. Cosca nevertheless has a variety of innovative play equipment on the hillside overlooking Lake Louise.

During the summer months and on spring and fall weekends you can rent rowboats and paddle boats or take a 15-minute train ride around the park. There are hiking and riding trails (no stables), a campground, picnic areas, tennis courts and athletic fields. You can even fish in the 15-acre lake, but a license is required for those over 16. The lake is stocked with bass, bluegill and catfish. There is no charge for Prince George's and Montgomery County residents; others pay a parking fee from Memorial Day through Labor Day.

If the fish aren't biting at Lake Louise you can head over to **Cedarville State Forest,** a 3,500 acre protected forest just about 15 minutes from Cosca. Here you'll find a stocked four-acre pond as well as four trails, campgrounds (reservations are required for all campsites at (301) 888-1410 or (800) 784-5380), a picnic area and playground. The brown trail, accessed from the pond parking lot, is one of the most interesting because it passes through the headwaters of the Zekiah Swamp, Maryland's largest freshwater swamp. John Wilkes Booth fled through this swamp in April 1864, after assassinating Lincoln.

Cedarville is open to the public daily from sunrise to sunset. A park bulletin board has brochures and hiking trail maps. Other activities at the park include horseback riding (although there are no livery facilities), dog training, hunting and birdwatching.

While you're headed south on Route 301, consider continuing 14.2

miles past Waldorf. After a short detour off Route 301, you'll find one of the most authentic crab houses in the state—many enthusiasts believe it's the best! The crowds, which are always seated rapidly, certainly testify to the popularity of **Capt' Billy's Crab House and Restaurant** at Pope's Creek. George W. Robertson, who is far better known as Capt' Billy, moved to Pope's Creek when still a young child and worked the river with his uncle. He had his first boat at age 14 and began crabbing and fishing. He also helped his grandmother at the Pope's Creek country store. By the mid-1940s Capt' Billy had opened the first of his restaurants and some of his employees are still with him.

He now has two restaurants on the water at Pope's Creek. From the restaurants' porches, diners can see the Potomac River Bridge and the many boaters who tie up at the adjacent dock so they can enjoy the fresh seafood. The restaurant serves about 80 to 90 bushels of crab daily (there are about six dozen crabs in each bushel). The "all you can eat crabs" are perhaps the most popular menu item, but there is a wide range of seafood as well as other options. (If you are traveling with someone allergic to seafood, the chicken in the basket, another Maryland specialty, is a tasty treat.) Lunch and dinner are served seven days a week on Sunday through Thursday from 11:00 A.M. to 10:00 P.M. On Friday and Saturday closing is at 11:00 P.M. For more information, call (301) 932-4323.

Directions: From Baltimore take 1-95 south to the Washington Beltway and continue south on I-95 toward Andrews Air Force Base. At Exit 7A (Route 5, Branch Avenue) head south toward Waldorf. Go straight for several miles and turn right onto Route 223, Woodyard Road. At the second light, turn left onto Brandywine Road, Route 381. Go to the second light about 1½ miles on Route 381 and then make a right turn onto Thrift Road. Go two miles (following the signs) to the Clearwater Nature Center. For Cedarville State Forest take Route 5 to Route 301 and go south on Route 301 to Cedarville Road and turn left. Follow Cedarville Road for three miles to the entrance to the park on the right (Bee Oak Road). For Capt' Billy's Crab House and Restaurant continue on Route 301 past Waldorf, LaPlata and BelAlton. You will take a right on Pope's Creek Road (which is marked by a big sign for the restaurant) and head down until you see the signs.

Fort Washington

On the Ramparts

In 1794 George Washington selected this bluff overlooking the Potomac River as the site of the first fort to be built to protect the country's new capital. Fort Warburton, as it was originally called, was destroyed only five years after its completion, during the War of

1812. Ten years later its replacement, the present Fort Washington, began a much longer life as capital defender and military post.

Fort Washington (its name was changed by 1810) was destroyed without firing any shots at the British. So how did it meet its fate? Some reports imply that's what the army asked fort commander Captain Samuel Dyson before he was stripped of his commission. Dyson's verbal orders were to destroy the fort if it came under land attack from British troops during the War of 1812. The United States government did not want Fort Washington to fall into enemy hands. But it was from the Potomac River that the threat was posed on August 27, 1814. A British fleet of seven ships under Captain Gordon had with great difficulty—the ships ran aground 22 times—made its way up the Potomac. Positioned off the fort, the ships opened fire. Dyson and his men were under fire for two hours before he destroyed all of the equipment and spiked the cannons. As he and his men were leaving the fort they laid a powder trail and blew up almost 3,000 pounds of black powder to prevent the British from seizing it.

The British threat prompted quick action, and barely 12 days after the fort was destroyed Secretary of War James Monroe commissioned Major Pierre L'Enfant, architect of the nation's capital, to rebuild it. The French engineer ordered 200,000 bricks and a large quantity of stone and lumber. But work proceeded slowly, so slowly that after the Treaty of Ghent ending the war was signed on February 13, 1815, the need for defense was tempered by the desire for economy.

L'Enfant was insulted when requested to submit reports on the work in progress and his plans for the fort's construction. He simply ignored the request. Work was then halted, and he was dismissed. On September 6, 1815, Lt. Col. Walker K. Armistead took over. When the new Fort Washington was finally completed on October 2, 1824, the total cost was more than $426,000.

Little has changed since 1824, as you will see when you cross the drawbridge over the dry moat and enter the walled fort. From the sally port entrance there is a panoramic view of the construction design, which incorporates three levels of defensive positions. The lowest level is the V-shaped water battery, positioned 60 feet below the main fortifications. This battery was started under L'Enfant's direction. Next are the casemate positions, bombproof gun sites from which defending soldiers could fire upon ships on the Potomac. From the high ramparts two half bastions commanded the river above and below the fort.

Uniformed guides will explain the advantages and disadvantages of these three-gun positions. On Sunday afternoons costumed volunteers re-create military life of the mid-1800s. The men show you around the offices and soldiers' barracks, and on selected occasions a cannon is fired on the parade ground. To obtain more background on the fort, stop at the visitor center, located in the historic Commanding Officer's House.

A different perspective is gained by touring Fort Washington during the Torchlight Tattoo ceremonies. These are presented several times each summer on Saturday evenings (call (301)763-4600 for schedule and information). You'll be briefed before the ceremony begins; then the clock is turned back to the tense Civil War days. You will be treated as visiting Washingtonians anxious about southern attacks on the capital. Fort Washington, manned by only 40 marines in January, 1861, was the sole fort protecting the city. By February units of the Regular Army and Militia took over. When Fort Foote was built on the Maryland side of the Potomac in 1864, the military significance of Fort Washington was eliminated. The masonry fort was closed in 1872, but the reservation remained an active military post until 1945.

Fort Washington is open daily year-round from 8:30 A.M. to 5:00 P.M. Picnicking is encouraged.

Directions: From Baltimore take I-95 south to the Washington Beltway and proceed south (still on I-95) to Exit 3A (Route 210, Indian Head Highway). Take Indian Head Highway south for four miles to Fort Washington Road. Turn right and go three miles to the fort.

Montpelier Cultural Arts Center and Mansion

Elegant Quakers

The **Montpelier Cultural Arts Center** has something in common with the mythical phoenix, having arisen from the ashes of a 1976 fire that destroyed the old barn on the Montpelier estate previously earmarked for the arts center. The blaze reduced all but the cylindrical glazed-block silo to rubble.

A state grant and hard work salvaged the project, and the Montpelier Cultural Arts Center opened in August 1979. Artists and craftsmen display their work in the center's three galleries, and anywhere from 20 to 30 artists rent studios. Painters, sculptors, printmakers, photographers, cabinetmakers, basketweavers and ceramists all work and display at Montpelier. Classes, workshops and performances are regularly scheduled; for information call (301) 953-1993. Visitors are welcome to drop in between 10:00 A.M. and 5:00 P.M. daily, except holidays.

If you visit on Sunday from NOON to 4:00 P.M., you can include a tour of the 18th-century Montpelier Mansion, which was built by Thomas and Ann Snowdon around 1783. When Thomas and Ann married in 1774, their combined wealth was so great that they were forbidden to attend Quaker services until they divested themselves of a portion of their bounty. They sold 100 slaves to satisfy the Quaker requirements.

At Montpelier you will see indications of the Snowdon wealth in the gracious and lavish Georgian architecture and indications of their religious commitment in the interior and exterior design. The door design suggests a wooden cross, with the bottom panels representing Bible pages.

The religious motif is continued in the garden, where the boxwood is planted in the shape of a cross. The boxwood allee, or path, leads to the only surviving 18th-century belvedere, or summer house, in Maryland. Indeed, it is one of the few to survive from this early period in America.

Directions: From the Washington Beltway take Exit 22, the Baltimore-Washington Parkway, to the Laurel exit, Route 197. Proceed north toward Laurel for a short distance to the Montpelier Shopping Center on your right. At the light turn left on Muirkirk Road and then right into the parking lot for the Montpelier Cultural Arts Center and the Montpelier Mansion.

NASA's Goddard Visitor Center and Museum

Neighborly NASA

As a Trivial Pursuit question it would be a guaranteed puzzler: when, where and who launched the first successful rocket? The answer: March 16, 1926, in Auburn, Massachusetts, by Robert Hutchings Goddard. The flight of Goddard's liquid fuel rocket, though only a brief 2½ seconds, prepared the way for man's ventures into space.

You'll see a full-scale sculpture of Dr. Goddard and his rocket as you enter **NASA's Goddard Visitor Center** in Greenbelt. The facility named in honor of the Father of Modern Rocketry was established by the National Aeronautics and Space Administration. As you would expect from a space-age agency, the technology at the visitor center is state-of-the-art, with some refreshingly humorous exceptions. Families will want to bring a camera to get a shot of young space enthusiasts with their heads stuck in a space-suit cutout, more carnival than Canaveral.

Push button interactive exhibits allow you to design and build your own computer simulated spacecraft. You can test your knowledge of space flight using the visitor center's interactive quiz computers. You can also view the Gemini XII spacecraft and then have a seat in a full-scale Gemini mock-up and imagine yourself an early NASA astronaut.

Be sure to visit the visitor center's earth science gallery. This new exhibit offers interactive multi-media kiosks that help you explore the mysteries and wonder of our home planet, Earth. Live real-time weather statistics and warnings are available throughout the day from

Among numerous mind-expanding exhibits at NASA's Visitor Center is a sculpture of the liquid fuel rocket and its inventor who prepared the way for man's ventures into space.

a down link station on the roof of the visitor center. Those traveling from out-of-state can check the current weather in their home town. The visualization theater continuously demystifies such earth science phenomena as: volcanoes, tornadoes, the ozone layer and El Niño. These and other popular topics are explained and envisioned using the latest data from Earth-orbiting satellites.

Surrounding the visitor center are examples of the sounding rockets that are critical to Goddard's data collection. NASA annually launches roughly 50 sounding rockets with payloads weighing from 12 to 2,500 pounds. There are Nike-Tomahawk sounding rockets, the earliest Iris, the large javelin and the two-stage Nike Black Brant. You'll also see a full-scale model of an Apollo spacecraft and an early Delta Launch Vehicle. If you want to see rockets launched, stop by on the first and third Sunday of each month at 1:00 P.M., when model rockets are fired from the hilltop behind the Goddard Visitor Center.

The Center is open at no charge daily from 9:00 A.M. to 4:00 P.M. Public tours are offered Monday through Friday at 11:30 A.M. and on Saturday at 11:30 A.M. and 2:30 P.M. These tours are for groups of fewer than 15 people and no reservations are required. Tours visit the Hubble Space Telescope Operations Control Center and Goddard's Communication Management Center, the nerve center for NASA's orbiting satellites.

Directions: From the Washington Beltway take Exit 22 (well-marked for NASA/Goddard). Bear to the right for Greenbelt Road. Head down Greenbelt Road past the main entrance to Goddard Space Flight Facility; signs will indicate route for visitor center. Turn left on Conservation Road and then left again onto the Goddard grounds and into the parking lot for the visitor center.

National Colonial Farm

Harvesting Your Roots

The **National Colonial Farm** is growing more than crops; the site itself is growing. It has added farm buildings, additional fields and trails and the **Robert Ware Straus Ecosystem Farm**. Visitors to this farm, created by the Accokeek Foundation within the 4,700-acre **Piscataway Park**, get a strong sense of being part of America's evolving history.

Imagine standing along the farm's Potomac River bank in March 1634, watching the first Maryland settlers sail past on the *Dove*. Governor Leonard Calvert was on his way to meet the "Emperor of the Piscataway" to obtain his "permission" to settle in Maryland. This exchange marked the beginning of European settlement and the beginning of the end for the Piscataway tribe.

Move the clock forward to March 1799, the last year of George

Washington's life. If you were standing on this farm looking through powerful field glasses, you might spot George relaxing on the porch of Mount Vernon. What is amazing is that the farm Washington would have seen across the river from his home has remained unchanged through all the subsequent years!

What he saw then and what you see today is an 18th-century free-holder's farm. The colonial farm site includes a circa 1780 farm dwelling, an 18th-century tobacco barn, smokehouse, necessary and out-kitchen. Workers in 18th-century attire till the fields and prepare food in the rustic out-kitchen using handmade tools and implements. Many of the kitchen tools are carved from gourds that, like the ingredients for the meals, are grown at the farm. A few steps away from the kitchen is the **Museum Herb Garden** featuring hundreds of varieties of vegetables, herbs and even wild plants. All of these crops have a long history in Maryland. There are four sections to the garden: Crops of the Americas, Crops Brought from Europe, Crops of Africa and Gathered Plants. Corn and squash were cultivated by the Piscataway Indians, while cabbage and carrots were brought from Europe's cooler areas. Okra and watermelon originated in Africa. The garden is a living reminder of how these crops relate to both the environment and the people from many cultures who have shaped Maryland.

The fields at this farm are planted, tended and harvested as they would have been during colonial days. One departure from bygone days is that some animals, once allowed to roam, are now penned. Tobacco was the cash crop but corn and wheat were, and are, also planted. An orchard, like the one here, provided fruit for wine and cider (the colonists did not drink the water).

If time permits, take one of the farm's five nature trails that lead through the woods and along the Potomac shore. From the farm's riverbank you can see Mount Vernon across the river. Walking these trails is indeed walking back into history. Archeologists have found reminders of five prehistoric groups who crisscrossed this land. The Piscataway Indians settled here in a town Captain John Smith called Moyaone.

The Persimmon Trail takes you to the wildfowl pond where if you're lucky you might spot a bald eagle. An island in the pond is a nesting place for geese, ducks and in the spring a variety of nesting birds. The Ken Otis Bluebird Trail, with more than 50 bluebird houses, borders the Native Tree Arboretum, with 128 species of trees and shrubs native to Southern Maryland. The Pawpaw Trail begins at the Arboretum. Narrow and somewhat primitive, it proves rewarding in April and May when the columbines and Jack-in-the pulpit bloom. The Pumpkin Ash Trail is named for the northernmost stand of these trees in the country. A boardwalk along this trail takes you over a fresh water tidal swamp to the Robert Ware Straus Ecosystem Farm, which can also be accessed from the Blackberry Trail (often very wet and demanding of old shoes or hiking boots).

The Ecosystem Farm, named after one of the founders of the

National Colonial Farm Museum in Accokeek, across from Mount Vernon, provides settings for exhibits and demonstrations of women's and men's work on 18th century Tidewater farms.

Accokeek Foundation, is a certified organic demonstration farm that provides a practical demonstration to visitors of what it really means to practice land stewardship along with agricultural practices. The farm follows the principles of SHARE—Sustainable Harvest, Adaptive Research and Education. The surrounding community can purchase shares of the harvest before planting and the harvest is distributed each week during the growing season. The farm has ongoing research projects such as studying a solar powered irrigation system that moves water from the Potomac River to the fields, innovative tillage practices that improve soil structure, modifying insect habitats to promote beneficial insect populations and controlling insects and diseases by growing resistant varieties and carefully using biological insecticides.

You can explore the National Colonial Farm Tuesday through Sunday from 10:00 A.M. to 5:00 P.M. A nominal admission is charged. The farm offers daily tours; call (301) 283-2113 for specific times and information on their special event weekend craft and cooking demonstrations. There is a pier at the farm where boaters on the Potomac River may dock while they visit. Those with fishing licenses may try their luck from the pier.

Directions: From Baltimore take 1-95 south to the Washington Beltway and proceed south (still on 1-95/495) to Maryland Exit 3, Indian Head Highway. Go south on Indian Head Highway for ten miles. At the light for Bryan Point Road turn right and proceed four miles to the entrance to the National Colonial Farm.

Oxon Hill Farm

Your Kids Will Love These Kids and Piglets, Too

The bib overalls and long cotton work dresses worn by the staff of **Oxon Hill Farm** help establish a late 1890s time frame. The farming methods they use at the 512-acre Oxon Cove Park also reflect that era. This living-history farm encourages both young and old to find out more about America's rural past by looking, touching and doing.

Visitors may help with the milking, if they want. Youngsters are often amazed when they discover that milk comes from cows, not cartons. Of course, this milk is not pasteurized and is fed only to the pigs. And speaking of pigs, they are the brains of the barnyard. Those at Oxon Hll have learned to turn on the water spigot to get a drink, something cows or goats don't do.

Spring is when you find the most young animals, although family planning is not foolproof on the farm, and you will see some kids and piglets born in other seasons. Traditionally the sheep get a haircut each May. Visitors watch this tricky maneuver, amazed at how naked the sheep look without their winter coats.

While the animals are of greatest interest to young visitors, they learn a lot about the food they eat by examining the well-marked rows of vegetables—playing "I spy" as they spot ripening tomatoes, squash, eggplants, peppers, peas and beans. Another reason excursions to Oxon Hill are so popular with young visitors is that on weekends they may get a chance to ride in a wagon or climb on one of the good-natured horses.

As on any operating farm, there's always something interesting happening at Oxon Hill, such as the sorghum cane-cutting in the fall. Once cut, the cane is stripped and mashed, and the runoff boiled to make sweet syrup. Winter, the slowest time of year, is when tools are repaired and fences mended.

There are many special programs at the farm, including square dancing. To get up-to-date information on the full schedule, call (301) 839-1176. Oxon Hill Farm is open daily, without charge, from 8:00 A.M. to 4:30 P.M. and is closed only on New Year's Day, Thanksgiving and Christmas. The Barn Book Shop, open Sunday through Friday 9:00 A.M. to 3:45 P.M., is closed on Tuesday and Thursday. On other weekdays it stays open only until 1:00 P.M.

A final word must make mention of the half-mile blazed Woodlot Trail, a steep path that takes visitors through a wooded ravine. Visitors may also hike along the lower fields or bring bicycles and enjoy the bike path along Oxon Cove. If you bring your own snack or lunch have a picnic at the designated area.

Directions: From Baltimore take I-95 south to the Washington Beltway, I-95/495. Take the Beltway south to Exit 3A, Indian Head Highway south. From Exit 3A, bear right immediately onto Oxon Hill Road and right again after about 100 yards onto the farm road.

Patuxent River Park and Merkle Wildlife Sanctuary

Walk on the Wild Side

Tucked out of the way in Prince George's County's rolling farm country is Jug Bay Natural Area's 2,000 acres of undeveloped wilderness. This is just one of 11 limited-use areas that compose **Patuxent River Park.** The park was established to allow visitation and use of the river without disturbing the natural environment. To achieve this objective, special-use permits for activities like hunting and fishing are issued, and advance reservations are necessary for many planned activities. Call (301) 627-6074. The park, however, is always open to first-time visitors who wish to discover the diverse activities and appeal of this marvelous natural area.

Nature study and environmental education take place in an outdoor classroom, the **Black Walnut Creek Area**, under the learned eye of a park naturalist. Boardwalks allow hikers to cross the marshy wetlands as well as penetrate the surrounding forest. The free 45-minute guided hikes must be pre-arranged.

Not everyone comes empty handed to the wilderness. Bird watchers never visit without their binoculars, and photographers come ladened with cameras to the marshland blind at the river's edge, a vantage point for nature shots.

For those who want to get out on the river there are 50-minute pontoon ecology tours. The pontoon program runs from mid-April to mid-October. Trips highlight various aspects of the ecology; one focuses on aquatic life while another is designed for bird watchers. The Possum and Muskrat trips are normally scheduled for groups, but families can often be added to pre-existing parties. Children must be over 13 to go on these tours.

A less structured way to see the river is to rent a canoe and explore Mattaponi Creek and the Jug Bay area (do call ahead and check on availability). There are also scheduled downriver canoe trips that give you a chance to see the river's transition from woodland stream to tidal wetlands.

Other recreational options at Patuxent Park include eight miles of horseback riding trails (there are no horses for hire, alas), two fishing areas, six miles of hiking trails, two boat ramps, a primitive campsite for backpackers and a group campsite.

The river has historical as well as ecological significance. It has contributed to the social history of Prince George's County for more than 300 years. The park's **Patuxent Village** shows what it was like to live along the river a hundred years ago. You'll see a rough-hewn log cabin. With old tools, park naturalists demonstrate pioneer skills, scoring the logs with a broad ax and finishing them with the adze. Patuxent Village contains a smokehouse, hunting and trapping shed, and a packing house with a tobacco prise. (See Tobacco Prise selection.)

Those interested in old tools should be sure to pre-arrange a visit to the **W. Henry Duvall Memorial Tool Collection**, which is open on Sunday afternoons from 1:00 to 4:00 P.M. Mr. Duvall collected more than 1,200 antique tools and farm implements; obviously the two buildings at Patuxent can only exhibit a small portion of them. Tools of the trade surround a carpenter's workbench, and cobblers' and wheelwrights' tools are also displayed. The cumbersome implements of a country dentist illustrate just how far we've progressed in that field. One entire building is devoted to agricultural tools.

Your visit to Patuxent Park should be combined with a stop at the nearby **Merkle Wildlife Sanctuary,** where a visitor center and observation deck help visitors appreciate the many species of birds. Merkle is best visited during the spring and autumn migratory seasons. If your timing is right, you will see the fields crowded with visiting Canada geese. Birds of prey and a wide variety of waterfowl stop here on their north-south journeys. Unlike the eastern shore wildlife refuges, Merkle is close enough to allow visiting in the early morning before the birds begin their day's foraging or at dusk when they return.

There are three hiking trails that encompass five miles of forested uplands and fields. Trails lead along the stream valley for Lookout Creek as it flows toward the Patuxent River. Mounds Trail is particularly popular with birdwatchers and also offers the chance to spot beavers. A four and a half-mile Critical Area Drive Tour (CADT) connects Patuxent River Park and Merkle Wildlife Sanctuary. This hard-packed one-way loop is open to cars on Sundays from 10:00 A.M. to 3:00 P.M. year round and to hikers and bikers on Saturdays at the same hours from January through September. Along the loop road there is a 1,000-foot bridge over the Mattaponi Creek with an observation platform and a boardwalk.

Merkle Wildlife Sanctuary's Visitor Center is open weekdays from 10:00 A.M. to 4:00 P.M. Monday through Friday and weekends 10:00 A.M. to 5:00 or 6:00 P.M. depending on the season. There is a per vehicle charge year round. Park personnel offer interpretative programs and a summer day camp for children 8 to 14. For details call (301) 888-1410 or (800) 784-5380.

Not far from these sites is a related spot worth visiting, the **National Wildlife Visitor Center** at the 12,750-acre Patuxent Research Refuge. This science and environmental education facility has state-of-the art interactive exhibits that explain how wildlife research helps preserve the earth's vital resources. Exhibits focus on subjects such as migratory bird routes, wildlife habitats and endangered species recovery efforts. A large picture window with spotting scopes, binoculars and tracking equipment encourages visitors to watch for wildlife. More than 200 species of birds have been sighted at the refuge. There are also walking trails and seasonal tram tours through forest, wetlands and meadows. The center is open without charge daily 10:00 A.M. to 5:30 P.M. There is a nominal fee for the guided tram tour. For more information, call (301) 497-5760. A shop is stocked with gifts, environmental books and other educational materials.

The visitor center is in the refuge's South Tract; there is also a North Tract, which is located off Route 198, just 1.4 miles east of the Baltimore-Washington Parkway. The Visitor Contact Station marks the entrance to the North Tract. This section is also open daily (except for Thanksgiving, Christmas and New Year's Day). The Baltimore Gas and Electric Company has contributed to a wetland and wildlife viewing area at the North Tract where you are apt to spot waterfowl, shorebirds, raptors and songbirds.

Hunting and fishing are permitted within the refuge with appropriate licenses. For details on hunting, call (301) 317-3825 or, during hunting season, (301) 317-3819. Fishermen can try their luck at Lake Allen, New Marsh, Cattail Pond, Rieve's Pont, Bailey Bridge Marsh or the Little Patuxent River.

Directions: From Baltimore take Route 3 and Route 301 south to Upper Marlboro. Four miles south of Route 4 make a left turn on Croom Road (Route 382), and follow to Croom Airport Road where you turn left (there will be a sign for Patuxent River Park). For Merkle, continue down Croom Road to St. Thomas Church Road and turn left. Follow St. Thomas Church Road for 2.8 miles, where the name of the road changes to Fenno. Follow across the bridges and look for sanctuary entrance on the left. For the National Wildlife Visitor Center, from Route 301 head east on Route 197 which will take you to the Patuxent Research Refuge just south of Laurel. If you are coming from Baltimore, take the Baltimore-Washington Parkway, exit on Powder Mill Road and drive two miles east to Route 197 to the visitor center.

Paul E. Garber Facility

The Right Stuff

Aircraft conservators responsible for taking old planes apart prior to restoration at the Smithsonian's **Paul E. Garber Facility** have discovered some unusual messages from the past.

Staffers working on the Enola Gay, the B-29 that dropped the uranium bomb on Hiroshima, found one of the three original arming plugs behind a piece of heavy equipment. In a Chance Vought F4U Corsair, the U.S. Navy carrier-based fighter plane that first exceeded 400 mph, a conservator was dismantling the engine when he found a faded scrap—probably placed there by a fun-loving crew chief during a 1940s maintenance check. It read: "What in the hell are you looking for in here, you silly..."

At the Paul Garber Facility you can readily see what it is they're looking for in these old planes—the blueprints of past designs. In the five buildings open to the public at Silver Hill, the Smithsonian has roughly 140 aircraft on display, compared with 75 at the Mall museum in downtown Washington. The remainder of the 322 aircraft in the collection are on loan, in storage or undergoing restoration. In an average year two or three aircraft are restored, each requiring between 5,000 and 13,000 man-hours of labor.

Touring the Garber warehouses gives you an inside look at the world of aviation. A typical tour group of 15 to 30 will consist mainly of pilots or aviation buffs. The conversation tends to sound like Hollywood outtakes with talk of "auguring in," the "outside of the envelope" and "hangar queens." No two tours are exactly alike because the docents tailor the 2½- to 3-hour tours to the participants.

Grown men become enthusiastic youngsters as they crowd around vintage biplanes and one-of-a-kind experimental models. A fre-

The Paul E. Garber Facility gives wings to Hemingway's words: "You love a lot of things if you live around them, but there isn't any woman...or any horse...that is as lovely as a great airplane."

quently asked question is "Can these planes fly?" Many can, but none does. Once the Smithsonian acquires a plane it is grounded to prevent additional damage.

As you tour the workshop you'll see planes still unrestored and wonder how what appears in some cases to be rubble can be restored to mint condition. Providently, aviation developed simultaneously with photography, and there was always someone with a camera to rush out to the field when a barnstorming show came to town. Thus there is excellent photo documentation of even the earliest aircraft. All restorers need is one small piece clearly visible in a photo, and the remaining pieces can be drawn to scale. Similarly, if parts from only one side of a plane survive, the other side can be reconstructed.

At the Smithsonian the planes are restored exactly as they were; if the insignia had been painted on with a brush, a brush will be used, not a spray gun. On the Bellanca CF every screw head on the wooden section has the slots lined up just as they once were. Such a lineup enabled the pilots to tell when a screw was loose. If restorers cannot locate an original part, it is made to match, then carefully labeled to indicate that it is not authentic. Old-timers have come through the Garber Facility and commented that the planes here look better than the originals.

In addition to learning a good bit of aviation history, you'll discover why the early pilots wore flowing white scarves, why the Messerschmitt killed more friends than foes, what one airplane was on the military inventory the day WWII started and the day it ended, and why German fighter pilots had an edge over the WWII Lightning.

After a visit you may agree with the Ernest Hemingway quote prominently displayed over a desk in the reception area: "You love a lot of things if you live around them, but there isn't any woman and there isn't any horse ... that is as lovely as a great airplane. "

To arrange a visit call (202) 357-1400 weekdays between 9:00 A.M. and 5:00 P.M., or write the Tour Scheduler, NASM, Smithsonian Institution, Washington, D.C. 20560. Free tours are given Monday through Friday at 10:00 A.M. and on weekends at 10:00 A.M. and 1:00 P.M. Wear comfortable walking shoes and note that the cavernous warehouses have neither heat nor air-conditioning.

Directions: From Baltimore take I-95 south to the Washington Beltway (I-495/95) and go south on I-95 to Exit 7B (Branch Avenue, Route 5, Silver Hill). After exiting make a left on Auth Road and proceed one block to the traffic light at the junction with Route 5. Turn right and follow Route 5 north one mile to St. Barnabas Road, Route 414. Make a right on St. Barnabas and go ½ mile to the Paul Garber Facility on the right directly across the Silver Hill Road intersection.

Riversdale

A.K.A. Calvert Mansion

Riversdale felicitously blends the New World with the Old. The five-part stucco-covered brick mansion was built between 1801 and 1807 by Henri Joseph Steir, a Flemish financier, who fled Flanders with his family during the French Revolution just before French troops invaded his country. Steir was a descendant of Peter Paul Rubens and brought with him an outstanding art collection, including a number of paintings by his famous relative.

After a little more than a year in Philadelphia, by the end of 1797 the Steirs family moved to the William Paca House (see selection) in Annapolis. While staying in the Maryland capital, the family made the acquaintance of George Calvert, a descendant of the family who founded the colony and served as the first governor. On June 11, 1799 Steir's youngest daughter, Rosalie Eugenia married Calvert.

Although the Steirs had hoped to return to Flanders, by April 1801, they had purchased 740 acres just north of Bladensburg. The house plan was in the Palladian five-part style favored in the mid-Atlantic, but the three ground floor parlors were reminiscent of the Chateau du Mick, built in 1790 and the newest of the Stier family homes in and around Antwerp. When you tour the house you will see the fine plaster work in the central salon with the triple-arch motif on each wall and the heavy mahogany doors.

When the Steir family returned to Belgium in the spring of 1803, Rosalie and George Calvert, with their first two children, made Riversdale their home. Although Rosalie corresponded with her family until her death in 1821 and received architectural and horticultural advice as well as numerous art objects to embellish the house, they were never reunited. Steir's art collection was sent back to Belgium in 1816, but before it was packed for transport there was a two-week exhibit at Riversdale for artists and politicians. Auctions in 1817 and at Mr. Steir's death in 1821 have dispersed the collection.

Rosalie Calvert is buried at Riversdale with four of her nine children. Her tombstone was carved by an Italian sculptor who was embellishing the U.S. Capitol under Latrobe's direction. George Calvert died in 1838 and one of his two sons, Charles Benedict, made his home at Riversdale with his wife Charlotte A. Norris and their six children.

Charles B. Calvert represented his county in the state legislature and was the principal founder of the Maryland Agricultural College, which became the University of Maryland. The school was situated on Calvert's 428-acre "Rossburg Farm." The cannon on the lawn at Riversdale was a gift to Charles Calvert from St. Mary's City. It was said to have come from either the *Ark* or *Dove* (see Historic St. Mary's selection). Calvert was a close friend of Henry Clay, the noted political figure and presidential candidate, who often stayed at Riversdale. Local legend claims that he drafted the Compromise of 1850 at the mansion. Calvert died in May 1864 and his estate was divided among his heirs with the mansion going to his eldest son, George Henry. He lived there with his family until 1887 when he and his brother, Charles Baltimore, sold the mansion and 475 acres to a New York real estate syndicate. The syndicate created the community of Riverdale Park, which became the nucleus of the town of Riverdale.

In 1912, the mansion, which had fallen into disrepair, was renovated by Thomas H. Pickford. The east hyphen and wing was converted to a two-story banquet hall and the west wing became a garage. Pickford also filled several rooms with period furnishings. The house was then leased from 1916 to 1929 to Senator Hiram Johnson, one of the founders of the Progressive, or Bull-Moose, party. He was Teddy Roosevelt's running mate on the national ticket in 1912.

Pickford sold the house to Arkansas Senator Thaddeus Caraway. When Caraway died in 1931, his wife Hattie was chosen to finish his term and she was elected in her own right in 1932, the first woman elected to the United States Senate. She served until early 1945. A mortgage default enabled Pickford to regain the house, and he sold it in 1933 to former Oregon congressman Abraham Lafferty. It was Lafferty who sold the mansion and grounds in 1949 to the Maryland National Capital Park and Planning Commission.

Tours of Riversdale are given on Sundays from NOON to 4:00 P.M. from March through December. A nominal admission is charged and there is a gift shop in the mansion. The mansion can also be rented for special events. Call (301) 864-0420 or on Sundays (301) 864-3521.

Directions: From Baltimore take the Baltimore Washington Parkway south to the Washington Beltway, I-495/95. Head northwest on the Beltway to Exit 23, Route 201, Kenilworth Avenue south. Continue for approximately three miles and turn right on East West Highway, Route 410. Proceed ½ mile and follow Maryland History signs to the mansion, which is off East-West Highway at 4811 Riverdale Road.

The Surratt House

Step Back to the Victorian Era

The Victorian era greatly influenced modern times. At **The Surratt House** in Clinton, visitors can find out just how by viewing ever-changing exhibits and taking part in special events. You may see lacy Valentines of the Golden Age (1840-1900) or somber mourning memorabilia. Other exhibits have included a photographic history of "Washington of Yesteryear" and a festive look at Christmas traditions of the Civil War era.

Surratt House is the mid-Victorian home of Mary Surratt. It has a tragic history. Although the extent to which Mrs. Surratt was involved in the criminal conspiracy to assassinate Lincoln is still debated, it was sufficient for the government to execute her, the first of her sex to suffer that fate at the hands of the federal government.

Mary Surratt was widowed in 1862, ten years after her husband, John Surratt, built a house and tavern in Clinton. From the beginning the tavern served as a gathering spot for the community. As the country grew ever more bitterly divided, Southern dissidents gathered here to repudiate Maryland's Northern alignment. When John Jr. left college to help his widowed mother run the family business, he quickly fell in with Confederate sympathizers and became a party to a scheme to kidnap President Abraham Lincoln.

The tavern also became a safe house for Southern agents. John Wilkes Booth was one such agent who knew he could find help here. As Booth made his way south after shooting the President, he stopped at the Surratt House to pick up his field glasses, left for him earlier in the day by Mary Surratt, and the "shooting irons" that had been hidden in the ceiling as part of the earlier kidnaping plot. His accomplice took one of the guns, but Booth decided against carrying any because his injured leg made it difficult for him to ride. Testimony that Mary Surratt had indeed helped Booth led to her conviction by a military court and her death by hanging on July 7, 1865. Two years later when her son, John Jr., was tried on similar charges in a civil court, the jury could not reach a verdict.

In the spring and fall the Surratt Society sponsors a full day's excursion along the route John Wilkes Booth took from Ford's Theatre to present-day Fort A.P. Hill, where he was finally cornered and shot. To reserve a spot on the next **John Wilkes Booth Escape Route** tour write the Society at 9110 Brandywine Road, P.O. Box 427, Clinton, MD 20735, or call (301)868-1121.

The Mary Surratt House can be toured from March through mid-December on Thursday and Friday from 11:00 A.M. to 3:00 P.M. and Saturday and Sunday from NOON to 4:00 P.M.

Directions: From the Washington Beltway (I-95) take Exit 7A (Route 5, Branch Avenue) south to Woodyard Road (Route 223) in Clinton. Turn right on Woodyard Road and continue to second traffic light, where you turn left onto Brandywine Road. The Surratt House is on the left at 9110 Brandywine Road.

Central Maryland
Introduction

I f Maryland is America in miniature, then the six counties of Central Maryland help make that distinction possible. Many of the points of interest in this region have national significance, from the Maryland State House, where in 1783 George Washington resigned his commission as Commander-in-Chief of the Continental Army, to Fort McHenry, where an anxious Francis Scott Key watched during a pivotal battle of the War of 1812 to see if his country's flag still flew. At the nearby Star-Spangled Banner House you'll hear about the young mother, daughter and niece who created the oversize flag. At Baltimore's Inner Harbor you can see the U.S.S. Frigate *Constellation,* launched in 1797 and the first official ship of the U.S. Navy. Also at the harbor is the National Aquarium, one of the country's most exciting aquatic exhibits with huge ocean tanks alive with reef fish, sharks and stingrays. The bottle-nose dolphins are put through their paces in their 1.2 million-gallon tank. Baseball, our national pastime, is celebrated at the Babe Ruth Birthplace and Baseball Center, which also serves as the official Baltimore Orioles Museum.

In addition to its two significant cities Baltimore and Annapolis this region is also blessed with rolling farmland, verdant vineyards, quiet towns and pastoral back roads. Boordy Vineyards has a special place in the history of wine making, not just in Maryland but across the country. If Baltimore is a modern metropolis, the 13th largest city in the country, towns like Ellicott City and Havre de Grace transport visitors back to bygone eras. Ellicott City continues the story begun at the B&O Railroad Museum, the birthplace of the American railroad and the oldest railroad station in the country. The first trains ran from Baltimore's Mount Clare station to the Ellicott City station which now houses the B& O Station Railroad Museum.

A number of the state's most outstanding gardens can be discovered in this region. The whimsical Ladew Topiary Garden and Harvey Ladew's equally delightful home is a favorite with garden fanciers and among the best not only in the state but in the country. In Annapolis there is the formal splendor of the William Paca Gardens and outside the city, the informal charm of the blooming hillsides of London Town Publik House and Gardens. And finally, unexpectedly you can even spend a day at the beach in this Maryland's central region at Sandy Point State Park.

CARROLL COUNTY

Carroll County Farm Museum

Down on the Farm

Over the years Hollywood has turned its spotlight on rural America with movies such as *Places in the Heart, Country* and *The River*. But this kind of attention is not as personal and hands-on as the **Carroll County Farm Museum** in Westminster, which has been depicting the life of 19th-century independent farmers since 1966.

This is not a museum in the traditional sense. Although there are a few display cases filled with carefully labeled articles, this is primarily a recreation of the way of life of a land-owning farm family in the 19th century. On such farms the farmer planted enough to feed his family and his livestock. He acquired mechanized equipment very gradually, relying primarily on horse power. His wife preserved and canned the excess crop, and the seeds were saved for the next year. Market days were major events for the entire family.

The house at the Carroll County Farm Museum was built in 1852 to serve as the County Almshouse. In the 19th century it was customary to house the poor in such a community dwelling. The house, which opened in May 1853 was called the "County Home." It was run by a "steward of Almshouse" who was paid $400 annually. There were for a time as many as 50 people living here with the women on the third floor, the stewards on the second and a separate men's dormitory. At times hobos and tramps stayed in the house and it wasn't uncommon to have criminals or mentally impaired individuals housed here. Able residents worked on the farm to raise food.

The farm was worked from the late 1850s until 1965 when it became this museum. Six rooms of the house are now furnished (many would say over-furnished) in the Victorian style of the late 19th century. The layered look is definitely in—tables are covered with not one but three decorative cloths. Ornate picture frames are draped with swags to draw the eye from one picture to the next.

As you tour the house, the only building where a guided tour is offered, it becomes evident that although the days were long and the life hard, farming did enable a family to acquire a few of the finer things. While you're exploring, see how many objects you can name. The kitchen offers a treasure trove to be identified. Few can pin a name on the whipped cream churner, though most can identify the apple corer.

The guides, dressed in period costumes, will direct you to the outbuildings where blacksmiths, weavers, spinners, quilters and tinsmiths demonstrate their skills and wares. After watching these artisans, you

The Carroll County Farm Museum re-creates the way of life on a family farm in the 19th century. In one barn, blacksmiths, tinsmiths, weavers and others demonstrate skills.

can check out the farm support buildings, which include a bank barn, blacksmith shop, broom shop, spring house, smokehouse and one-room school house. There are farm animals and a fish pond. The farm is just part of a 140-acre park. Two pavilions in the garden are popular for reunions, wedding receptions and other private functions. There are nature trails, including a Bluebird Trail, to hike if you have the time and a place to picnic under the trees surrounding the pond.

The Carroll County Farm Museum is open weekends NOON to 5:00 P.M. May through October and every day except Monday from 10:00 A.M. to 4:00 P.M. during July and August. Throughout the year the farm sponsors a series of festivals (see Calendar of Events). The

General Store, which suggests the 1800s, sells items crafted by museum artisans as well as penny candy and souvenirs.

Directions: From Baltimore take Route 140 northwest to the Westminster area. One mile south of Westminster turn left off Route 140 onto Center Street. Go 1½ miles and the Carroll County Farm Museum is on the right off Center Street.

Hard Lodging, Strawbridge Shrine and Uniontown

A Piece of the Rock

Hard Lodging, the name Solomon Shepherd gave his home in the 1790s, could easily refer to the solid rock foundation on which it rests. Shepherd actually named his estate after a nearby land grant. The townsfolk, however, called the house on the rock top Solomon's Folly.

When you tour this house, which is now on the National Register of Historic Places, one of the first areas you'll be shown is the basement. The floor on this lower level is the irregular rock ledge on which the house stands. The house is a typical English style house with a brick belt course (a distinctive brick design that separates the first and second floors) and a water table (a strong molding beneath the front windows to throw off rainwater).

The main section, now the dining room and overhead bedrooms, was built in the 1790s. A service wing was added later, which is currently decorated as an Early American den and living room. The last owner, Mrs. Thelma Littlefield Shriner, had an informal wing with sun porch built on in 1950.

Much of the furniture is from the Empire Period, 1815-1820, although some pieces are older. Some of the furnishings have an interesting history. In the entrance hall the Empire secretary, or desk bookcase, belonged to the Jerome family, who were friends of Mrs. Shriner's grandfather. Jenny Jerome was Winston Churchill's mother.

Mrs. Shriner amassed an eclectic, but interesting, collection of furnishings. The silver service in the dining room also belonged to the Jeromes. Decorative pieces in the dining room include Limoges plates and a Currier and Ives lithograph. One piece that delights visitors is the five-faced cookie jar. Tours are given by the Historical Society of Carroll County. To make arrangements call (301)848-6494 or 848-9531.

There are two additional points of interest north and south of New Windsor that can easily be combined with a stop at Hard Lodging. On the south is **Strawbridge Shrine** where you'll see a replica of the 1764 meeting house of the first American Methodist congregation and a rustic cabin. There is also the home of John Evan, Methodism's first American convert. Robert Strawbridge, for whom the shrine is named, came to America from Ireland after being converted to Methodism by John Coughlin, one of John Wesley's preachers. The homestead where Robert Strawbridge lived is privately owned and cannot be toured. However, you are free to explore around the Shrine.

North of New Windsor lies the village of **Uniontown,** whose main street hasn't changed since the turn of the century. There are no chic boutiques or elegant eateries here. A walking-tour brochure gives architectural details of the picturesque private homes lining Uniontown Road. Those who really like to get away from the hustle and bustle should try the Newel Post, a Victorian bed and breakfast in town. Call (301)775-2655 for details.

One last spot you should include on your day's itinerary is the International Gift Shop at the New Windsor Service Center. Handicrafts from around the world are sold under the auspices of the Church of the Brethren World Ministries Commission. The Gift Shop is open Monday through Saturday from 9:00 A.M. to 5:00 P.M. Closed on holidays.

Directions: From the Baltimore Beltway (1-695) take Route 26 west 20 miles to Route 27 and turn right. Go left at the intersection with Route 407 and then right on Route 31, New Windsor Road. Turn right on Wakefield Valley Road and right on Strawbridge Lane for Strawbridge Shrine. For Hard Lodging return to Route 31 and head north. Turn left on Route 75 for a short distance.

Piney Run Park and Cascade Lake

Natural Selection

Two natural treats await you in Carroll County. One of your choices is **Piney Run Park.** The park's 300-acre lake provides a picturesque setting for picnickers and boaters and multiple options for fishermen. The lake is stocked with rainbow trout. Other fish include large and small mouth bass, crappie, bluegill, channel catfish, freshwater rockfish and tiger muskies. You can either fish from the shore or rent a canoe or rowboat and try your luck farther out. From November through March fishing is allowed from the shore only.

For fun on the lake you can rent paddle boats or enjoy a pontoon ride, available hourly on weekends June through August from 1:00 to 5:00 P.M. A nature center introduces you to the region's flora and fauna, and five miles of nature trails crisscross the park. During the winter the trails are used by cross-country skiers. When the lake freezes, ice skating is permitted.

Piney Run Park's main season is April through October weekdays

9:00 A.M. to sunset and weekends 6:00 A.M. to sunset. From November through March park personnel are available at the nature center. Visitors can park outside the gate and still take advantage of the hiking, fishing, skating and skiing.

Not too far away, just outside the town of Hampstead in the hamlet of Syndersburg is **Cascade Lake**—a six-acre lake surrounded by 20 acres of park land. Dating back to the 1920s, Cascade Lake has been updated by the addition of water slides, paddle boats and a number of decks overlooking the lake. Visitors may swim, slide, picnic and enjoy the game room and playground. This privately-owned family-oriented park is open to the public from Memorial Day to Labor Day. Admission is charged. For current hours call (410) 374-9111 or (410) 239-4708.

Directions: From the Baltimore Beltway, I-695, take 1-70 west, exit 8D on Route 32 north, then turn left on Route 26 for Piney Run Park. When traveling from Baltimore to Cascade Lake take Route 140 northwest to Route 30. Go north on Route 30 to Hampstead. Turn left on Route 482 and make a right on Snydersburg Road. Cascade Lake is at 3000 Snydersburg Road.

Union Mills Homestead and Gristmill

Shriver Family Saga

The Shriver family, founders of **Union Mills**, are savers. This becomes apparent as you tour the family homestead. In addition to the furnishings and memorabilia accumulated by six generations of Shrivers who have lived here, there are also diaries, accounts and records. Only the Adamses of Massachusetts have more detailed family records, but then their family had two presidents, John and John Quincy Adams.

The Shriver brothers, Andrew and David, came to Maryland in 1797. They each built a two-room log house separated by a "dog walk." The cost for building both houses was $86; the exact figure is listed in the accounts kept from the very beginning. On their 100 acres the brothers next built a sawmill, followed by the gristmill you'll see on your visit. Records show that 100,000 bricks were fired for the gristmill but only 70,000 were used. A tannery and shops for a blacksmith, cooper and carpenter were added later.

Once the family businesses were functioning smoothly, David Shriver moved to the Shellman House in Westminster, and then to Cumberland, on the National Road that he surveyed. Andrew stayed at Union Mills, where both his family and his home expanded over the years. Andrew fathered 11 children, and the house was eventually enlarged to 23 rooms. The various additions are easily seen from outside.

Possessions from six generations of Shrivers enrich their Union Mill Homestead. There are no period rooms; the furnishings are an eclectic mix reflecting a family that never threw anything away.

M.E. WARREN

Andrew Shriver campaigned for Thomas Jefferson. The grateful president rewarded Andrew with the postmastership of the Union Mills community. Andrew's original eight-slot postmaster's desk still sits in his office, one of the house's four original rooms.

The Civil War divided the country; it also divided the Shriver family. The second Andrew, son of Andrew Shriver, inherited the homestead and tannery. His brother William had a nearby house, called The Mills, and the gristmill. Andrew Kaiser was a Protestant, a Republican, and though he owned slaves he was a Northern supporter. Two of his sons served in the Union army. William, a convert to Catholicism and a Democrat, did not own slaves but he supported the South. Four of his sons fought for the Confederacy.

The tensions within the family reached their peak just before the Battle of Gettysburg when troops from both armies were fed at the homestead. On June 29, 1863, J.E.B. Stuart's 2,400 rebels camped in the farm's apple orchard, which has been replanted. At about 2:00 A.M. they were all fed pancakes prepared in the kitchen's huge fireplace by "Black" Ruth Dohr. Not long after the Confederates had departed, Union General Barnes arrived. He was given a bedroom at the homestead and he and his officers were entertained in the parlor by the Shriver daughters. They sang and danced. Accounts of the evening mention that one song heard that night was "When the Cruel War Is Over."

When the war was over the Shrivers returned to the business of business. The family tannery won an award at the 1876 Centennial in Philadelphia. The certificate, which still hangs at the homestead, commends their "oak sole leather from Texas hides." The house itself served as an inn for travelers along the coach road from Baltimore to Pittsburgh. Washington Irving stayed here, talking late into the night in front of the fire. James Audubon also enjoyed the hospitality of Union Mills Homestead while he was researching and writing about Baltimore orioles. Audubon watched an oriole build a nest in the willow tree outside his window.

Unlike other historic homes, Union Mills Homestead has no period rooms. Here you'll find an amiable lived-in mix of furnishings. As one of Andrew Shriver's descendants remarked, "No one seems ever to have thrown anything away!"

Across from the house is the restored water-powered gristmill. The mill operated from 1798 to 1942 and was one of the first mills to use the revolutionary designs of Oliver Evans. Evans's *The Young Millwright and Miller's Guide*, published in 1795, included the greatest innovations in milling since before the time of Christ. The first mill to incorporate these ideas was at Ellicott Mills (see selection). Both George Washington and Thomas Jefferson employed the new design. The Union Mills gristmill is one of the most accurate restorations of an Evans design in the country.

You can buy flour milled at Union Mills, as well as other items, at the gift shop in the restored Miller's House. Also restored is the Old Bark Shed where, on selected weekends blacksmithing, carpentry and woodworking are demonstrated.

Union Mills Homestead and Gristmill are open June until September, Tuesday through Friday from 10:00 A.M. to 4:00 P.M. and Saturday and Sunday from NOON to 4:00 P.M. They are open weekends only in May and September. Admission is charged.

Directions: From Baltimore Beltway, I-695, take Exit 19 to I-795 to Route 140 west to Westminster. Then head north on Route 97. Union Mills is on the right on Route 97 seven miles north of Westminster.

BALTIMORE COUNTY

Ballestone Manor and Heritage Society Museum

Manor on the Green

There is one spot on the Rocky Point Golf Course where golfers are not allowed: the carefully fenced grounds of **Ballestone Manor.** This historic 18th-century plantation house is built on land given to George Washington's maternal great-grandfather, William Ball. In 1659 Cecilius Calvert, the second Lord Baltimore, granted Ball 450 acres on Back River Neck.

Ball, a Virginian, considered this Maryland acreage an investment and never built on it or visited the property. It was the Stansbury family who built a 2½-story, three-bay Flemish-bond brick house in the post-Revolutionary period, around 1780. These were years of economic growth for Baltimore and the surrounding countryside because of the prosperous mercantile trade.

In 1819 the estate was purchased by the Leakin family, who expanded the house with a 1½-story brick addition, plus a two-story frame structure that is no longer standing. The final expansion was done by Edward Miller between 1850 and 1880. He raised the roof to a full two stories and added a columned portico with a Victorian millwork railing.

The house, built over a hundred-year period, fell victim to time, the elements and vandalism. It became a project of the Heritage Society of Essex-Middle River. This group advocated its restoration as a museum in 1974. Ballestone's restoration was a Bicentennial Project.

When you tour Ballestone, you will see the dining parlor filled with

Ballestone Manor, 100 years in the building, graces land given to George Washington's maternal great-great-grandfather, William Ball, by the second Lord Baltimore in 1659.

Federal pieces and the parlor representing the later Victorian era. Upstairs there is an 1840 Empire bedroom as well as a children's bedroom. After you tour the main house, do stop in the kitchen. Although the kitchen is a modern addition, it does suggest an 18th-century dependency.

Docents attired in period clothes conduct tours of Ballestone Manor on Sundays from 2:00 to 5:00 P.M. during May, June and September.

You'll find more regional history at the museum operated by the Heritage Society in the old firehouse in Essex (this is not in any way associated with Ballestone Manor). The walls are now lined with display cases; furniture and costumed mannequins fill the rooms. There are literally thousands of artifacts that tell the story of the Essex and Middle River area. One room has fire-related regalia, while another has a collection of memorabilia from the nearby Martin Marietta airplane plant. There is also an old drugstore and a 1920 vintage school room. An avenue of shops includes a toy store, music shop, general store, post office and the Essex Candle Company, which operated from 1932 to 1950. The **Heritage Society Museum** is at 516 Eastern Boulevard in Essex. It is open on weekends from 1:00 to 4:00 P.M.

Donations are welcome.

Directions: For Ballestone Manor take I-695, the Baltimore Beltway east, to Route 702. Take Route 702 toward Essex; turn on Back River Neck Road and continue to Rocky Point Golf Course. The entrance road will be on the left, then you will see Ballestone Manor on the right. For the Heritage Society Museum from Baltimore take I-695 to U.S. 40; turn right on Rossville Boulevard to Stemmers Run Road. On Stemmers Run Road proceed to the intersection with Eastern Boulevard in Essex and turn right. At the third traffic light there will be a sign indicating the Heritage Society Museum.

Boordy Vineyards

Lift Your Spirits

"Maryland's climate is eminently suited to the culture of the grapevine, but the state has never had a reputation as a wine producing area. The one notable exception is the admirably run **Boordy Vineyard** in Riderwood near Baltimore, where J. & P. [Jocelyn and Philip] Wagner... experimented widely with different types of grapes.... They also make wines, if only to demonstrate how good eastern American wines from hybrids can be, if properly handled. The result, so far as quality goes, is laudable, and their contribution to American winemaking is enormous."

Since Alexis Lechine wrote the above in the *New Encyclopedia of Wines and Spirits* in 1977, more Maryland vintners are taking advantage of the climate he praises. But Boordy continues to have a special place in the history of winemaking in Maryland and indeed across the country.

Philip Wagner had tried to cultivate California varieties on his Riderwood farm during the 1920s and 1930s, but the Maryland climate proved inhospitable for them. Wagner, a reporter for the *Baltimore Sun,* was sent with fellow correspondent and wine buff H.L. Mencken to France during World War II. Wagner did more than cover the conflict. He used the opportunity to persuade French farmers to part with cuttings of their hybrid grapes.

When Wagner returned to Riderwood, he established experimental plantings of these hybrids. When they proved ideal for the Maryland climate, he established not only a winery, but he also sold his newly discovered French hybrids to vintners across the country. Wagner once said, "There isn't a state in the union now, with the possible exception of North Dakota, that doesn't have them."

Wagner's Boordy Vineyards produced wine that was acclaimed from coast to coast. By 1965, demand exceeded output. Looking around for new fields, Wagner prevailed upon his friends, the

Defords, to plant grapes at their Long Green Farm in Hydes. In 1980, when he decided to retire, Wagner sold Boordy Vineyards to the Defords, who had to evict 150 cattle from their dairy barn to convert it into a winery. The grapes came in early that year, and changes were still being made on the barn when the first truckloads of harvested grapes arrived.

The Defords expanded and introduced up-to-date winemaking techniques while retaining the 19th century stone and wood barn that was so conducive to the aging of wine. White wines are cool-fermented in stainless steel to preserve the fresh fruit aromas, while the reds are barrel-fermented and the sparkling wines undergo the "method champenoise." Individual care is given from hand-harvesting the fruit through fermentation, aging and bottling. The result is award-winning wines that have won critical acclaim.

In Robert Parker's book, *Wine Buyer's Guide*, he wrote, "The most successful Maryland winery from a commercial and critical point of view is Boordy Vineyards whose wines have moved from strength to strength in the late 1980s and early 1990s." Michael Dresser, *Baltimore Sun* columnist, also recognized the vineyards quality. He wrote in his *Baltimore Sun* column, "Buying Maryland wine is not just a matter of home state pride. Boordy Vineyards, the state's oldest, is an especially good source of whites for under $10. If your purpose is to confound a wine snob, you couldn't do better." The whites are not the only Boordy selections to receive critical praise. *The Wine Advocate* judged the 1993 Grand Reserve Cabernet Sauvignon, "...impressive enough to be matched with the best from Europe and California."

You can judge for yourself, since visitors are welcome at Boordy for tours and tastings on the hour daily from 1:00 to 4:00 P.M. You can also call the winery at (410) 592-5015 for information about wine-related special events.

Directions: From the Baltimore Beltway (I-695) take Exit 29, Cromwell Bridge Road, and go northeast for 2.9 miles. Turn left on Glen Arm Road and proceed 3.2 miles to the intersection with Long Green Road. Turn left and continue 2 miles to Boordy Vineyards entrance on the left.

Fire Museum of Maryland and Valley View Farms

Pumping Iron

Over 42 fire-fighting vehicles dating from 1806, and an impressive array of support equipment, fill the 23,000 square feet of display and storage space at the **Fire Museum of Maryland,** one of the country's largest fire museums.

Although there are rows and rows of equipment, visiting the Fire Museum is certainly not dull. Clanging bells, fire sirens, ongoing fire calls, and the chance to operate an old pump engine combine to create a sensory barrage.

Fire-fighting procedure is explained at the firehouse watch desk. A desk similar to this could be found in firehouses across the country through the 1940s and 1950s. Volunteers demonstrate the alarm telegraph, and at the back of the museum you see a replica of the central alarm office. Both at the watch desk and in the alarm office there are alarm boxes that may be activated by visitors. But volunteers are careful to explain how vital it is to turn in alarms only when there is an emergency. (Check the schedule at the museum's movie theater; you might be able to catch a short film on fire safety and fire fighting.) In addition to learning how and when to use a fire alarm, visitors are permitted to ring one of the fire bells. Some of the larger bells produce an ear-piercing ring.

Also explained are the different types of fire alarms. You'll learn who and what determines whether a fire is a single-alarm fire. Then you'll see how that message is conveyed to the firefighters at the firehouse. Fire companies had ceremonial, as well as functional, equipment. One glossy parade piece on display is the 1875 L. Butler & Sons hose carriage. Nearby is an 1853 James Smith pumper that still works. You can try your hand at pumping water with this vintage model. It may seem easy, but those on the line had to keep pumping until the fire was out.

As you wander down the rows of equipment, you can see the evolution from hand pump to steam pumping engines, and from hand-drawn wagons to horse-drawn vehicles. The 1916 fire engine that Walter Christie revolutionized by installing a tractor engine marked another step forward. It was one of the first gas engine fire-fighting pieces.

Most of the pieces are big and most are painted bright red. Even companies that painted their trucks what one volunteer terms "slime lime" are now repainting them red. There are small display cases filled with fire hats and helmets, old speaking trumpets, and kerosene and whale oil lanterns.

The Fire Museum of Maryland was founded by Stephen G. Heaver in 1971. His substantial collection is the heart of the museum, although additional pieces have been added or loaned.

The museum is open weekends May through October and Wednesday, Thursday and Friday during the months of June, July and August. Hours are Wednesday through Saturday 11:00 A.M. to 4:00 P.M. and Sunday 1:00 to 5:00 P.M. Before leaving, don't forget to visit the museum gift shop with fire service-related souvenirs, books, t-shirts, jewelry, toys and birthday party supplies.

Just seven miles north on York Road in Cockeysville you can visit **Valley View Farms**, which boasts the "nation's largest, most complete and most unique Christmas shop." Under a twinkling canopy of lights, 100 decorated Christmas trees offer more than 6,000 decorations, displayed beneath the trees. You can also buy the materials to make your own ornaments.

The International Christmas Shoppe has decorations and handmade specialty items from around the world. There are exquisitely carved nativity creches; all but a special few may be purchased. There is an amazing array of music boxes and hand-carved German figurines that are also musical toys. Another Christmas favorite, the Nutcracker, is available in myriad forms. Angels come in spun glass, brass, wood, ceramic, pewter, papier-mache, crystal, porcelain and wax. These are only a few of the thousands of items gathered from around the world.

Valley View Farms has a floral design shop and a country deli. Beginning in early November from dusk to closing there is a huge outdoor light display. Valley Views' Christmas shops are open daily September 15 through December 24 from 7:00 A.M. to 9:00 P.M.

Directions: From Baltimore Beltway (I-695) Exit 26 go north on York Road, Route 45, for one block. The Fire Museum of Maryland is on the right behind the Heaver Plaza office building. For Valley View Farms continue north to 11035 York Road.

Gunpowder Falls State Park

Maryland's Largest

Did you know Baltimore County has 173 miles of Chesapeake Bay shoreline? The idea that there are a number of scenic beaches (including a Miami Beach) north of Baltimore surprises even some long-time Marylanders. Both Miami and Rocky Point Beach are part of the county's Department of Recreation and Parks. But the largest park in the county, and indeed in Maryland, is **Gunpowder Falls State Park.** Within its 15,000 acres you can swim, fish, boat, tube, white-water canoe, hike, ride, camp and picnic.

Big and Little Gunpowder Rivers meet in Baltimore County for the last eight miles of their journey to the Chesapeake Bay. There's a wonderful, but probably apocryphal, legend about how the rivers were named. When European settlers gave gunpowder to the Indians, so the story goes, the Indians planted the black powder along the riverbanks in hopes it would grow.

You can find reminders of America's colonial past within Gunpowder Falls State Park. A popular colonial fording spot can be seen where the Old Post Road passes Long Calm Ford in historic **Jerusalem Village.** The only double-dormed mill in the United States, Jerusalem Mill, is on Jericho Road. David Lee built the mill in 1772.

(Today the restored mill houses a museum, open weekends from 1:00 to 4:00 P.M. and park offices open weekdays 8:00 A.M. to 5:00 P.M.) Lee also built a two-story building, also restored, in which he produced guns for the Revolutionary army. A little farther south (a round trip hike is less than one mile), downriver on Jericho Road, you'll see the picturesque **Jericho Covered Bridge** over the Little Gunpowder River.

There are several separate sections of the park. Two of the most popular are the Hammerman/Dundee area and the more northern Hereford area. Visitors often think the water that they see at Hammerman is the Chesapeake Bay, but it is actually the Gunpowder River. Dundee Creek Marina is on a tributary of the river. Since the days when Indians fished these waters, sportsmen have flocked to this area. The blue crab, a Chesapeake Bay delicacy, can be found from late summer through early fall. At the mouth of the Gunpowder River, licensed fishermen can fish for striped bass, perch and pickerel. The Hereford area is noted for its excellent fly fishing in the Big Gunpowder. The catch along the river in this area includes bass, carp and catfish.

Near the area known as Sweet Air there are 1,155 acres of hiking and horseback trails. There are also trails in the central area along the Big and Little Gunpowder Rivers. The **Northern Central Railroad Trail** is the most historic section; hikers, bikers and horseback riders enjoy this 21-mile trail along an abandoned railroad bed. The Monkton Train Station on this trail has been restored and serves as a ranger station, museum and gift shop (open Wednesday through Sunday from Memorial Day to Labor Day and on weekends in the spring and fall). Also on the trail is the Sparks Bank Nature Center, open on weekends from 1:00 to 3:00 P.M. The trail continues into Pennsylvania and as of 1999 extends more than 20 miles to the city of York.

The central area is noted for the **Sweathouse Branch Wildlands Area**, a popular area for birders and wildflower enthusiasts. Trails take visitors through a lush hardwood forest on the banks of the Big Gunpowder. The parking lot that accesses these trails is adjacent to the Route 1 bridge over the Big Gunpowder, north of Perry Hall.

Gunpowder Falls State Park is open year-round during daylight hours. Only the Hammerman area has an entrance fee.

Directions: From I-695 take I-95 north and proceed to the first exit, White Marsh Boulevard. Take White Marsh Boulevard to Route 40 north. Continue on Route 40 to Ebenezer Road and continue 4.5 miles to the Hammerman area of the park. For the Hereford Area take I-83 to Exit 27, Mt. Carmel Road. For the park's central area take Route 1 exit off I-695. This will provide access to the hiking trails on the Big Gunpowder and Little Gunpowder Rivers.

Hampton National Historic Site

Ridgelys Right on the Money

The Ridgely family always seemed to be at the right place at the right time. The first to emigrate to America from England was Robert, who held several governmental positions including Deputy Secretary of the Colony. Two more Ridgely generations were planters in the rich farmland of Anne Arundel County. After the family was in Maryland for about one hundred years, they moved to the frontier of Baltimore County. Here they developed an iron furnace that supplied cannons and shot to the Continental Army and Navy

Captain Charles Ridgely took the vast fortune he acquired during the Revolutionary War and built what was the largest mansion in the United States. **Hampton Mansion**'s opulence survives today almost unchanged. The eye-catching design pulls your eye up the white columns at the front door, past the second floor balcony to the octagonal white dome cupola, 86 feet above the ground. The mansion's distinctive pink color comes from iron oxide in the sand used to mix the stucco.

There were those who questioned Captain Ridgely's judgment when he began the seven year project of building his house. Built deep in the woods, 11 miles from Baltimore, the neighbors, believing it an impossible task, called it "Ridgely's folly." Captain Charles, the builder, died approximately six months after the mansion was finished, leaving behind a childless widow. His nephew inherited the property on the condition that he change his name from Charles Ridgely Carnan to Charles Carnan Ridgely. Young Charles had a distinguished career as a Representative in the Maryland General Assembly, Senator in the Assembly and Governor of Maryland. He and his wife, Priscilla, had 13 children.

It was Charles Carnan Ridgely who undertook the landscaping that is as spectacular as the mansion itself. The famous landscape architect Henry Winthrop Sargent said: "It has been truly said of Hampton that it expresses more grandeur than any place in America." The gardens are laid out in huge parterres, or falls, planted in a formal geometric style. Bulbs, boxwoods and flowers adorn some of the parterres, while others feature heirloom rose varieties. The estate reached its peak under the second owner, who amassed some 24,000 acres. Over 300 enslaved African-Americans, as well as indentured servants and craftsmen lived on the estate and contributed to its wealth.

If the first owner built it and the second owner landscaped it, the third owner and his wife spent a fortune and a lifetime furnishing Hampton. Eliza Ridgely, whose famous portrait hangs in the Great Hall, traveled Europe acquiring art treasures and furniture for her grand Maryland home. The park today has about 40,000 original items, many of which were purchased by Eliza. Present plans are for each room to reflect a decorative period popular during the lifetimes of the seven generations who lived at Hampton. One of the most striking rooms is the dining room, painted a brilliant Prussian blue. The blue is picked up in the curtains, where it is combined with gold and trimmed with gold and orange tassels—quite a striking window treatment!

After your house tour, take a walking tour of the grounds and gardens. Five trees on the site are Maryland state champions. Slave quarters, stables and other buildings remain from the heyday of the estate.

The grounds are open daily from 9:00 A.M. to 5:00 P.M. Tours of the mansion are offered on the hour from 9:00 A.M. until 4:00 P.M. Admission is charged. A tea room serves lunch every day except Monday. Hampton is a part of the National Park Service.

Directions: From the Baltimore Beltway (I-695) take Exit 27B, Dulaney Valley Road. From Dulaney Valley Road make an immediate right onto Hampton Lane, proceed one-half mile. Hampton is on the right.

BALTIMORE CITY

Babe Ruth Birthplace and Baseball Center

A Guaranteed Hit!

If the cry, "Play ball!" stirs your blood, you're sure to enjoy the **Babe Ruth Birthplace and Baseball Center.** George Herman "Babe" Ruth was born at this Baltimore rowhouse on February 6, 1895.

The narrow rowhouse at 216 Emory Street, just 12 feet wide by 60 feet long (the museum encompasses three adjacent houses as well), belonged to Babe Ruth's grandparents. The Babe did not have an easy childhood, and his wild ways didn't help. At seven he was sent to St. Mary's Industrial School for Boys, part reform school for incorrigible boys and part orphanage. The school offered much that George Herman Ruth didn't like, but it did introduce him to the love of his life: here he learned to play baseball. One of the most poignant items in the museum is the school hymnal, inscribed, "World's worse [sic] singer, world's best pitcher," signed George H. Ruth.

George's finest hour as a pitcher came in the 1916 World Series, two years after he entered the major leagues. He pitched scoreless innings for the Boston Red Sox, a record not beaten until Whitey Ford's streak in 1961.

Ruth went on to set batting records with the New York Yankees. He

Babe Ruth and Jimmie Foxx star at the Baltimore Orioles Museum. At the Babe's birthplace nearby, one hears that the great pitcher/hitter learned to play baseball at a reform school.

hit 60 home runs in 1927, a feat no player equaled until 1961, when Roger Maris knocked 61 balls out of American League parks. Only one player, Hank Aaron, ever hit more total home runs than the Babe's 714. Aaron soared beyond with 755. The museum has a 714 Home Run Club Wall with a plaque for each of the Babe's home runs. Here also is career information on the only 15 players to hit more than 500 homers. It includes the most recent, Eddie Murray, whose 500th home run ball, which was purchased for an unprecedented $500,000 then donated to the museum, is on display.

Since this is the official **Baltimore Orioles Museum**, fans can see photographs and memorabilia on the hometown team. From the 1895 International League Orioles mascot's uniform to the 2131 banners that hung on the warehouse at Camden Yards when Cal Ripkin broke Lou Gherig's record, more than 100 years of Orioles history is chronicled.

Hours at the Babe Ruth Birthplace are 10:00 A.M. to 5:00 P.M. daily, April through October. There are extended hours when the Baltimore Orioles have home games and closing is at 7:00 P.M. From November through March hours are 10:00 A.M. to 4:00 P.M. daily. Closed Christmas Eve and Day, Thanksgiving and Easter. Admission is charged.

Directions: Babe Ruth Birthplace is located on Emory Street, two blocks south of Pratt Street, just two blocks west of Oriole Park at Camden Yards.

B&O Railroad Museum, Mount Clare Mansion and City Fire Museum

Train of Thought

The story of the American railroad begins at Mount Clare in Baltimore, when Maryland's Charles Carroll laid the first stone for the Baltimore and Ohio Railroad on July 4, 1828 (coincidentally on the same day President John Quincy Adams turned over the first shovel of soil for the building of the Chesapeake and Ohio Canal just outside Washington, D.C.). Carroll said about his involvement in the B&O Railroad inauguration, "I consider this among the most important acts of my life, second only to the signing of the Declaration of Independence, if second even to that."

At the **B&O Railroad Museum** you can explore this pivotal transportation revolution. Fifty locomotives and full size models are housed in the museum's Mount Clare station roundhouse. The station is considered the birthplace of the American railroad and the oldest station in the United States. The first American trains ran from this spot to Ellicott City (see selection), and it was here that Peter Cooper built the engine he called his Teakettle, nicknamed by others Tom Thumb.

Cooper's Tom Thumb is known as the early locomotive that lost a legendary race with a horse. As sometimes happens with such stories, fiction has clouded fact in this tale. Although a race evidently did take place, just when and where have never been firmly established. It might have been on August 28, 1830, during the engine's inaugural 13-mile run between the Mount Clare station and Ellicott City. However, no horse could have matched the engine's time of 26:22 minutes, and the many news accounts of the run do not mention a race. It is far more likely that the race took place in 1831, during the celebration of Charles Carroll's 94th birthday. The fan belt broke during this run, slowing the train enough for a horse to beat it.

The B&O Railroad Museum is known worldwide for the size and scope of its collection. Many of the prize railroad cars rest on the roundhouse's 22 turntable tracks. There are vintage Pang born engines, Imlay coaches, trains from the Civil War (when the military first used railroads) and later wars. From World War I there are "40 and 8" trains, so called because they carried 40 men and eight horses.

Trains overflow to the front and back of the museum. These are popular with young visitors who play conductor and engineer on the vintage engines. The museum is open Wednesday through Sunday from 10:00 A.M. to 4:00 P.M. Admission is charged.

The ten acres on which Mount Clare Station was built was virtually given to the B&O Railroad by James MacCubbin Carroll for the bargain price of $1. Carroll's nearby family home, **Mount Clare Mansion**, is also open for tours. This pre-Revolutionary Georgian estate is the oldest in Baltimore, circa 1756, and the oldest house museum in the state. It was built by Charles Carroll the Barrister, who helped write the Declaration of Rights for Maryland and the Maryland State Constitution. Carroll's first wife, Margaret Tilghman Carroll, who was Mount Clare's longest resident, was responsible for much of its expansion. The estate's greenhouse, which has been excavated, was the model for the greenhouse at George Washington's Mount Vernon estate. The house is furnished with Carroll family pieces. Mount Clare is noted for its portrait collection including works by Charles Willson Peale, Robert Feke and John Hesselius. You can tour the house Tuesday through Saturday from 11:00 A.M. to 4:00 P.M. and Sunday from 1:00 to 4:00 P.M. It is closed on Mondays and holidays.

Baltimore has another small museum that focuses on transportation. The **Baltimore Streetcar Museum** at 1901 Falls Road has an audio-visual program and exhibits in the visitor center and offers unlimited streetcar rides on its one-mile track. The museum is open year-round on Sunday from NOON to 5:00 P.M. From June through October it is open on Saturday as well at the same time. For December hours and special events call (410) 547-0264. Admission is charged. (See National Capital Trolley Museum selection.)

Loosely related to the subject of transportation, getting firemen to the fire is part of the story at the **City Fire Museum** near Belair Market (see Markets selection). The museum has a few examples of antique

America's love affair with trains began on Mount Clare with the start of the Baltimore and Ohio Railroad on July 4, 1828. It is kept aglow by the B&O Museum's world-famed collection.

equipment, fire department insignias and badges and photographs of the great Baltimore fire of 1904. It is open at no charge Monday through Friday 9:00 A.M. to 4:00 P.M. A more comprehensive collection of fire engines and equipment can be found at the Fire Museum of Maryland in Lutherville.

Directions: The B&O Railroad Museum is located at 901 W. Pratt Street, a few blocks west of Martin Luther King Jr. Boulevard in downtown Baltimore. For the Mount Clare Mansion take Pratt Street to Lombard Street west. Take a left on Martin Luther King Boulevard and turn right onto Washington Boulevard. Turn right into Carroll Park; the mansion is at the top of the hill in the center of the park.

Baltimore Maritime Museum

Ship to Shore

Three very different ships comprise the **Baltimore Maritime Museum** at the Inner Harbor's Pier 4. The U.S.S. *Torsk* was the head of a submarine wolf pack; the *Chesapeake* was a floating lighthouse and the

U.S.C.G. *Taney* is the last surviving ship from the Japanese attack on Pearl Harbor.

On August 14, 1945, the *Torsk* sank two Japanese men-of-war. The next day word came that the war had ended. Thus it was the *Torsk* that fired the last torpedoes of World War II. The submarine holds another record: it is the "diving-est" ship in the world, with 11,884 submersions.

After World War II the *Torsk* was converted to a snorkel-equipped GUPPY submarine. It was involved in operations during the 1960 Lebanon crisis and the naval blockade of Cuba in 1962. The *Torsk* was transferred to Maryland in 1972 and now affords visitors a real feel for life aboard a submarine.

Visitors may find even a short stay claustrophobic in the crew's 14- by 30-foot quarters. It is sobering to realize the conditions under which 26 men lived; no movie or book adequately conveys the entombed feeling you'll get as you explore this submarine. You'll leave with a new respect for submariners.

The second ship of the Baltimore Maritime Museum is the lightship *Chesapeake* built in Charleston, South Carolina, in 1930. Lightships were used where traditional lighthouses could not be constructed, near harbors or channel entrances. Seven years before the *Chesapeake* was built, a lightship began guarding the approach to New York Harbor.

The *Chesapeake* is on the National Register of Historic Places, but it's a "place" that doesn't stay put. This is one of the few lightships that is still operational, and it visits other cities as a representative of the city of Baltimore. When the *Chesapeake* is in port, it can be toured on a combination ticket with the *Torsk*.

The *Taney*'s 50 years of naval service included serving as command ship at Okinawa and serving as fleet escort in the Atlantic and Mediterranean. Before being decommissioned in 1986, the *Taney* provided medical relief during Vietnam. She also has the distinction of being the last ship afloat that participated in the search for Amelia Earhart. There is a museum store aboard the *Taney*.

Included in the museum's collection is the seven-foot **Knoll Lighthouse**, which marked the entrance to the Baltimore Harbor for 135 years before it was moved to the Inner Harbor. Built in 1855, this is the oldest "screwpile" lighthouse in the state.

The Baltimore Maritime Museum, operated by the Living Classrooms Foundation, is open daily 9:30 A.M. to 4:30 P.M. Admission is charged.

While you're in the area, take the elevator to the top of the World Trade Center for a view of the Baltimore Maritime Museum, the harbor area and indeed the entire city. The panoramic gallery is called the Top of the World, and it affords one of the best views in Baltimore. Telescopes and detailed maps help you pinpoint the city's main attractions. The World Trade Center at Pier 2 is the tallest pentagonal building in the United States. It is open 10:00 A.M.. to 5:00 P.M. and admission is charged.

Directions: From I-95 take Exit 53 (I-395, Downtown). From this exit, bear left, following signs to the Inner Harbor. Continue in the left or center lane until the third light. Make a right onto Pratt Street and continue four blocks to the Inner Harbor. The three ships of the Baltimore Maritime Museum are docked at Pier 3 next to the National Aquarium at the Inner Harbor. When you leave the Inner Harbor to return to I-95, take Pratt Street to President Street and turn left. Continue for one block to Lombard Street and turn left. Take Lombard for nine blocks to Howard Street, following signs for I-395, Stadium. Make a left onto Howard Street, which will become I-395. Continue on I-395 to I-95.

Baltimore's Municipal Markets

To Market, To Market...

Baltimore's markets could be called moveable feasts—you do the moving and they provide the feast. This market system is the oldest institution in the city. It was set up in 1765 when the Maryland General Assembly approved a lease for the Commissioners of Baltimore Town to establish and regulate a market. This was before the establishment of a Mayor's office, Health Department or other city agencies.

In 1752 Baltimore was a community of roughly 250 residents, with 25 homes, two taverns and one church. These townsfolk needed a market where they could purchase fresh produce. The oldest market in Baltimore (indeed, the oldest continuously operated market in the country) is the **Lexington Market,** established in 1782 when General John Eager Howard donated some of his land so that outlying farmers could meet there and sell their wares. Conestoga wagons and farm carts rumbled to market with harvested crops, fresh meat, fowl and even seafood. General Howard named the market Lexington, after the Revolutionary battle.

By 1803 sheds appeared; more and more were added until the market spread onto another block. The reputation of Lexington Market also spread, and colonial leaders stopped here, including George Washington and Thomas Jefferson. Baltimore, too, was growing. In the mid-1800s it was the second largest city in the country, and the markets were where the crowds congregated to shop and gossip. More than 600 wagons from Maryland, Virginia and Pennsylvania rolled into the city on Saturday mornings to serve a crowd of 50,000. Oliver Wendell Holmes paid a visit to Lexington Market in 1859. Its size and selection so impressed him he dubbed

Baltimore "The Gastronomic Capital of the Universe."

On March 25, 1949, a six-alarm fire destroyed Lexington Market. It was rebuilt on the original site, re-opening in 1952 even bigger than before with three block-long sheds sheltering more than 130 merchant stalls. The market is now housed in two large permanent brick structures, augmented by the arcade (with an adjacent multi-level parking garage). Fresh meats and produce, a complete seafood spread including a raw bar, and home-baked goods are augmented by 22 ethnic eateries in the glass-enclosed market arcade. The Lexington Market at Lexington and Eutaw streets is open Monday to Saturday 8:30 A.M. to 6:00 P.M.

Although Lexington is the most well-known market in the city—it claims to be "world famous"—six other markets provide old-fashioned shopping experiences in neighborhood settings. These are not tourist markets but the daily stop of in-town natives. Because the original Lexington Market burned to the ground, the oldest market structure in the city is the more than 200-year-old **Broadway Market** at 1640-41 Aliceanna Street, originally constructed in 1785. This hub at Fell's Point (see selection) is set among newly refurbished shops, pubs, fashionable restaurants and ethnic eateries. It is a neighborhood that maintains maritime ties.

Broadway Market's two buildings have stalls selling meat, poultry, seafood, bakery goods, spices, plants and flowers, as well as fresh fruit and vegetables. Market stalls were the goal of European immigrants to Baltimore who wanted to move up from a streetside produce cart. Descendants of these early immigrants still own stalls in the city markets. The Broadway Market is open Monday through Thursday 7:00 A.M. to 6:00 P.M., Friday and Saturday 6:00 A.M. to 6:00 P.M.

There are two other East Baltimore neighborhood markets, the **Northeast Market** and the **Belair Market.** The former is located at 2101 East Monument Street, near the Johns Hopkins Hospital. Northeast Market was originally built in 1885. Today, in addition to fresh produce, you'll also find lunch counters, a delicatessen and a bakery here. It is open Monday through Thursday 7:00 A.M. to 6:00 P.M., Friday and Saturday 6:00 A.M. to 6:00 P.M. Operating during the same hours is the Belair Market, built in 1835, at Gay and Forest Streets in the **Oldtown Mall.** It is an unglorified neighborhood market selling food staples and baked goods.

Visitors can enjoy the chance to mingle with the hometown crowd at **Cross Street Market,** easy to reach via trolley from the Inner Harbor. Cross Street Market, built in 1845, is at 1065 S. Charles Street. It is the neighborhood market for Federal Hill and South Baltimore. The food here is not pre-packaged; you'll find a wide selection of fresh meat, poultry and fish. The raw bar is a popular meeting spot and the stalls sell everything from hand-dipped chocolate to European cheeses. As in all the markets, specialization means better selection and better service. The butcher cuts the meats to order and can advise just how much you'll need for dinner guests. Meanwhile the cottage cheese is scooped per request and the steamed crabs can be packaged to go. Cross Street Market is open Monday through Thursday 7:00 A.M. to 6:00 P.M., Friday and Saturday 6:00 A.M. to 6:00 P.M.

These markets reflect Baltimore as a "melting pot" of ethnic origins; they even provide the produce for the pot. One well-known Baltimore resident who habitually haunted West Baltimore's **Hollins Market** was H.L. Mencken. Mencken shopped at the market near his home and often rhapsodized in his column on "the whole incomparable repertoire of Maryland masterpieces—beaten biscuits, soft crabs, oysters, fried chicken and blackberries." Hollins Market still carries all this and more; it is open Tuesday through Thursday 7:00 A.M. to 6:00 P.M., Friday and Saturday 6:00 A.M. to 6:00 P.M.

The last of the municipal markets is **Avenue Market** (formerly called the Lafayette Market), 1700 Pennsylvania Avenue. It too serves West Baltimore residents. It was originally built in 1869 and has served discriminating natives over the years. Hours are Monday through Thursday 7:00 A.M. to 6:00 P.M., Friday and Saturday 6:00 A.M. to 6:00 P.M.

The city has one additional market that is not part of the municipal system but does offer fresh produce from nearby farmers. It is the **Farmers' Market** at Holiday and Saratoga streets beneath the Jones Falls Expressway. From late June through mid-December, farmers from Maryland and Pennsylvania sell their goods on Sunday mornings from 8:00 A.M. until they sell out. Thus they continue a practice that began in the late 1700s, producing not decades but centuries of satisfied customers that have shopped at Baltimore's markets.

Directions: To help you plan your marketing pick up a city map at the Baltimore visitor kiosk at the Inner Harbor. You can also call the Baltimore Municipal Markets at (410) 276-9498.

The Baltimore Museum of Art

Old Masters Are Waiting in the Wings

Have you ever wondered what it would be like to live amid the splendor of great art? In the newly renovated and expanded Cone Wing of **The Baltimore Museum of Art,** two rooms from Claribel and Etta Cone's Marlborough Apartments have been replicated and filled with paintings by Henri Matisse. The furnishings look like those Matisse used in his work, so the feeling in these rooms is not only of being around the art—it's as if you are actually in it.

The Cone sisters began seriously collecting art in 1901 under the

A museum visitor enjoys the American Paintings Gallery at the Baltimore Museum of Art. The museum's Cone Collection, a stunning selection of early 20th-century French art, is an unparalleled treat for the senses.

CHARLES FREEMAN

tutelage of their friend Gertrude Stein and her brother Leo. The Cones amassed a stunning selection of early 20th-century French art by Picasso (in addition to several oils, they collected 113 of his works on paper), Cezanne, Gauguin, Van Gogh, Renoir and Matisse. Etta met Henri Matisse in 1906 and they became lifelong friends. This special relationship developed a passion in the sisters for Matisse's art, and they acquired an outstanding collection of his works—42 oils, including one for each year starting in 1917 and going to 1940; plus 18 sculptures, 36 drawings, 155 prints and seven illustrated books.

The Cone Wing alone makes a visit to The Baltimore Museum of Art rewarding. In fact, William Rubin, Director of Painting and Sculpture of New York's Museum of Modern Art, said, "Seeing the Cone Collection is one of the truly great experiences available to the public for modern art." The museum, however, is known as a "collection of collections," and the Cone sisters are just two of several art devotees who have donated substantial holdings.

Numerous Baltimore collectors have contributed works by Mondrian, Miro, O'Keefe, Giacometti and others that hang in the post-World War II collection in the West Wing for Contemporary Art. Sixteen galleries display a collection the museum has been amassing since its founding in 1914. This is the largest collection of post-1945 art in the state of Maryland. Among its highlights are 15 pieces by Andy Warhol. Architecturally this wing is interesting because of its three-story concrete rotunda with a spiral staircase leading to the upper galleries.

For those who prefer the Old Masters there is the Jacobs Wing, with works by Botticelli, Titian, Rembrandt, Frans Hals, Fragonard, Van Dyck and Raphael. There are also the fabled Antioch Mosaics, dating from the early Roman Empire. These mosaics were part of a group of stone pavements excavated at Antioch-on-the-Orontes in Northern Syria.

The recently renovated John Russell Pope Building encompasses galleries on three floors and includes landscapes, portrait work, a study section for Maryland decorative arts from 1730-1840 and a comprehensive array of American furniture. All these arts are combined in the nine period rooms, which include a room from 18th-century Eltonhead Manor, a Baltimore Federal parlor from Waterloo Row, the Weston Bed Chamber and a 1771 room from the Abbey, or Ringgold House, in Chestertown, Maryland.

There are also galleries filled with the art of diverse cultures from Africa, the Americas and Oceania. Many of the items were used in ritual ceremonies marking harvests, funerals, coronations, coming of age rites and marriages. African masks, miniature stone carvings, mortuary carvings, intricately detailed household items, woven baskets, jewelry and other objects are displayed in large glass cabinets that offer a 360-degree perspective.

Because there is so much to savor, you'll want to spend several hours exploring. Donna's at the BMA, the museum's restaurant, is a delightful venue in which to enjoy a midday break. The restaurant overlooks the Wurtzburger Sculpture Garden, and during the summer you can eat outside on the garden patio. The fountain and reflecting pool provide a cool oasis on the hottest day.

The Baltimore Museum of Art is open Wednesday through Friday 11:00 A.M. to 5:00 P.M., Saturday and Sunday from 11:00 A.M. to 6:00 P.M. It is also open on the first Thursday of each month from 5:00 to 9:00 P.M. It is closed on Monday, Tuesday and major holidays. Admission is charged except on Thursday. For general museum information, you can call (410) 396-7100 or visit the BMA's web site at www.artbma.org.

Directions: From downtown Baltimore take Charles Street north and turn left on 29th Street. Go right on Art Museum Drive. The Baltimore Museum of Art is three miles north of the Inner Harbor at North Charles Street and 31st Street. Metered parking is available on Art Museum Drive and in the museum's east parking lot.

Baltimore Museum of Industry

A Working Museum for a Working City

Baltimore's work ethic—the people and industry that built the city—is celebrated at the **Baltimore Museum of Industry**. If to you industry means only steel and smokestacks and workers in overalls, a visit to this museum will be a delightful surprise. You'll find it fascinating and full of hands-on fun.

The Baltimore Museum of Industry is appropriately located on the working side of Baltimore's harbor in an old oyster cannery, the 1865 Platt Packing Company. The weekday bustle of the Baltimore-Locust Point Industrial District is matched by the weekend bustle within the museum.

The turn-of-the-century machine shop still turns out replacement parts for the museum's antique industrial equipment. Huge belts extending from floor to ceiling turn the big flywheels that power the machine tools. If you are familiar with Rube Goldberg's cartoon contraptions, you'll recognize these machines as the real thing.

Another work area is an old-time print shop where visitors can help "pull the devil's tail." The heavy lever on the vintage printing press is indeed a devil to pull, and after one try you'll understand why so many printers developed muscular arms. You'll also have the opportunity to work the 1900 Poco Proof Press and print your own souvenir, which reads: "I Printed This." Several American expressions may have evolved from these early printing methods. A printer had to "mind his Ps and Qs" as he picked the correct type from his composite case. (Another explanation for this phrase involves bartenders carefully pouring pints and quarts.) The expression "hot off the press" makes sense when you learn printers dried the wet ink on the freshly printed pages by holding them over a candle flame.

The garment workshop also lets you get the feel of the job. You can try your hand—and your foot—working the 80- to 100-year old treadle sewing machines. Many young girls spent all their daylight hours in Baltimore lofts working these machines, some of which were quite specialized for the day: a belt looper, for example, a large and small basting machine and a hand-operated button sewer.

Other museum displays remind visitors of Baltimore's canning and shipping industry. In the Kids Can, children are transported back to 1883 and become oyster shuckers and canners. Young visitors also work at a Children's Motor Works Assembly line and build a cardboard replica of a 1914 truck. During your visit you'll discover that Baltimore was the first city in the country to have a gas company, which used the gas lamp, or "ring of fire," invented by painter Rembrandt Peale. A re-created tinsmith's shop is lit and powered by gas. There is also an 1895 Baltimore drugstore that once stood on the corner of Eastern Avenue and Conkling Street, and an elaborate electric repair shop full of old-fashioned household appliances.

Moored at the dock just outside the museum is the historic 1906 S.S. *Baltimore*, one of the last steam engine tugboats on the East Coast. Recovered from the bottom of the Sassafras River, this boat is in the process of being restored. The museum is also restoring the Glenn L. Martin Company's 1937 *Tadpole Clipper*, a prototype seaplane. You can watch the restoration work in the museum's back gallery.

The Baltimore Museum of Industry is open on Saturday 10:00 A.M. to 5:00 P.M. and Sunday NOON to 5:00 P.M. Admission is charged.

Directions: In downtown Baltimore go south past Harborplace on Light Street. Make a left on Key Highway; the museum is on the left at 1415 Key Highway. From I-95, get off at Key Highway Exit. Turn left at light, go under the underpass and turn left on Key Highway. The museum is immediately on your right.

Baltimore Public Works Museum

Down Under

Day and night, all year round, there is a working world beneath the city streets; that's what the **Baltimore Public Works Museum** is all about. Located on the eastern fringe of the Inner Harbor, this unusual facility—the only one of its kind in the country—faces glitzy competition from the National Aquarium and Harborplace. It can easily be included on a day trip to its more well-known neighbors. The museum provides a behind-the-scenes—and even under them—glimpse of how a large city provides the utilities services its citizens need.

Youngsters are immediately attracted to the museum's outdoor **Streetscape** sculpture. This gives you a look down under, beneath the streets. You'll see the connections for street lights, phone lines, conduits, storm drains as well as a network of pipes for water, sanitation and gas.

The museum is housed in the Eastern Avenue Pumping Station, built in 1912 as part of Baltimore's sewage system. Despite its utilitarian purpose, the building has a number of architectural embellishments, including a copper-trimmed roof and decorative gables and cupola.

Many people have only a fuzzy idea of what constitutes public works. The museum's exhibits acquaint visitors with such diverse services as street lighting, road maintenance, sewer service, trash removal and water service. A 15-minute slide presentation encapsulates the history of public works in Baltimore. You may not learn all the technicalities of how a pump works, but rather, how it changes your life.

The Baltimore Public Works Museum is open Tuesday through Sunday 10:00 A.M. to 5:00 P.M. Admission is charged.

After learning all about city plumbing, you can visit the **B. Olive Cole Pharmacy Museum** and see how folks got their interior plumbing, among other things, fixed the old-fashioned way. Those interested in medicine will appreciate the museum's collection of early pharmaceutical paraphernalia. Old medicine bottles, pill crushers, prescription scales and a selection of 19th- and 20th-century mortars and pestles fill the shelves. Downstairs there is a complete turn-of-the-century pharmacy, its cabinets still stocked with vintage potions and yellowing prescription book. This museum is in the Kelly Memorial Building at 650 West Lombard Street on the University of Maryland at Baltimore campus. Hours are 10:00 A.M. to 4:00 P.M.; there is no charge.

For those with medical interests the **National Museum of Dentistry** is also on the campus of the University of Maryland at Baltimore (31 S. Greene Street at Lombard). This unique museum has quite a collection including George Washington's "not-so-wooden" teeth, a tooth jukebox and a life-size model of a circus "iron jaw" performer. Exhibits include equipment and gadget associated with dentistry. The museum is housed in a 1904 architectural gem that was home to a dental school for 25 years. This campus is the site of the world's first dental college. Museum hours are Wednesday through Saturday from 10:00 A.M. to 4:00 P.M. On Sunday it opens at 1:00 P.M. Admission is charged.

Directions: In downtown Baltimore take Pratt Street past the Inner Harbor and turn right on East Falls Avenue. The entrance to the Baltimore Public Works Museum is on East Falls Avenue, at the corner of Eastern Avenue, across the pedestrian bridge from Pier 6.

Baltimore Zoo

Animal House

When the **Baltimore Zoo** opened in 1876, its collection of captive animals included 17 species. Among the residents were 215 deer, 15 white rats, 3 swans, 2 black bears, 1 tiger cat and 1 three-legged duck. At that time there were only three zoos in the country; the others were in Philadelphia and Cincinnati. Today, the zoo's 180-acre Druid Hill Park is home to more than 2,250 mammals, birds and reptiles—many of which are threatened and endangered species. The zoo's pastoral setting contrasts with the bustling of nearby downtown.

Among the zoo's most popular exhibits are the Chimpanzee Forest, featuring troops of chimpanzees, African monkeys, crocodiles and other tropical forest species. Another favorite is the African Watering Hole with rhinos, zebras and gazelles. In the African Plains Lion exhibit lions roam the perimeter of their large grassy enclosure. One sector is separated from visitors by a heavy stockade fence with a picture window. The window provides nose-to-nose confrontations that leave visitors wondering about the strength of the glass.

Though not majestic like the king of the beasts, the prairie dogs seem to enjoy playing king of the mountain as they chase one another around their hillside homes. Children always enjoy watching their antics. Another area popular with young visitors is the eight-acre Lyn P. Meyerhoff Children's Zoo with its 48 innovative exhibits. In its two main areas, the Children's Zoo offers a tour through habitats of animals native to Maryland—including a marsh aviary, beaver lodge, limestone cave, tree and meadow and a Maryland farmyard with hands-on animal exhibits. A variety of activities in this special area are designed to give youngsters a new perspective on nature. These include a groundhog exhibit, where children burrow right next to the animals, and a submerged plexiglass tunnel for underwater exploration. There is also a giant turtle shell for youngsters to climb in, a walk-through aviary and a huge man-made tree kids enter through the roots and climb from the inside. Climbers will also enjoy playing on the jungle gym shaped like a woolly mammoth's rib cage.

The zoo is divided into major animal exhibit areas. When you enter you'll get a park map with an explanation of the symbols used at each exhibit. These symbols provide a wealth of information about each animal. You'll learn their native habitat, their diet, the hours they are most active and how they live with others of their species in the wild.

The Baltimore Zoo is open daily 10:00 A.M. to 4:00 P.M. It is closed on Christmas and one day in June for the annual fundraiser. Admission is charged, but on the first Saturday of the month children are admitted free before NOON. Children under two are always admitted without charge.

Directions: From downtown Baltimore take Martin Luther King Boulevard north. Turn left on McCulloh Street to Druid Hill Park. Follow signs for the Baltimore Zoo. From north of Baltimore take the Jones Falls Expressway (1-83) south to Exit 7. Follow Druid Park Lake Drive; signs will direct you to the zoo. Parking is free.

Churches of Baltimore

Freedom of Choice

Baltimore, celebrated for its baseball team, ethnic restaurants and colorful Inner Harbor, is also known as the "city of 1,000 spires." A tour of Baltimore's churches provides an overview of various religious denominations and a wide range of outstanding ecclesiastical architecture. The Mother Churches of American Methodism and Catholicism are found in Baltimore as is the third oldest synagogue in the country, an early Lutheran and an Episcopalian church.

The **Lovely Lane Methodist Church and Museum** is an architectural gem, listed on the National Register of Historic Places as the first church designed by Stanford White. A leading architectural scholar calls it "a national treasure." Leaving aside for a moment its religious significance, this Romanesque church with Etruscan detailing is a fascinating place to explore. The massive grey stone walls and 186-foot tower built of Port Deposit granite loom impressively over St. Paul Street.

Interior interest focuses on the vaulted ceiling above the sanctuary. It was painted to show the heavens, complete with 719 planets and major stars, as they were at 3:00 A.M. on November 6, 1887, when the church was dedicated. The sky was charted by Dr. Simon Newcomb, the first professor of astronomy at Johns Hopkins University. The beautiful wooden staircases and doors, the Tiffany glass in the chapel and the organ especially captivate visitors. If you are lucky enough to hear the organ, you will understand why some have called the sanctuary "the finest small concert hall in the area."

The Lovely Lane Museum in the church basement traces the history of American Methodism from the founding Christmas Conference, which took place at the Lovely Lane Meeting House in 1784. The present church was built as a centennial symbol of that meeting. Lovely Lane is open Monday through Friday from 10:00 A.M. until 4:00 P.M. and there are Sunday tours at NOON. The address is 2200 St. Paul Street.

The **Basilica of the Assumption** is the Mother Church of Roman Catholicism in the United States. Begun in 1806, this church was designed by Benjamin H. Latrobe (architect of the Capitol under Thomas Jefferson) and is considered one of the finest examples of neoclassical architecture in the world. One architectural historian,

Designed by Benjamin Latrobe, the Basilica of the National Shrine of the Assumption of the Blessed Virgin Mary is considered one of the finest examples of neoclassical architecture in the world. It is the Mother Church of Roman Catholicism in the United States.

Nicholas Pevsner, calls it "North America's most beautiful church." Its interior spaciousness is much admired, as is the central dome supported by segmented vaults. It, like many of Baltimore's churches, features stained-glass windows, which add luminous color to the interior on sunny days. In May, 1996 Mother Teresa visited the Basilica and that same year in October, Pope John Paul II visited. The Basilica, at Cathedral and Mulberry Streets, is open Monday through Friday from 7:00 A.M. to 5:00 P.M. and on weekends until 6:30 P.M. Guided tours are given every Sunday after the 10:45 A.M. Mass (tours begin approximately at NOON). There is no charge but donations are appreciated. Parking is available in the Franklin Street Garage, between Charles and Cathedral Street.

The first synagogue built in Maryland (the third oldest in the nation) was erected in 1845 at 11 Lloyd Street in Baltimore (the visitor center is at 15 Lloyd Street). Now restored as a museum and historic site, the **Lloyd Street Synagogue** is noted for its Star of David window and matzo oven. The architect, Robert Cary Long, Jr., built it in a Greek classical style at a time when the classical revival in Baltimore was ending. The synagogue is open year-round Sunday, Tuesday, Wednesday and Thursday from NOON to 4:00 P.M. A guided tour takes place at 1:00 P.M. and on Sunday at 2:30 P.M. as well.

The **Zion Lutheran Church** at Holiday and Lexington streets is one

151

of Baltimore's first Lutheran churches. It was built in 1807. The stained-glass windows make this worth visiting. It is interesting to compare these windows with those you will see at the Basilica.

Baltimore's first Episcopal Parish was established in 1692, and **Saint Paul's Parish and Church** at Charles and Saratoga streets was begun in 1854. It was designed in an Italian Romanesque basilica style to replace an earlier church that burned to the ground. This church is noted for its Tiffany stained-glass windows, exterior bas-relief panels and the garden. The church is open Monday through Friday from 11:30 A.M. to 1:30 P.M. and on Sunday from 8:00 A.M. until 1:00 P.M.

These five only skim the surface of the many houses of worship to be seen in Baltimore. On another visit you may want to see the **Old Otterbein United Methodist Church** at Sharp and Conway streets, which is the oldest church in continuous use in Baltimore. The **Mother Seton House** at 600 North Pratt Street can be seen by appointment. The beautiful **Cathedral of Mary Our Queen** at 5200 North Charles Street has a series of lovely stained-glass windows.

Directions: In order to help you plan your own church tour you may wish to pick up a city map available free at the Baltimore visitors kiosk at the Inner Harbor.

Cylburn Arboretum and Sherwood Gardens

Floral Double Feature

Those who complain about alternately freezing and sweltering during Maryland winters and summers can take some comfort from knowing those same variations make it possible to grow flowers indigenous to both cold and warm climates. Maryland's cornucopia includes a rich array of wildflowers whose small, delicate blossoms are too often overlooked amid the color of spring.

Cylburn's wildflower preserve, which peaks in April and May, is just one part of the 176-acre **Cylburn Arboretum.** Nature's bounty can be enjoyed on the trails as well as in the more formal gardens near the Cylburn Mansion, built in 1863 by Jesse Tyson. Benches provide resting spots and vantage points from which to savor the sights, sounds and smells of the forest, field and gardens. Flowers and trees are labeled, but you'll need a field guide to identify the more than 150 species of birds that have been observed at Cylburn, a designated bird sanctuary.

There are several formal gardens planted with perennials; these are particularly appealing in June. Cylburn also has a vegetable garden, an herb garden, several small specialty gardens and an All-America Display Garden. The Display Garden is one of more than 200 across the country heralding new varieties of flowers and vegetables not yet ready for marketing. A Garden of the Senses is designed for those in wheelchairs and the visually impaired. Plants are chosen for their scent and texture and are labeled in print and in Braille. Cylburn Arboretum is open daily 6:00 A.M. to 9:00 P.M. at no charge. Like all parks the rule is, "Take nothing but photographs, leave nothing but footprints."

Not more than a 15-minute drive from Cylburn in the elegant Guilford section of Baltimore is the seven-acre, privately developed **Sherwood Gardens** (open free to the public). In mid-May it's worth combining these two floral attractions. Sherwood is a riot of colors when the 5,000 azaleas and 100,000 tulips bloom. Pansies, dogwoods and flowering spring trees add to its charm.

Directions: From the Baltimore Beltway, (1-695) take the Jones Falls Expressway (1-83) south and then take Northern Parkway west. Turn left onto Cylburn Avenue. Proceed to the left for Greenspring Avenue and immediately turn left into the Cylburn Arboretum at 4915 Greenspring Avenue. For Sherwood Gardens take Greenspring Avenue south to Cold Spring Lane and follow it east across Jones Falls Expressway. Approximately two miles past the expressway turn right onto Underwood Road and then right onto Stratford Road and the gardens will be on your left.

Edgar Allan Poe House

Mythic and Mysterious

"Ill-fated and mysterious man! Bewildered in the brilliancy of thine own imagination, and fallen in the flames of thine own youth!" Edgar Allan Poe could well have been speaking of himself in this passage from his story "The Assignation." He apparently could not confine his extraordinary imagination to the poetry and stories that have since established him as one of America's greatest writers. His tales of his heroic defenses of freedom in Greece and Russia, for example, were picked up as fact in the early accounts of his life. Later biographical research revealed that he had never traveled to these countries. Poe even gave a false name—Edgar Perry—to the U.S. Army. For Poe mystery was a way of life.

Several cities in the Mid-Atlantic lay claim to Poe; Philadelphia and Richmond both have houses associated with him. Poe's link with Baltimore is perhaps stronger, however, because his family is from here and his grandfather served as the Quartermaster General during the Revolutionary War. Poe, himself, lived and died in Baltimore. His years in Baltimore were not happy, despite the fact that it was during this period that he met and courted his young cousin, Virginia Clemm.

Edgar Allan Poe lived here as a struggling poet with his aunt, grand-mother and cousin from 1831 to 1835. He married the cousin in Richmond in 1836 when she was but 13.

Although Poe romanticized his forebears, he was without family support from a young age. His parents were itinerant actors and his father disappeared while Poe was still an infant. It is not known whether he died or deserted his family, but after he vanished there was no mention of him, though likely even a mediocre actor would have been mentioned somewhere. His mother died when he was two. Poe was raised by the Allans, a Richmond family. He gambled while in college to earn money to pay for necessities. The gambling, the death of his foster mother and the remarriage of his foster father all contributed to the severing of ties between him and Allan. From the age of 22, Poe was completely on his own—and for the most part constantly in debt and struggling to eke out a living.

When Poe left West Point in 1831 he went to Baltimore to live with his father's sister, Mrs. Maria Poe Clemm, and her daughter Virginia. Previously he had published two volumes of poetry, and now he began writing prose stories. From Baltimore Poe wrote to Allan that he feared debtor's prison, because of a debt incurred by his deceased brother Henry, but he received no help. He stayed in Baltimore until 1835 when he moved to Richmond to edit the Southern *Literary Messenger.* Just 13, Virginia lied about her age and married him in Richmond in 1836.

The Baltimore house where Poe lived and struggled from 1831 to 1835 is still in a struggling neighborhood. During Poe's era it was virtual country, on the western edge of the city. Poe, who had rarely seen his blood relations, was now surrounded by family. In addition to Maria and Virginia, his grandmother and his cousin Henry lived in the house. The family welcomed the addition of the $240 annual widow's pension his grandmother received from the government because of her husband's service in the Revolution and the War of 1812. Poe's grandmother died in the upstairs bedroom.

The house is small and the upstairs barely more than a garret. There is not much furniture and none is original. The kitchen is furnished to represent the 1820s. The house does have a number of Poe artifacts including china and crystal from the John Allan estate, a lap desk from his college days and the 1849 obituary by Rufus Griswold. There is also a full-size color reproduction of Virginia's death portrait. During January, you can attend *The World's Largest Edgar Allan Poe Birthday Celebration.* Whenever you visit you can watch video presentations of Poe's poems and stories. The **Edgar Allan Poe House** at 203 N. Amity Street is open Wednesday through Saturday from NOON to 4:00 P.M. During July, August and September hours are Saturday only, NOON to 4:00 P.M. The Poe House is closed January, February and March. A nominal admission is charged. For more information you can call (410) 396-7932.

At the time of his death, Poe was en route from Richmond to New York and had stopped off in Baltimore. He did not, as some stories would have it, die in a gutter. Some reports claim that he was found in a doorway violently delirious and taken to a hospital where he died on October 7, 1849. Although rumors intimated he was under the influence of drugs or alcohol, later research indicates the probability of diabetes and pneumonia. The condition of his body and his clothes also suggest that he had been beaten and robbed.

Poe was buried in Baltimore's Westminster Cemetery. The church is on the National Register of Historic Places and can be toured by appointment; call (301)328-2070. Poe was not even buried in peace: biographers disagree about his funeral, some claiming that only a few attended services and others reporting that hundreds followed his cortege. After the first burial, his remains were reburied in 1875 in a more prominent position at the front of Westminster Churchyard, a position that can be seen from the street.

Directions: In downtown Baltimore take Paca Street north to Fayette Street, where you turn left. (Poe's grave is at the corner of Fayette and Greene streets.) Proceed west on Fayette Street and turn right at Schroeder Street. Go two blocks and turn right at Saratoga Street and turn right again almost immediately at Amity Street. The Poe House is at the far left end of Amity Street.

Fell's Point

Point Worth Taking

Fell's Point is unique; it is the only one of the three colonial settlements that made up Baltimore Town that has survived. It is also one of the East Coast's few remaining original urban waterfront communities. A visitor can easily sense the early American flavor of this seaport that contributed so much to Baltimore's growth during the Revolutionary War. The architecture and physical characteristics have changed very little over the years.

Edward Fell, a Quaker shipbuilder, purchased this point on the Patapsco River in 1731. The Fell family divided the land into building lots. By 1763 these lots, with their deep water frontage, were in great demand. By 1804 there were more than 20 shipyards at Fell's Point. Among the ships built and launched here were the historic frigate U.S.F. *Constellation* (see selection) and many of the classic Baltimore Clippers. Sailors, settlers and European immigrants filled the taverns, restaurants, streets and docks.

There are 350 residential structures from the American Federal architectural period. But only the **Robert Long House** is restored to its 18th-century appearance and open to the public. Long, a young merchant, purchased three lots from Edward Fell in 1765. On his waterfront lot Long built a four-story brick warehouse. He built his home on the Ann Street lot, now 812 S. Ann Street.

The house that Long built was not typical of 18th-century Baltimore architecture. In fact, no other surviving home is designed in a similar style. Long's house follows the Quaker floor plan, two-and-one-half stories with a pent-roof across the second floor front. The interior design is simple, and the small rooms are furnished to reflect occupancy by the Longs from 1765-81. The Robert Long House, the oldest surviving urban residence within the boundaries of old Baltimore Town, is open on Thursdays for tours at 10:00 A.M., 1:00 and 3:00 P.M. Admission is charged. Groups may arrange tours by appointment; call (410) 675-6750. The Robert Long House Garden, an L-shaped recreation of a colonial garden, is open at no charge on weekdays from 9:00 A.M. to 5:00 P.M.

You can obtain a walking tour guide to Fell's Point from various establishments in the area. The Fell's Point brochure provides information on the buildings you will pass as you stroll around the historic neighborhood. Be sure to stop at the **Broadway Market** (see selection), where you'll be tempted by the array of deli items that can make up a picnic lunch. Or you might want to try one of the ethnic cafes or bistros so popular with Baltimoreans.

One lunchtime or overnight option is **The Admiral Fell Inn** at 888 South Broadway (call 410-522-7377). This was once a hotel for seafarers but now is an elegantly decorated inn. Each room has a distinctive style ... and a jacuzzi.

The specialty shops scattered around Fell's Point are yet another attraction. One of the popular spots is The China Sea Marine Trading Co., Inc. on Fell Street. The shop, an old stable and rope establishment, carries a wide range of maritime curiosities. Fell's Point also has an old book shop, antique emporiums, art galleries and boutiques. A brochure listing the restaurants and stores is available in any of the shops.

Directions: Fell's Point is in downtown Baltimore east of the Inner Harbor and south of Pratt Street. From Pratt Street, turn right on Broadway for this quaint neighborhood.

Fort McHenry National Monument and Historic Shrine

A Real Star

The play of history is often sensed best in the places where our forebears lived and fought. At **Fort McHenry** the cannons and walls stand in silence, but once they spoke out in defense of liberty. The sight of the 30x42 foot American flag triumphantly waving over the fort inspired Francis Scott Key to write the *Star Spangled Banner*, our national anthem. The September 13, 1814 battle was a turning point in the War of 1812 and led to the cessation of hostilities with Great Britain five months later.

Lt. Clagett and the 1,000 other soldiers and sailors manning Fort McHenry that September night had the job of defending the fort and saving Baltimore from the fiery fate suffered by Washington when the British captured that city. Rain made it difficult for the British to keep their powder dry, but the Americans had a greater problem—their guns could not reach the British ships. The British were in range to bombard the fort with their guns and the new Congreve rocket; they fired between 1,500 and 1,800 bombs, rockets and shells. It is amazing that the heavy barrage resulted in only four deaths and 24 men wounded. Despite the strength of their firing position, the British could not subdue the fort, and thus the attack on Baltimore failed.

The gallant defense of the fort is captured in a 16-minute film that is shown at the Fort McHenry Visitor Center. The film packs an emotional wallop: it ends with a stirring rendition of the national anthem as the window curtain is slowly withdrawn to reveal the oversize flag still flying over the fort.

You'll get more out of your walk around the fort if you see the film. The present fort is not the first to stand on this pivotal ground guarding the approach to Baltimore. Fort Whetstone protected the city during the American Revolution. The star-shaped fort you'll explore was built between 1798 and 1803. The design was chosen to make surprise attacks impossible, each point of the star being visible from the points on either side.

As you explore the star fort you'll notice along the base of the walls the remains of the dry moat that once encircled it. The fort is entered through an arched doorway, or sally port, which is flanked by bombproof underground rooms built immediately following the bombardment. Across from the sally port is a ravelin, consisting of angled embankments used to protect the powder from enemy attack. Guardhouses, barracks and junior commanding officers' quarters have been re-created. This fort was used not only during the War of 1812, but the Civil War, World War I and World War II.

During the summer months members of the Fort McHenry Guard, in replica U.S. uniforms of 1812, perform drills and military demonstrations in the fort. Make sure you check out the electric map. This sound and light display illustrates the troop movements during the Battle of Baltimore.

Fort McHenry is open daily at a nominal charge from 8:00 A.M. to 5:00 P.M. (in the summer it is open until 8:00 P.M.). Closed Christmas and New Year's Day. From mid-June through Labor Day ranger-guided activities are offered daily. Check the directory board behind the information desk in the visitor center for the schedule. On some Sundays in June, July and August at 6:30 P.M. military tattoos (programs of music and drill) are performed. Each September there is a Defenders' Day program to celebrate the anniversary of the Battle of

At Fort McHenry, a guard member and a park ranger lower a replica of the flag that flew during the War of 1812 when Francis Scott Key wrote the words to the national anthem.

Baltimore with a mock bombardment, military drills, music and fireworks. For details on the schedule you can call (410) 962-4290.

Those who want a different perspective on Fort McHenry should take the *Baltimore Patriot* when it sails from the U.S.F. *Constellation* dock at the Inner Harbor (see selection). The 1½-hour narrated boat tour lets you see the fort from the vantage point of the British ships anchored off Baltimore. Boat tours are given spring, summer and fall. The schedule for mid-April through May and October is 11:00 A.M., 1:00 and 3:30 P.M. From June through September boats depart hourly 11:00 A. M. to 4:00 P.M. During the summer two additional boats, the *Defender* and the *Guardian*, also sail from the Inner Harbor to Fort McHenry. For more information call (410) 685-4288.

Directions: From the Inner Harbor area go south on Light Street. Proceed past the Light Street Pavilion and the Maryland Science Center and turn left on Key Highway. Take Key Highway for one mile then turn right on Lawrence Street. Take Lawrence Street to Fort Avenue and turn left and proceed to Fort McHenry National Monument. From I-95, take the Fort McHenry exit and follow the signs.

Maryland Historical Society

Preserving the Heritage of the Free State

Where would you expect to find the original draft of the Star Spangled Banner? Appropriately, it is one of the prized possessions of the **Maryland Historical Society**. Their headquarters houses a museum as well as the Library of Maryland History. This is a museum for history buffs who want to be thorough in their coverage of Baltimore's historic sites.

The Maryland Historical Society's collection is the largest single repository of the state's cultural heritage. Begin exploring at the Radcliff Maritime Museum on the museum's basement level. There you'll see rigged models of Baltimore clippers, as well as paintings of steamboats and other Chesapeake Bay craft. A 13-minute audiovisual presentation delves into the life of Maryland's watermen and Maryland's maritime heritage. There is also an exhibit on ship chandlery and ship building.

On the first floor you'll see exhibits on early Maryland. Artifacts are displayed from those who inhabited the land before European settlement. Contributions made by the first settlers are recognized. The newly renovated Darnell Children's Museum is also on the first floor.

On the museum's second floor more recent Maryland history is presented. Here you'll find the Library of Maryland History. The library includes more than 50,000 books plus manuscripts, maps, prints and photographs dealing with Maryland and its citizens from the earliest years to the present. You do not have to be engaged in academic research to consult this collection. Those researching their family genealogy and those simply interested in wiling away an afternoon reading for pleasure are welcome. Plans are underway to expand the library and add classroom and workshop space for the society's popular lectures and programs.

The museum, which has a fine collection of furniture built and designed in Maryland, is also linked to the adjacent 1847 **Enoch Pratt House**, which has 19th-century period rooms. In the Pratt House the rooms provide a complete picture of 19th-century life. In the bright orange parlor, mannequins wearing day dresses are arranged around the tea table. The front room mannequins wear visiting dresses. The upstairs bedrooms are not open to the public but the lower level has a collection of doll houses on display.

Recently added to the museum, is the Dorothy Wagner Wallis Furniture Gallery which showcases Maryland furniture and innovatively examines its relationship to the state's history, culture and other decorative arts. Baltimore's well-known painted furniture is prominently exhibited. Also new is the Claire McCardell Textile Gallery and an architectural garden.

The Maryland Historical Society acquired 300,000 items from the unfortunate closing of the Baltimore City Life Museums. They will eventually be housed in a new facility. In the interim, items from the collection are again being included in special exhibits. The merger of these two collections make the Maryland Historical Society the largest holder of Peale—Charles Willson Peale, his niece Sarah Miriam Peale and Rembrandt Peale—family items and paintings in the nation.

A former Greyhound bus garage in the historic Mount Vernon neighborhood has been donated to the society by the City of Baltimore and renovated into a large exhibition space. National and local exhibitions are mounted here.

The Maryland Historical Society's museum is open Tuesday through Friday from 10:00 A.M. to 5:00 P.M., Saturday from 9:00 A.M. to 5:00 P.M. and Sunday from 11:00 A.M. to 5:00 P.M. It is closed on Mondays, major holidays and Sundays in July and August. Admission is charged. There is no charge to visit the museum shop and bookstore.

Directions: The Maryland Historical Society is located at 201 West Monument Street in downtown Baltimore. From the Inner Harbor go north on Charles Street, staying in the left lane. Take a left on the second Mt. Vernon Place. Turn left on Cathedral Street and make an immediate right turn onto West Monument Street. From I-95 take Exit 53 (I-395) to Martin Luther King Blvd. Turn right on Druid Hill Avenue, left on Howard Street and right on Monument Street. (The museum is approximately 2.5 miles from the I-395 exit.)

The Maryland Historical Society is the largest single repository of the state's cultural heritage. Exhibits include items like the masthead figure from Breton Bay, St. Mary's County.

Maryland Science Center

Gee Whiz Kids

The innovative **Maryland Science Center,** at Baltimore's Inner Harbor, is one destination where children should bring friends or count on an active assist from parents, because it takes two to carry out many of the center's experiments.

This scientific wonderland, like Alice's, invites visitors to "Try this!" Easy-to-understand instructions help you get involved with science. After you try the various experiments, you'll learn their scientific significance.

Plan to set aside a long morning or full afternoon because youngsters will not want to be hurried as they tackle the wide variety of participatory experiments, challenge the games in the computer center and marvel at the planetarium show. The admission is roughly that of an afternoon at the movies.

There are three floors to explore, with changing exhibits and permanent displays. The latter include a look at the Chesapeake Bay and the Hubble Space Telescope as well as an interactive exhibit that helps visitors discover the many ways math touches all aspects of our lives. The Maryland Science Center is without a doubt one of the best ways to introduce children to science—it's educational and never boring.

There is an educational fun house on the third floor with a room of distortion with a slanted floor and mind-confusing optical illusions that change visitors into midgets and giants. Special lenses, telescopes, lights, sound and optics turn science into a game.

Youngsters enjoy video games in the Computer Company, also on the third floor. The technology of the computer is explained so that terms like binary counter, logic gate and memory bank become more than the unfathomable jargon of a new age. The games continue in Energy Place where a metric tic-tac-toe game lets you convert one form of energy to another.

Staff members of the Maryland Science Center present live demonstrations throughout the day. One of the presentations focuses on energy as the center's Van de Graff Generator produces one million volts of electricity. In another, a staff member pulls a tablecloth from beneath a stack of dishes to illustrate Newton's first law of motion. In addition to these and other popular live demonstrations, there are science films and shows in the Boyd Theatre.

Finally, no visit to the Maryland Science Center should be considered complete unless it includes **The Davis Planetarium's** multimedia presentation. Although you can measure this 144-seat theater's dimensions—50 feet in diameter and 32 feet high—when the lights dim it seems to encompass all of space. The illusion is enhanced by the 125 projectors and four-channel sound system. Traditional astronomy shows are also offered. During a typical 30- to 35-minute show, 500 to 700 visual effects are used and might include a star-filled universe, flaring comets, falling meteors and spinning galaxies. The effects are all brilliantly employed to tell a scientific story.

And that's not all—the Science Center also boasts a five-story IMAX movie theater. For those not familiar with the term, it is the name for the world's biggest motion picture system. Screens are more than 55 feet high and 75 feet wide, more than five times the width of the average movie screen. Viewers have the vivid sensation of being *in* the picture as astronauts blast into space, divers probe the ocean's depths and explorers cover the far corners of the globe.

During the winter, spring and fall the Maryland Science Center is open Monday through Friday from 10:00 A.M. to 5:00 P.M. Hours on Saturday and Sunday are 10:00 A.M. to 6:00 P.M. The IMAX performances are Monday through Friday at NOON, 1:00 and 3:00 P.M., Saturday on the hour from 11:00 A.M. to 5:00 P.M. and Sunday on the hour from 1:00 to 5:00 P.M. The planetarium schedule is Monday through Friday at 2:00 P.M., Saturday at 11:00 A.M., 1:00, 2:00, 3:00, 4:00 and 6:00 P.M. and Sunday on the hour from 1:00 to 5:00 P.M. From mid-June through Labor Day weekend, the Science Center hours are 10:00 A.M. to 6:00 P.M. Monday through Thursday. On Friday, Saturday and Sunday it stays open until 8:00 P.M. The planetarium and IMAX performances are on the hour from 11:00 A.M. until closing. There is a special K.I.D.S. (Key Into the Discovery of Science) Room to encourage children ages four to seven to get involved with science. It is open during the summer daily, NOON to 4:00 P.M. For additional information call the Science Center at (410) 685-5225.

Genuine science enthusiasts may also want to visit the **Historical Electronics Museum, Inc.**, that is less than 30 minutes away from the Inner Harbor near Baltimore Washington International Airport (beside the BWI Marriott at West Nursery & Elkridge Landing Roads). Here you find an intriguing collection of breakthrough electronic equipment. On the museum grounds is the large SCR-270 radar, like the rotating device that first detected Japanese planes as they approached Pearl Harbor on December 7, 1941. Inside the museum, from the early 1900s there is an Edison cylinder player belt that still belts out *Alexander's Ragtime Band* and other tunes. Visitors hear a different message when they try sending Morse code. Messages were enciphered during World War II on the infamous German Enigma. Visitors can encode a message using this cipher machine. The first electro-mechanical computer was built to crack the Enigma problem. Moving to a more modern age is the lunar TV camera, one of only two models surviving that were used on July 20, 1969 to transmit Neil Armstrong's first steps on the moon. The museum is open at no charge Monday through Friday from 9:00 A.M. to 3:00 P.M. and Saturday from 10:00 A.M. to 2:00 P.M. For more information you can call (410) 765-3803.

Directions: In downtown Baltimore take Light Street south past Harborplace; the Maryland Science Center is on the left at 601 Light Street. You can park in the adjacent hotel parking lot or at Piers 5 and 6 near Harborplace.

Mother Seton House

The Bells of St. Mary's

The austere simplicity of the small house on North Paca Street in downtown Baltimore reflects the lifestyle of its most significant tenant, Elizabeth Ann Seton, the first American-born canonized Roman Catholic saint. She lived here for one pivotal year in her life, arriving on the very day, June 16, 1808, that the Old Saint Mary's Seminary Chapel was dedicated.

The future saint, raised a non-Catholic, married William Seton when she was 19 and they had five children. His declining health prompted William and Elizabeth to take a voyage to Italy in 1803. They hoped his health would improve. However, soon after they arrived he died of tuberculosis. Elizabeth and her daughter, Anna, who had accompanied her parents, were left in Italy without funds but not without friends. The Filicchi family, devout Catholics and old acquaintances, invited Elizabeth to stay with them until they obtained passage back to the States. It was while she waited to return to New York, under the wing of the Filicchi family, that Elizabeth became interested in the Catholic faith. She converted in 1805.

Elizabeth Seton's first efforts to establish a nonsectarian school in New York were not successful. Then Father William Dubourg invited Mrs. Seton to set up a Catholic boarding school for girls in Baltimore. He was a member of the Sulpician Fathers who established the first U.S. Catholic seminary.

In 1809, Elizabeth founded an order of nuns—the Sisters of Charity of St Joseph—and took her first vows of poverty, charity and obedience before Archbishop John Carroll in St. Mary's Lower Chapel on March 25, 1809. The Archbishop conferred on Elizabeth the title "Mother." The other young women who had joined her took their vows in Emmitsburg in Western Maryland. They formed the nucleus of the Sisters of St. Joseph.

For the year that Mother Seton lived and worked in Baltimore, the bells of St. Mary's framed her day. Angelus bells rang at 5:30 A.M. before she attended morning service; they rang again at midday and then at 7:45 P.M. In a letter to a friend, she described the chapel as "the most elegant chapel in America open from daylight till nine at night." When you visit her home be sure to include a stop at this historic church, included on the National Park Service list of national landmarks.

When Mother Seton was offered property in Emmitsburg (see Seton Shrine selection), she and her young teachers took some of their young boarders with them. Her inclusion of parish children in her school led to the establishment of the first parochial school in the country.

When you tour the **Mother Seton House** you'll see that it reflects the period but not the specific residency of Mother Seton. There are no original furnishings here, although there are some at the Emmitsburg house. Family pictures do cover one wall, and upstairs you will see a lap trunk that belonged to Elizabeth. In the bedroom closet there is a copy of the black habit, short black cape and white and black bonnets that Mother Seton and other Sisters of Charity of St. Joseph wore. The house also has a relic of Mother Seton.

You can visit without charge on Saturdays and Sundays, November through February from 1:00 to 3:00 P.M. From March through October the hours are 1:00 to 4:00 P.M. At other times you may visit by appointment. Call (410) 523-3443.

Directions: The Mother Seton House is at 600 N. Paca Street in downtown Baltimore. It is one short block north (right) off Route 40W (Franklin Street) at Paca or two blocks north (left) off Route 40E (Mulberry Street) at Paca. There is free parking on the property.

National Aquarium in Baltimore

Fish Will Lure You

The Inner Harbor is one of Maryland's most popular spots. While at the Inner Harbor most visitors include a stop at the **National Aquarium in Baltimore.** Since opening on August 8, 1981, the aquarium has quickly become the premier paid tourist attraction in the state, drawing an average of 1.5 million visitors a year.

The aquarium is a big water wonderland—the entire living collection includes 10,000 marine and freshwater animals—and you'll want to allow plenty of time for exploration. Most visits take two hours, but you can easily stay longer, especially if you watch the feedings.

Several feeding presentations, scheduled throughout the day, take place in the "Wings in the Water" exhibit. This 260,000-gallon pool contains the largest collection of rays in the world, as well as various species of small sharks.

The self-guided tour of the aquarium is arranged as a one-way trip. The objective is to give visitors an awareness of the importance of aquatic environments. On Level 1, the Caribbean Reef is a crystal clear, 775-gallon cylinder that showcases between 20 and 30 species of Atlantic Coral Reef fish and invertebrates. The diverse patterns and colors of jewel-like fish—butterflyfish, angelfish, drums and wrasses—can be viewed from all angles and from other levels.

Level 2, Maryland Mountains to the Sea, starts with a mountain pool and traces the various water habitats of Maryland. The killdeers you'll see in the Coastal Beach section stand so still it's always startling when they move, but records show that these birds are indeed active. They've raised two chicks in their glassed-in home. That's nothing compared with the gray-necked wood-rails in the Rain Forest, who have reared 56 offspring!

On Level 3, some very exotic animals help demonstrate various facets of adaptation. You're not likely to forget the yellowhead jawfish, featherduster worms or red-backed cleaning shrimp. In the "feeding" exhibit visitors are delighted with the striking color of the clownfish and sea anemones.

Spectators at the Living Coral Reef exhibit have the rare chance to examine colonies of delicate coral—tiny animals that are relatives of jellyfish and sea anemones. These animals are seldom seen alive in the wild except by divers. Coral is not only difficult to transport, but also for most institutions to maintain. Other unusual creatures in this third level exhibit include giant clams and long-spined sea urchins.

You reach the heights at Level 5, the glass-roofed South American Rain Forest. On a cold winter's day its warmth, colorful feathered inhabitants, and constant activity prompt visitors to linger, enjoying this bit of the tropics. Try to spot the lizard that walks on water and the large scarlet ibis. The large iguana periodically tumbles down from its precarious roost, causing momentary consternation among passing visitors. It's fun to stand on the observation deck, which affords a bird's eye view of the Inner Harbor, and try to spy the numerous birds residing in the rain forest.

Exiting the rain forest you'll see the tiny and colorful poison arrow frogs whose brilliant hues warn enemies of their poison. The aquarium has bred more than 20 species, more than any other institution in the country.

As you begin your descent back to Level 1, remember you can always retrace your steps or get your hand stamped and return later in the day. On the way down you will again see the Atlantic Coral Reef, one of the aquarium's best exhibits. This multilevel, 335,000-gallon donut-shaped tank provides a diver's view of the denizens of the reefs. Their placid circular progress is interrupted several times daily when a diver enters the tank to feed the fish. They are hand fed to prevent the more aggressive fish from consuming all the food.

Beneath the coral reef is the 220,000-gallon Open Ocean ring. Here you can have a close encounter with three varieties of sharks—lemons, sand tigers and nurses—and a number of large game fish. This is just one of the tanks that together contain more than two million gallons of city water the aquarium has transformed into sea water by the addition of a blend of more than a dozen sea salts.

The aquarium also includes a Marine Mammal Pavilion with a

1,300 seat amphitheater. Each day, bottlenose dolphins demonstrate their grace and agility in an educational exhibit that highlights the importance of environmental awareness. In "Explorations Station," visitors can probe a collection of high-tech attractions at their own pace. Participatory exhibits probe the life and lore of marine mammals by videos, graphics and computer technology.

Although the admission is steep, it is certainly good value for dollar spent, and various discount opportunities are available. For information call (410)576-3800. Hours during July and August are Sunday through Thursday from 9:00 A.M. to 6:00 P.M. and Friday and Saturday until 8:00 P.M. From September through June the aquarium is open Saturday through Thursday from 10:00 A.M. until 5:00 P.M. and Friday until 8:00 P.M. From March through October the aquarium opens at 9:00 A.M.

During the summer and on weekends there is often a long waiting line for aquarium admission tickets. This wait can be avoided by purchasing advance tickets through Ticket Center outlets. There is a nominal charge for this service. In Baltimore call (410) 481-SEAT, in Washington call (202) 432-SEAT and elsewhere call (800) 551-SEAT. On the day you plan to visit you can also purchase coupons for specific entry times from the aquarium's outdoor reservation booth.

Directions: Traveling from points south, take I-95 north to I-395 to Pratt Street. Turn right on Pratt Street to Pier 3. From points north take I-95 south through the Fort McHenry Tunnel to Exit 53, I-395 to Pratt Street. Again turn right on Pratt Street. Parking is available for a fee at Pier 5 and 6 and at the Inner Harbor Center Garage on Pratt Street across from the Aquarium.

Star-Spangled Banner Flag House

Spirits that Never Flagged

Oh, say can you see by the dawn's early light,
What so proudly we hailed at the twilight's last gleaming?
Whose broad stripes and bright stars, thro' the perilous fight,
O'er the ramparts we watched were so gallantly streaming?
And the rockets' red glare, the bombs bursting in air,
Gave proof thro' the night that our flag was still there,
Oh, say does that star-spangled banner yet wave
O'er the land of the free and the home of the brave?

On September 14, 1814, Francis Scott Key wrote these stirring words, which became the first stanza of our national anthem. Key was trying to negotiate the release of his friend, Dr. William Beanes, who was taken hostage after the British burned Washington during the War of 1812. From his position aboard an American truce ship anchored outside Baltimore's harbor, Key witnessed the British attack on Fort McHenry, and he anxiously awaited the coming of dawn to see if the flag still flew and the fort still held.

The flag he searched for had been designed with visibility very much in mind. Major Armistead, Commandant of Fort McHenry, had wanted a giant flag so big "that the British will have no difficulty in seeing it from a distance." He commissioned Mary Pickersgill to fashion the oversize flag. Mary, with some help from her teenage daughter and niece, worked for ten hours a day for six weeks to make the 30- by 42-foot flag. It was the largest battle flag ever designed and weighed 80 pounds. Eleven men were needed to raise it.

Mary Pickersgill, a young widow, had moved from Philadelphia in 1807 to this rowhouse at 844 East Pratt Street with her seven-year-old daughter, Caroline, and her mother, Rebecca Young, also widowed. Mrs. Young had worked as a flag and banner maker in Philadelphia and had made the first flag of the Revolution at the request of George Washington. That flag, the Grand Union or Continental colors, was raised by General Washington on January 1, 1776, at Cambridge, Massachusetts.

The furnishings in Mary Pickersgill's home are from the Federal period, popular when she lived here. In the parlor there is a Charles Willson Peale portrait of Mary's uncle, Colonel Flower, who was George Washington's Commissary General. The upstairs front bedroom is where Mary and her daughter and niece spent hours working on the giant flag. Keeping it all in the family, the material they used was probably purchased at the Fells Point dry goods store of Captain Jesse Fearson, Mary's brother-in-law. It was Mary's military connections and her mother's reputation as a flag maker that prompted Major Armistead to choose her to make the Fort McHenry flag.

Visitors enter the **Star-Spangled Banner Flag House** by way of a small building, which is both a gift shop and a small 1812 War Military Museum. A short audiovisual program serves as a background for understanding the War of 1812 and the part played by Mrs. Pickersgill's flag: a symbol of defiance to the British and a source of inspiration for Francis Scott Key. Guided tours of the house are given after the program.

Mary Pickersgill's tattered flag is displayed at the Smithsonian Institution's National Museum of American History in Washington. A replica may be seen at Fort McHenry (see selection). Mrs. Pickersgill's receipt for the flag is owned by the Flag House; a photostatic copy is on display. She received $405.90.

The Star Spangled Banner Flag House and 1812 War Military Museum are open Tuesday through Saturday from 10:00 A.M. to 4:00 P.M. A nominal admission is charged.

Directions: Take Pratt Street east past the Inner Harbor to the 800 block. The Star Spangled Banner Flag House is on the left at the corner of Pratt and Albemarle streets. A large sign for Little Italy on the left provides a landmark for locating the Flag House. Parking is available on Albemarle Street.

U.S. Frigate *Constellation*

Sea-Link with History

Britannia indeed ruled the waves during the War of 1812. When the newly established United States Navy challenged her sea it was akin to David attacking Goliath. England had some 400 large warships, 350 of which were outfitted with 50 or more cannon. She also had smaller brigs, sloops, schooners and cutters. Against this the United States had three 44-gun frigates: the *Constitution*, the *President* and the *United States*; and four frigates with between 32 and 38 guns. Among the latter was the 38-gun *Constellation*, the first official ship of the U.S. Navy, which had been launched from Baltimore's Fells Point on September 7, 1797.

The *Constellation* was a seasoned veteran by the time the young country became involved in the War of 1812. She had the distinction of being the first U.S. Navy ship to engage and defeat a man-of-war from Europe. In 1799, the *Constellation*, reacting to attacks on American ships by French privateers and men-of-war, triumphed over the French frigate *L'Insurgente* off Nevis in the Caribbean. She had also engaged the Barbary pirates (and would continue to do so after the war). Unfortunately she was unable to contribute during the War of 1812 because the Yankee Race Horse, as she was called, was penned up in Hampton Roads, Virginia, for the duration of the conflict by a seven-ship British fleet under Admiral George Cockburn.

The *Constellation* was to achieve other distinctions. It was aboard this ship that the U.S. Navy signal book was written by the ship's first captain, Thomas Truxtun. The signals and regulations he wrote still serve as basic operating guides. Later in the *Constellation's* service, while circumnavigating the globe in 1842, she became the first U.S. ship-of-war to enter China's inland waters.

The *Constellation* is one of the only surviving American warships that saw action in the Civil War. Recognizing the *Constellation's* historic significance, President Franklin Roosevelt ordered her back to active duty during World War II as the flagship of the U.S. Atlantic Fleet. It was the only sailing ship to hold this honor. Fleet Admiral Chester Nimitz called the *Constellation* "perhaps the most important link that the United States Navy and the American people have with our early historic efforts to preserve our liberty."

The *Constellation's* long career means that she has the longest record of service of any U.S. warship. She is also the oldest ship in

170

the world that has been continuously afloat. Purists may argue that the extensive rebuilding undermines this distinction, but most Americans are grateful that this historic link with our past has been saved.

The *Constellation* has been undergoing significant restoration efforts. Plans call for a summer 1999 reopening. Admission is charged.

Directions: The U.S.F. *Constellation* is docked at the Inner Harbor.

Walters Art Gallery and Evergreen House

Art of the Ages

It isn't surprising that the young William Walters, who claimed he spent the first five dollars he earned on a painting, should go on to amass one of 19th-century America's most eclectic art collections. Thomas Hoving, former director of the Metropolitan Museum of Art, lists William Walters and his son Henry among the top five private collectors in the country's history.

The Walters, pere and fils, are lauded not so much for the number of works they acquired as for the breathtaking diversity of their collection. A day spent at the **Walters Art Gallery** provides the same scope as a semester-long course in art appreciation. Among its thousands of treasures, the Walters Art Gallery holds the finest collection of ivories, jewelry, enamels and bronzes in America and a spectacular reserve of Medieval and Renaissance illuminated manuscripts. The Walters' Egyptian, Greek and Roman, Byzantine, Ethiopian and western Medieval art collections are among the best in the nation, as are the museum's holdings of Renaissance and Asian art.

Sheer breadth of range is no guarantee of a collection's quality, but among the Walters's 30,000 pieces are numerous acknowledged masterpieces. The impressionist works *At the Cafe* by Manet and Monet's pastel-hued *Springtime* are but two of the great paintings. More somber is the ivory sculpture *The Virgin with the Standing Christ Child,* carved around 1400. The Walters's Raphael *Madonna of the Candelabra* is a prized Renaissance canvas; the 5th-century Rubens Vase, exquisitely carved from a single piece of agate, is another treasure. You should be sure to see the magnificent K'ang Hsi Peach Bloom Vase. Ferreting out these art works can be something of an adventure. The five-story wing added in 1947 has circles within circles for you to explore.

The Renaissance sculpture court located in the 1908 wing, built by Henry Walters as a private gallery, is modeled on the Palazzo Balbi in Genoa, Italy. It has state-of-the-art lighting and is covered with rich brocade. Art is displayed as it was for the Renaissance princes, with

Artist Alice Warden Garrett's paintings are displayed on the walls at Evergreen House. Her house also exhibits the largest private collection of work by her friend Raoul Dufy.

paintings, furniture, sculpture and decorative pieces combined for total visual pleasure.

The gallery's attention turns next to the adjacent Hackerman House, which John Russell called "the epitome of the mid-nineteenth-century American town house." It is in this gallery visitors see the Asian collection.

"The most important privately assembled general museum in the U.S.," in the opinion of art authority M.S. Young, the Walters Art Gallery is open Tuesday through Friday from 10:00 A.M. to 4:00 P.M. and weekends from 11:00 A.M. to 5:00 P.M. The gallery hosts ongoing special exhibitions and has a full schedule of public programs, including family days, lectures and concerts. Admission is charged.

The home of another Baltimore collector, Alice Warden Garrett, and her husband, John Work Garrett, is also open to the public. Their home, **Evergreen House,** was bequeathed to Johns Hopkins University and is the location of many university functions. It was the scene of many glittering social events during the first half of this century, when the Garretts entertained the political and artistic elite. Mrs. Garrett dabbled in the arts (her paintings are hung at Evergreen), but she also acquired a number of outstanding works that have never been exhibited elsewhere. The walls of Evergreen House display the works of Picasso, Utrillo, Dufy, Modigliani, Vuillard, Bonnard and Rivera. Alice's collection of paintings by her friend Raoul Dufy—17 watercolors and two oils—is perhaps the largest private collection of Dufy's work in the United States.

Art aside, the house is worth touring because it affords a glimpse of the lifestyle of the rich and famous. There is a Victorian bed chamber, an ornate gold bathroom, a library that could well serve as a set for Masterpiece Theater, as well as a marvelous private theater designed for Mrs. Garrett by Leon Bakst, set designer for the Ballet Russe de Monte Carlo, who also designed the dining room.

The house is open the second Tuesday of each month. Tours are given at 10:00 and 11:00 A.M. and 2:00 and 3:00 P.M. at no charge. Do call before visiting to make sure the renovation work is finished, (410) 338-7641.

Directions: The Walters Art Gallery is at 600 North Charles Street at Centre Street, one block south of the Washington Monument. Evergreen House, farther north, is at 4545 North Charles Street.

HOWARD COUNTY

Historic Ellicott City

Main Street-Main Attraction

Unlike Humpty Dumpty, Ellicott City was put back together again—
and again. In 1868 the town was flooded, causing the death of 50
inhabitants and $1 million in damages. Then in 1972, the town was
flooded in the wake of Hurricane Agnes. The community was next
devastated by a fire on the night of November 14, 1984, which
destroyed a number of Main Street shops. If all that is the bad news,
the good news is that Ellicott City is better than ever!

Bustling specialty boutiques, artists' galleries, antique shops and
old country stores line Main Street. The more than 50 shops include
the Stillridge Herb Shop, where aromatic fragrances waft out the
door, and the Maryland Wine Cellars, where wine buffs can find all
of the Maryland-produced vintages. Many of the shops are housed in
buildings, constructed in the early 1800s, that are built right into the
granite hills. At the Forget-Me-Not Factory's upstairs galleries, the
handmade pottery and sculpture sits on the rocky outcroppings. You
can even see seepage from underground streams moistening the
rocky wall. You can celebrate the holidays year round at the
Christmas Company. Find special magic for Disney fanciers at the
Margaret Smith Gallery which has hand-painted one-of-a-kind character cels and drawings used in the production of Disney's television
series. There are customarily 3,000 cels created for each episode and
a small percentage of these are offered at special galleries like this
one at 8090 Main Street.

You can take a guided walking tour of **Historic Ellicott City**, whose
history dates back to the Colonial era. Tours are given from April
through late fall on Saturday and holidays at 2:00 P.M. and Sunday at
3:00 P.M. Tickets can be purchased at the Howard County Visitor
Information Center at 8267 Main Street. At 8:30 P.M. on the first
Saturday of the month there is a special Ghost Tour that recounts stories about the haunting of Ellicott Mills.

Ellicott City, originally called Fllicott's Lower Mills, was established
in 1772 by three brothers from Bucks County, Pennsylvania. Joseph,
John and Andrew Ellicott purchased 700 acres of wheat land, plus
the water rights so that they could power a gristmill. The Ellicott
brothers began a road, that later was expanded into the National
Road, from Ellicott's Lower Mills to the markets in Baltimore and out
to Frederick to service their customers. They also built a wharf in the
harbor at Baltimore from which they shipped their products. Ellicott
Mills became firmly linked with Baltimore in 1830 when the city

174

On Tongue Row in Ellicott City, the original stone buildings, built in the 1840s by Mrs. Ann Tongue as living quarters for millhands and their families, are now specialty shops.

became the first railroad terminus in the United States.

The first historic run of Peter Cooper's engine, later called the Tom Thumb, took place on August 28, 1830. The daring riders who made the inaugural trip jotted down notes to prove that the human mind could function while traveling at the dizzying speed of 14 miles an hour. Before Cooper built his engine, trains were pulled by horses. This led to the expression "iron horse." It was die-hard supporters of the old ways against proponents of the newfangled engines that led to the legendary race between the Tom Thumb and a horse.

The Ellicott City **B&O Railroad Station Museum,** located in the 1830 granite stone station, is filled with railroad memorabilia and has an HO scale model railroad layout covering the first 13 miles of track between Baltimore and Ellicott City. The route comes alive when museum lights dim and track lights glow.

There is also an 18-minute audiovisual presentation on the early days of the B&O Railroad.

You'll see reconstruction of the Freight Agent's Quarters, where he lived and worked. The agent's $400 annual salary did not go far, even in the 1830s. Days and hours of operation change seasonally. Call (410)461-1944 for information. Admission is charged.

Another spot to explore is the **Patapsco Female Institute Historic Park**. Just two blocks from Ellicott City's Main Street, you can walk through the stabilized ruins of one of the country's most famous 19th-century girls school. The school's granite Greek Revival mansion with its four huge Doric columns was built on the town's highest hill overlooking the Patapsco River Valley. Elevated walkways permit access to the 8,000 square foot building at this active archaeological site. Plans call for the addition of a 19th-century garden. The park, at 3691 Sarah's Lane, is open from April through October on Sunday from 1:00 to 4:00 P.M.; guided tours are given at 1:30 and 3:00 P.M. Admission is charged.

Ellicott City recalls the small towns of yesterday and is filled with old-fashioned finds. Those who favor the lace and jewelry of earlier eras will love the specialty shops. It is not a town to hurry through; take your time and browse. If you arrive early you can have breakfast at Main Street Blues, 8098 Main Street, where you can try Texas style French toast or Creole omelets. For lunch you can enjoy the rustic charm of Cacao Lane where, if you're lucky you can sit by a window on Main Street. Fine dining is available at Milltowne Tavern, in the old stables on Old Columbia Pike. Tersiguel's Restaurant offers a French country ambience, while at the Phoenix Emporium the atmosphere is that of a turn-of-the-century cafe. If you just want to snack, try the fresh baked goods at Fisher's Bakery, the dessert treats at Scoop du Jour, or the micro-brew at Ellicott Mills Brewing Company, once a lumber store and yard and now the producer of fine German lager beer. Ellicott City has something for everyone.

Directions: From Baltimore take I-70 toward Frederick and then head south on Route 29. From the Washington Beltway, I-495/95, take Route 29 north. From Route 29 take Route 40 east, at Rogers Avenue, turn right and follow signs to the Historic Ellicott City. Turn right on Ellicott Mills Drive and go to the bottom of the hill and turn left onto Main Street.

Savage Mill

Maryland's Warp and Woof

Listed on the National Register of Historic Places, **Savage Mill** combines history, shopping and peaceful woodland trails. You'll weave your way through studios and specialty shops and past reminders of Savage Mill's significant contributions to Maryland's economic history.

In 1820, the Williams brothers—George, Amos and Cumberland—began building a dam and millrace to harness the power generated by the 52-foot Little Patuxent River falls. It was named for John Savage, a friend who loaned them money to launch their textile weaving business. This was one of many Maryland mills that prospered due to the proximity of the port of Baltimore. Raw cotton imported at Baltimore was turned into cloth at the mills and then shipped to other states. Savage Mill operated from 1822 through 1947.

Savage Mill specialized in manufacturing cotton duck, or canvas, a heavy material often used for clipper ship sails. The material woven here was also used for tents, cannon covers and other Civil War products. From 1890 to 1900, Hollywood producers purchased canvas in large sheets 208 inches in width and weighing 17 pounds per yard. These were painted and used for silent movie backdrops. During World War I and II, the canvas was used for tents, cots, truck covers and soldiers' transport bags. In World War II, the mill had 400 workers and turned out 400,000 pounds of cloth each month.

After 1947, the mill, which encompassed 12 buildings, was purchased by Harry Heim who turned it into a Christmas Display Village. Heim enjoyed portraying Saint Nick and even imported reindeer to graze in the orchard. The elaborate operation went bankrupt in 1950.

Nine buildings dating back to 1820 are part of the current Savage Mill. These interconnecting buildings ranging from one to five levels have been renovated and are used as specialty shops, fine art and craft studios and antique and collectible outlets. Historical displays have been placed between boutiques and art galleries. Photographs and exhibits tell the story of the workers at the old Savage Mill. You'll see a picture of the mill workers' houses. These were homes to families that earned all of four dollars a month for working six-day weeks of 10-12 hour days. Other photographs show the 1919 company store, the class of 1924 at Savage High School, and the mill superintendent's house (which has now been purchased and is being renovated to serve as a venue for special events and a permanent decorator's showplace highlighting the merchandise of the Historic Savage Mill Merchants). As you climb the winding old stairs in the Spinning Building, notice the metal nubs along the handrail; they were added to discourage the youngest mill workers, some of whom were barely eight, from sliding down the banister.

Many of the artists who work at Savage, as well as many visitors, find the historic Bollman Truss Bridge a tempting subject for photographs and paintings. Its picturesque suspended iron framework is dramatically framed by the verdant landscape. This type of bridge once could be seen all across the United States and Europe but the wrought and cast iron used to make the bridge rusted out. This is the sole surviving semi-suspension bridge.

There are several eateries overlooking Little Patuxent River. The surrounding landscape is part of Savage Park. Savage Mill, with approximately 265 vendors, is open Monday through Wednesday from 10:00 A.M. to 6:00 P.M. and Thursday through Saturday from 10:00 A.M. to 9:00 P.M. On weekdays between 9:30 A.M. and 3:00 P.M. you can take an escorted hour-long tour of the mill; call (410) 228-5342 for additional information and tour reservations.

Directions: From Baltimore take I-95 south to Route 32. Take Route 32 east to Route 1. Go south on Route 1 to Gorman Road and turn right. Signs will direct you to the parking lot of Savage Mill.

ANNE ARUNDEL COUNTY AND ANNAPOLIS

Banneker-Douglass Museum of African-American Life and History

Maryland Roots

The **Banneker-Douglass Museum**, Maryland's official museum of African-American history and culture, is appropriately located in Mt. Moriah A.M.E. Church, built in 1874 by its parishioners. The congregation, many of whom had been freed from slavery only ten years earlier, were proud of their ability to build this small-scale Victorian Gothic Church. It served the community for 98 years before being

178

sold to Anne Arundel County in 1971.

Scheduled for demolition, this historic church was saved by heroic efforts of local preservationists and the Maryland Commission on African American History and Culture, who converted it to a museum. They named it for two prominent black Marylanders—Benjamin Banneker (1731-1806), pioneer scientist and surveyor, and Frederick Douglass (1818-1895), abolitionist, newspaper editor and civil libertarian.

The museum's collections include ethnological and scientific findings of Arctic explorer Herbert M. Frisky, as well as historical records on black Marylanders donated by historian and attorney Azzie Briscoe Koger. There are also photographs, equipment and personal effects of Annapolis photographer, Thomas Baden. These items and thousands of other artifacts and photographs reveal the everyday and personal lives of black Marylanders in the 19th and 20th centuries. The museum houses African-American paintings, sculptures, prints, rare books, and archival materials such as an original letter by Benjamin Banneker dated 1795.

The museum sponsors craft demonstrations, lectures and films and hosts special traveling exhibits. There is also a reference library on African-American history in Maryland.

The Banneker-Douglass Museum at 84 Franklin Street is open Tuesday through Friday from 10:00 A.M. to 3:00 P.M. and Saturday NOON to 4:00 P.M. No admission is charged but donations are welcome.

Directions: From Baltimore take I-97 south to Route 50 east. Turn right on Route 50 to the Rowe Boulevard exit. Take Rowe Boulevard into Historic Annapolis and turn right on College Avenue to Church Circle. Turn right on Franklin Street off Church Circle; the museum is located in the church on your left.

Chase-Lloyd House and Hammond-Harwood House

Best Laid Plans

Two lovely Georgian homes sit on opposite sides of Annapolis's Maryland Avenue. Both begun by men whose dreams were never fulfilled, both were nevertheless beautifully built by master builder William Buckland.

In the 1770s legal firebrand Samuel Chase, described by the Mayor of Annapolis as "an inflaming son of discord," wanted to build a dream house. It turned into a nightmare for Chase when business reverses forced him to sell the uncompleted house to wealthy Eastern Shore planter Colonel Edward Lloyd IV. Lloyd's opulent lifestyle

179

earned him the nickname Edward the Magnificent. When he acquired the unfinished Chase House, he employed William Buckland to oversee its completion. Buckland, too, had a sobriquet: he was called the Taste Maker of the Colonies for his influential style. The combination of Buckland's talent and Lloyd's wealth produced one of the finest 18th-century interiors in America.

The exterior of this three-story Flemish bond brick mansion has a decorative cornice, projecting pedimented pavilion and what is called a Venetian doorway. But it is the lavishly decorated interior that marks this as one of Buckland's finest achievements. It begins in the main hall, where you see graceful Ionic columns separating the entranceway from the grand staircase. On the first level of the stairway there is a Venetian window and the staircase divides, forming a much-photographed architectural delight.

The **Chase-Lloyd House** remained in the Lloyd family for 73 years and then ironically was purchased by Chase's descendants. The last surviving Chase niece arranged for the house to be preserved as a home for elderly ladies. It is, however, open to the public on afternoons from 2:00 to 4:00, except on Sundays and Mondays. A small entrance fee is charged to support the upkeep.

Chase's fortunes did not improve after he sold his Annapolis home. He went bankrupt in 1789. In 1805 his legal career ended in ignominy when he was impeached as an Associate Justice of the Supreme Court, though in the end he was not convicted.

If Chase's dreams foundered for financial reasons, Mathias Hammond's foundered on the shoals of the revolution brewing in the colonies, and the end of his legislative career.

William Buckland was also the master builder for the splendidly ornamented **Hammond- Harwood House**. This was to be his last creation; he died before the house was finished. But it was also the first and only house he both designed and built. The house is a classic five-part Georgian mansion, considered by some experts the finest example of the style in America. Ionic pilasters, like those Buckland used in the interior of the Chase-Lloyd House, flank the front door. The columns support an elaborately carved pediment and frieze.

Inside, a wealth of details embellish the formal rooms. The dining room and drawing room are particularly fine examples of Buckland's work and they reflect the culmination of years of craftsmanship. The Hammond-Harwood House is not a mere decorative shell, either. The house is exquisitely furnished with 18th- and early 19th-century pieces. Maryland craftsmen are well represented, and there are several portraits by Charles Willson Peale. Appropriately, there is a copy of his portrait of William Buckland that shows in the background the drawings for this very house. There is also an original Peale portrait of Buckland's daughter.

The house came to be known as the Hammond-Harwood House after 1834, when it was given to the daughter of its second owner and her husband. The man she married was William Harwood, the great-grandson of William Buckland, the man whose vision and artistry had given birth to the beautiful house.

The Hammond-Harwood House is open March through December, Monday through Saturday from 10:00 A.M. to 4:00 P.M., and Sunday from NOON to 4:00 P.M. In January and February, hours are Monday through Saturday from 11:00 A.M. to 4:00 P.M. and Sunday NOON to 4:00 P.M. Closed on New Year's Day, Thanksgiving and Christmas. Admission is charged.

Directions: From Baltimore take Route 97 to Route 50 east. Take Route 50 to Rowe Boulevard exit. Follow to College Avenue (at "T" in road). From Rowe Boulevard turn left onto College Avenue, then right at the first light, King George Street. Proceed on King George Street to the first light and turn right on Maryland Avenue for both houses. Chase-Lloyd House is on the right corner and Hammond-Harwood on the left.

London Town Publik House and Gardens

Public House and Public Figures

Doors as enormous as those at the **William Brown House**, part of Edgetwater's **London Town Publik House and Gardens**, seem built to accommodate giants. Fittingly, some historic giants did pass through these portals. George Washington, Thomas Jefferson and Francis Scott Key were among the well-known figures who noted in their diaries crossing on the ferry at London Town.

This once-bustling town on the South River was one of the major ferry stops for travelers between Williamsburg and Philadelphia. It was also a point of departure for Europe and, after 1683, the port of entry for tall-masted ships carrying cargoes of European and East Indian goods to the colonies and taking tobacco back to England.

A log tobacco barn built in 1790 on a Maryland plantation has been moved to the grounds at London Town, but the William Brown House, now a National Historic Landmark, is the only town building to survive. Its extra thick walls were built to last. The bricks were laid in an all-header pattern, which you'll see on a number of colonial houses in nearby Annapolis. This pattern was costly, requiring far more bricks than the more traditional lengthwise pattern. The all-header pattern insured a greater depth and thus improved insulation. The publik house sits on a bluff overlooking the river, so it needed protection from the elements. As an additional deterrent to drafts each room was raised one step. All of the exterior doors, woodwork, hardware and even some windows are original. The sturdy furniture has been collected to reflect 18th-century styles.

181

According to records, the inn was built on land deeded to Colonel William Burgess by Lord Baltimore in 1651. The publik house served as both an inn and post house. It was to the inn that town folk flocked for news. The innkeeper frequently had more than one job. From 1764 to 1781 William Brown ran the publik house, operated a cabinetmaking business, served as ferry keeper and owned farm land nearby.

The trees and flowers of the London Town Gardens entice visitors to return to enjoy the site in different seasons. Spring is a particularly popular time to explore the eight-acre woodland gardens. There is a spring walk that features bleeding heart, Lenten rose, primrose, May apple and phlox, with a separate area for azaleas and viburnums. The wildflower walk is also at its best in the spring. The garden has one of the largest magnolia collections in the east.

During the summer months the day lilies provide the main attraction, but see the herb garden as well. Waterfowl, which can be seen at London Town's pond year round, are abundant during their autumn migration. The winter garden features dwarf conifers.

London Town Publik House and Gardens' hours are year round Monday through Saturday from 10:00 A.M. to 4:00 P.M. and Sunday NOON to 4:00 P.M. Admission is charged.

Directions: From Baltimore take I-97 south to the Annapolis area. Go west on U.S. 50/301 to Parole and exit, following Route 2 south. At the second traffic signal past the South River (Veterans Memorial) Bridge turn left on Mayo Road, Route 253. Take Mayo Road for one mile and then turn left onto Londontown Road, which leads to the grounds of the London Town Publik House.

Maryland State House and
Old Treasury Building

Stately Presence

When Francis Nicholson replaced Sir Lionel Copley as Royal Governor of Maryland in 1694, he immediately took steps to move the capital from St. Mary's City to Arundel Towne (it was renamed Annapolis to honor Queen Anne) on the Severn River at Todds (now Spa) Creek. The town's designation as the provincial seat of government prompted Nicholson to choose a Baroque town plan with streets radiating from two major circles, rather than the more common grid plan. The highest point of land was selected for Public Circle, now called State Circle, following Nicholson's directions to "survey and lay out in the most comodius [sic] and convenient part and place of the said town six acres of Land intire [sic] for the erecting of a Court House and other buildings as shall be thought necessary and convenient."

The Maryland State House in Annapolis is the oldest state capitol building in continuous legislative use. It served as the Capitol of the U.S. from November 1783 to August 1784.

State Circle was never quite the six acres Nicholson ordered but it did become the visual and actual hub of the new town. The first **Maryland State House** was built between 1696 and 1698. When fire destroyed all but sections of the brick walls and foundations in 1704, it was rebuilt from the standing remains. The second State House, completed in 1707, was by 1772 so derelict it was described as an "emblem of public poverty."

The cornerstone of the third State House was laid in March 1772. Work was slow because of the Revolutionary War. When George Washington came to Annapolis in December 1783 for the Continental Congress, it was still unfinished. The state legislature had been meeting in the half-built edifice since 1779. It was eventually completed, and the marble addition you see today was added between 1902 and 1905.

Annapolis was the first peace time capital of the United States from November 26, 1783, until June 3, 1784. It is the oldest State House in continuing legislative use in the country.

In the last weeks of 1783, George Washington bade farewell to his Continental Army officers in New York and traveled to Annapolis to resign his commission before the Continental Congress. The evening prior to the ceremony, December 22, a lavish dinner was held for 200 guests. After 13 convivial toasts were drunk, the guests moved to the State House to dance by the light of eight pounds worth of candles, an expensive indulgence. It is said Washington danced with every lady present.

The next morning in full military uniform, General Washington walked to the State House. In the Old Senate Chamber, he emotionally resigned the commission issued by the Congress on June 15, 1775. A mannequin now stands where he is thought to have stood for this dramatic leave-taking. A painting, hanging over the Governor stairway, purporting to capture this moment shows Martha Washington watching from the Senate floor. Actually, women were not permitted on the floor, and Martha had remained at Mount Vernon. Washington left immediately to join her for the Christmas holiday.

Another moment of history at the State House was the January 14, 1784, ratification of the Treaty of Paris by the Continental Congress. This treaty officially ended the American Revolution. In this, America's first peace treaty, Great Britain formally recognized the independence of her former colonies. This is worth remembering when you view the copy of the Declaration of Independence in the Silver Room. Portraits of the Maryland signers grace the walls. Here, too, is the Edwin White painting of Washington's resignation. On May 7, 1784, Thomas Jefferson was appointed as the first United States minister to a foreign government.

The State House is open daily 9:00 A.M. to 5:00 P.M., closed Christmas. Twenty-minute guided tours are given daily, at 11:00 A.M. and 3:00 P.M.

You may also want to stop by another of Annapolis's historic build-ings on State Circle, the **Old Treasury**. It is the city's oldest surviving municipal building, erected between 1735 and 1737. Local designer Patrick Creagh planned the building to offer security for the money it held in trust. There were iron bars on the windows, thick brick walls and even brick floors to reduce the risk of fire. Today the Old Treasury houses the Research Center of Historic Annapolis Foundation and is open by appointment; call (410) 267-7619.

The State House Visitors Center on the first floor of the State House is an excellent spot to pick up brochures on Annapolis and Maryland attractions and information on the state.

Directions: From Baltimore take I-97 south to the Annapolis area. Then take Route 50 east to Exit 24 and follow signs to Rowe Boulevard. Proceed into Historic Annapolis to Church Circle, then around to State Circle via School Street.

Sandy Point State Park

A Beach for All Seasons

Sandy Point State Park, on the western shore overlooking the Chesapeake Bay Bridge, is ideal for spontaneous beach outings any time of the year. It is roughly 30 minutes from the Baltimore Beltway and 40 minutes from the Washington Beltway.

Summer is the most popular season but not necessarily the most interesting. Warm weather brings out the sunbathers, waders and swimmers. The calm bay water is ideal for youngsters until the sea nettles arrive in mid-summer. Fishermen also flock to Sandy Point, where the catch includes perch, spot and bluefish. There are ramps to launch your own boats and a marina where you can rent boats and purchase bait and tackle. There is surf fishing and crabbing as well. During summer, naturalists are on hand at the park to conduct pro-grams, give talks and lead walks.

It is fun to sit on the beach and watch the action on the Bay, and that too changes with the seasons. In summer pleasure crafts vie for attention with seagoing freighters. You will spot an occasional cruise ship bound for exotic ports.

During fall there are fewer recreational sailboats and more fishing boats as Maryland's oysterman, clammers and crabbers take to the water. Autumn brings migratory birds to Sandy Point, one of the few spots on the Atlantic Flyway on the western shore; another is Merkle Wildlife Refuge (see selection). Migratory geese and ducks can be seen in abundance. There are also native shore and land birds in the park's marshland.

There's nothing quite like a walk along the beach to blow away the cares of winter. Children delight in an unexpected opportunity to play in the sand. The lapping water and rustling sea grass provide the perfect accompaniment to your walk, and white-sailed skipjacks can be seen on the bay.

Waterfowl winter over at Sandy Point, but in spring the migratory birds leave for the north. The pleasure boats return to the Bay; any breezy day brings a colorful array of sails all tacking in the wind. The intrepid can wade and the anxious can get a head start on their tans.

There is a nominal admission to the park in the spring and fall; it's slightly higher during the summer season. From December through February there is no charge.

Directions: From Baltimore take I-97 south. When it intersects with Route 50 head east on Route 50 to the Bay Bridge. Exit 32 from Route 50 east or west is the access road for Sandy Point State Park.

U.S. Naval Academy

Ship Shape

You'll be welcomed "aboard" at the **United States Naval Academy,** home of the Navy's undergraduate professional college since 1845. George Bancroft, President Polk's Secretary of the Navy, established this college at Fort Severn, an all but abandoned ten-acre army post. The fort had been built in 1808 to protect the thriving seaport of Annapolis from the dual threat of British and pirate attacks.

From this modest beginning the U.S. Naval Academy has grown to a 338-acre campus. The campus, or "The Yard," is best explored on an escorted walking tour, which is available through the Armel-Leftwich Visitor Center, located inside Gate 1 (King George Street). You can explore on your own with a self-guiding brochure, but you'll miss all the fascinating history, legends and stories about the high-spirited traditions of the Academy. The school, which began with seven professors and 50 students (midshipmen) now has a 600-member faculty. They teach more than 500 courses to approximately 4,000 midshipman.

The visitor center, which overlooks the Severn River and Annapolis Harbor, also features the film *To Lead and Serve,* interactive exhibits, a model of the U.S.S. *Maryland,* gift shop and galley. The visitor center is open March through November, 9:00 A.M. to 5:00 P.M. and December through February, 9:00 A.M. to 4:00 P.M. Tours are available daily. The center is closed Thanksgiving, Christmas and New Year's Day.

The Academy is a National Historic Landmark with the country's largest grouping of surviving turn-of-the-century Beaux Arts designs and modern architecture. The walking tour map provides information on 17 buildings and six monuments. One of the tour highlights is

Bancroft Hall, one of the world's largest college dormitories. Bancroft has 33 acres of floor space housing the entire student body, or brigade, as it is called. You can go in to see the rotunda, which is called Memorial Hall. In front of Bancroft Hall during the academic year, in good weather conditions, you can watch the Brigade Meal Formation. Brigade reports are given, the Drum and Bugle Corps performs and then the midshipmen march in to lunch. It is served in one of the world's largest dining rooms—55,000 square feet with 372 tables. But despite the room's size, lunch is always served within four minutes. Each day more than 12,000 hot meals are prepared and the students consume two tons of meat and 4,000 quarts of milk.

The next to the last stop on the tour is the **Naval Academy Chapel**, a building that resembles Les Invalides in Paris. Its copper-green dome can be seen above all the other buildings on campus. The cornerstone was laid in 1904. A stained glass window designed by Frederick Wilson and executed by Gorham honors four sea heroes—Mason, Porter, Farragut and Sampson. A Tiffany window is called the New Ensign Window, or Commission Invisible. A 12-foot model of a 15th-century Flemish sailing vessel hangs above the rear choir loft. Such models are traditional in churches serving communities of seafaring men.

Beneath the chapel is the crypt of American Revolutionary War hero John Paul Jones. Carved dolphins decorate the ark-like marble sarcophagus of the man who many call the father of the United States Navy. The names of the ships commanded by Jones are inscribed on the deck encircling the crypt. Jones' battlecry, "I have not yet begun to fight!" is one of the few quotes most of us remember from high school history classes.

Also interesting is Preble Hall, where 50,000 items are displayed in the **Naval Academy Museum**. Among these exhibits is the table from the mess deck of the U.S.S. *Missouri* on which the Japanese signed the surrender ending World War II. Additionally, you can see a fascinating collection of sailing ship models and an extensive group of maritime and naval paintings. One display reviews the life and accomplishments of John Paul Jones, another covers the Navy's role in global conflicts.

Before leaving the campus be sure to stop by the Robert Crown Sailing Center. The Academy's sailing program is one of the best in the world. The center has an impressive 120-craft fleet that ranges from ocean racers to windsurfers. The U.S. Naval Academy Museum is open Monday through Saturday 9:00 A.M. to 5:00 P.M. and Sunday 11:00 A.M. to 5:00 P.M.

Directions: From Baltimore head south on I-97 to the Annapolis area. Take Rowe Boulevard into Historic Annapolis and proceed to College Avenue. Make a left and drive two blocks to King George Street. Turn right. Go to the end of the street, through Gate #1 of the Academy. This is the Visitors Gate. Guards will direct you to the parking lot and the Visitor Information Center in Ricketts Hall.

In front of the U.S. Naval Academy's Bancroft Hall during the school year, visitors can watch the Meal Formation. Brigade reports are given, the Drum and Bugle Corps performs, and then the midshipmen march in to lunch.

Victualling Warehouse, Tobacco Prise House and the Barracks

Historic Annapolis's Trade and Troops

The 18th-century **Victualling Warehouse** brings back the days when Annapolis was a bustling commercial center, the principal seaport of the upper Chesapeake Bay as well as one of Maryland's tobacco inspection centers. This warehouse, at 77 Main Street, like others that once existed along the waterfront, was likely used as a victualling warehouse. Victualling (pronounced vit-alling) simply means provisioning. The term first referred to stocking up with victuals, or food, but later encompassed the supplies, sails, cordage and other equipment necessary for sailing. Annapolis was highly regarded for the quantity and quality of its ship chandlery, or provisioners.

The building currently houses Historic Annapolis Foundation's Museum Store where, in addition to antique reproductions and books on Maryland history, visitors will find a model of the Annapolis waterfront as it would have looked during the Golden Age of the 1750s and 1760s. It is open Monday through Saturday from 10:00 A.M. to 5:00 P.M. and Sunday NOON to 5:00 P.M.

Another building of this era is the **Tobacco Prise House** located on Pinkney Street, across City Dock from the Victualling Warehouse. This warehouse is far smaller and was possibly used to pack and store inspected tobacco. Small farmers close to town would have brought their tobacco already packed in hogsheads to such a warehouse for inspection. These hogsheads (or large barrels) were unpacked by the appointed inspectors who then assigned the tobacco a particular value. Slaves or laborers hired for the occasion would then repack the tobacco using a prise. At the side of the warehouse you'll see a prise, or wooden lever, that was used to compress the tobacco into the hogshead. These hogshead, weighing between 750 and 1,200 pounds, would then be stored at the warehouse until a ship could be arranged to carry the tobacco to a buyer. This building is open on special occasions.

Just up Pinkney Street from the Tobacco Prise House is one of the oldest surviving houses in Annapolis. The **Shiplap House**, named for the type of board siding that is on the rear of the building as well as the side addition, was built in 1715 by Edward Smith. Smith operated an ordinary, or tavern, on the property. When the building is open, visitors will find a recreation of Smith's Tavern in one of the downstairs rooms. Smith died in 1723, and the house subsequently had many owners and tenants. Just prior to the Revolution, Nathan Hammond owned this house and operated a small merchants shop here. Town residents could purchase nails, sugar, cloth and other necessities at Hammond's store. During the latter half of the 19th century, this house became the residence of noted artist Francis Blackwell Mayer. The building currently houses the headquarters of Historic Annapolis Foundation. The museum floor is open on some afternoons—check the sign on the door. There is no admission charged.

A bit further up the street at 43 Pinkney Street is a mid-18th-century, gambrel-roofed house. Known as the **Barracks,** this carpenter's house was typical of the many small homes leased to the state for use as Continental soldier barracks during the American Revolution. Housing was so scarce that even such small dwellings were pressed into service. Records from that period indicate that neither side was happy with the enforced troop quartering. The soldiers complained of the meagerly furnished rooms and lack of firewood. They retaliated by burning what furniture there was as well as structural portions of the houses—to the dismay of their reluctant landlords. The first floor of this building is open on special occasions.

Directions: From Baltimore take I-97 south to Route 50 east. Take Exit 24 (Rowe Boulevard) off Route 50 into historic downtown Annapolis.

William Paca House and Gardens

Picture Perfect

It is the colors you'll remember long after you visit the Annapolis home of William Paca (pronounced pay-ka). Five years of painstaking work peeled away 22 layers of paint and wallpaper to uncover the startling Prussian blue walls that have now been resplendently repainted. This sky-blue hue, so dramatically different from the muted Williamsburg shades that we think of as colonial, was the first commercially produced paint.

The restoration of the house was a remarkable achievement. The dramatic change can be seen in the before and after photographs displayed in the rear porch chamber. The additions made while the house was used as part of the Carvel Hall Hotel were all removed, and both the Georgian mansion and the 18th-century pleasure gardens were restored.

The house tour begins in the blue parlor which, like the rest of the house, has been furnished to reflect fashions ten years before the American Revolution. Because the house did not remain in the family, the furniture is not original, although one chair and several pieces of silver did belong to the Paca family. Each room shows a popular activity that the family might have enjoyed during that era. There is a card game spread out on the parlor table. You'll next move to the hall which, contrary to your expectation, is not a passageway but what we would call a family room, with the table set for tea. Again you'll see the bright blue, used here for trim. The table in the dining room is

The William Paca House and Gardens have been brilliantly restored to their original elegance of 1765. Paca is sometimes compared with his compeer, Thomas Jefferson.

M.E. WARREN

also set, but the guide explains that colonial families frequently had their meals served in whatever room they were using and only repaired to the dining room when entertaining company.

The back porch, not traditionally a part of Georgian homes, was added to the house by William Paca who, it can be conjectured, wanted a room where he could enjoy the garden on which he lavished so much time. You'll get your best overview of the garden from the upstairs window. Note how the terraces lead down to the wilderness garden, which is highlighted by a two-story octagonal pavilion. This pavilion and the Chinese Chippendale trellis bridge were included in the background of the Charles Willson Peale portrait of Paca. The pleasure gardens look as though they haven't been touched since the days when the portrait was painted. They were all restored after detailed excavation work uncovered the old garden foundations.

Paca's interest in gardening is but one of many similarities between Paca and Thomas Jefferson, with whom he was often compared. Both were lawyers, both served in the Continental Congress and both signed the Declaration of Independence. Paca went on to help draft the Maryland Constitution and served as Governor of Maryland from 1782-85 (Jefferson served as Governor of Virginia). At Paca's death in 1799 he was serving as the first U.S. District judge from Maryland, the position to which he was appointed by President Washington.

William Paca House and Gardens are open for tours. Many visitors return to enjoy his gardens as they change with the seasons. The house tours now also change every eight months, emphasizing different facets of 18th-century life. The William Paca House is open Monday through Saturday from 10:00 A.M. to 4:00 P.M. and on Sunday from NOON to 4:00 P.M. The William Paca Gardens are open at the same times except on Sundays, May through October, when it stays open an hour longer, until 5:00 P.M. Both house and garden are closed Thanksgiving, Christmas Eve and Christmas Day.

Directions: From Baltimore take I-97 to Route 50 east, then take Rowe Boulevard into Historic Annapolis. Turn left at the State House onto College Avenue, then make a right on King George Street, right again on East Street for one block to Prince George Street. Make a right on Prince George Street and you'll see the William Paca House at 186 Prince George Street.

HARFORD COUNTY

Havre de Grace

Amazing Grace

Though the British burned Havre de Grace on May 3, 1813, damaging 60 percent of its structures, the town today still has 800 buildings with "historic attributes." More than 60 are identified with date plaques. You can see the highlights on a self-guided tour beginning at the **Concord Point Lighthouse** and ending at the Lockhouse.

The most picturesque spot in town, the Concord Point Lighthouse, is open on Sundays from 1:00 to 5:00 P.M. May through October. Here you can pick up a brochure on the self-guided tours. (The brochure is also available at the Chamber of Commerce at the Mini-Mall on Washington Street Monday through Friday, 1:00 to 5:00 P.M.) If you arrive on Sunday, don't miss the chance to climb the lighthouse. You'll have an impressive view of the Susquehanna River flowing into the Chesapeake Bay. The lighthouse was authorized in 1826 and built of Port Deposit granite. Work was completed on May 21, 1829. One family, the O'Neills, served as light keepers until 1920—thus spanning the entire history of manual operation. The first of the light keepers, John O'Neill, who singlehandedly manned the town's hill battery, had been captured and imprisoned by the British in 1813. He was sentenced to be hanged, but was saved by the intervention of his daughter, Matilda. To arrange a lighthouse tour on a day other than Sunday, call (410) 939-1340 or (410) 939-2016.

From the lighthouse it's only a block down Market Street to the **Havre de Grace Decoy Museum**, overlooking the headwaters of the Chesapeake Bay. The museum has three main galleries. The first provides a background on decoys, how they are carved and various regional styles. There is a diorama of a carver's decoy workshop. The second gallery focuses on the different type of hunting that was done on the Susquehanna Flats including the boats and weapons that were used. There are also decoy collections grouped by carvers, including works by Madison Mitchell, Paul Gibson, Charles Bryan and others. On most weekends you will see carvers demonstrating and selling their work. Museum hours are 11:00 A.M. to 4:00 P.M. daily.

Continuing on your tour of Havre De Grace, the next stop is Tydings Park just past the 1920 Bayou Hotel. The park provides a lookout over the Susquehanna Flats, first viewed by Captain John Smith in 1608 on his voyage up the Chesapeake Bay.

Havre de Grace's long history is divided into six periods. The period from 1780 to 1830 is sketchily recorded because the fire laid waste to so much of the town. Only the Rodgers House at 226 N.

A self-guided tour of historic Havre de Grace takes you past many of the 800 buildings that survived the British burning of the town in 1813. The canal lockhouse dates from 1840.

Washington Street is conclusively dated as an 18th-century building. George Washington made note of stops at the Rodgers House in 1785 and 1795.

The period from 1830 to 1850, which brought the Susquehanna & Tidewater Canal and the concurrent railroad corridor, was probably the most interesting in the city's history. The growth slowed in the middle period, 1850-80, with the end of the canal era and the Civil War.

Then came the Victorian period, 1880-1910, with its gingerbread houses. Bay windows, towers, gables, turrets, stained glass, irregular windows and heavily carved porch trim are much in evidence on the tour. The city's late period, 1910-40, was marked by bungalows and weekend homes built by an influx of sportsmen. The contemporary period, 1940 to the present, accounts for a small number of new houses in the historic district.

All but four houses on the self-guiding tour can be seen as you drive up Union Street. Fourteen houses dating from 1801 to 1896 line this historic street. You'll also see some community churches and the Havre de Grace City Hall.

The in-town tour ends at the **1840 Lockhouse.** Once a combined office and living quarters for the locktender, the Lockhouse is now the home of the **Susquehanna Museum** and is open April through November on Sundays, 1:00 to 5:00 P.M. A short historical audio visual program on the Susquehanna & Tidewater Canal is shown. You'll learn that the canal was 45 miles long and had 19 locks, one of which you see directly in front of the house. There is also a pivot bridge that permitted wagons and mules to cross the canal to the river wharves. The parlor, kitchen and upstairs bedrooms have been furnished in the style of the canal era.

Directions: From the Baltimore Beltway (I-695) take 1-95 north to Exit 89, Havre de Grace- Churchville. Follow blue and white signs to hospital on Union Avenue. Continue on Union Avenue to Lafayette Street. Make a left on Lafayette to Concord Point Lighthouse, at the south end of town where the self-guided tour begins. To reach the lighthouse from the Lockhouse Museum, go south on Union Avenue to Commerce Street. Turn left and go east to Market Street and the lighthouse.

Ladew Topiary Gardens

I'll Be Seeing Yew

Harvey Ladew was an international jetsetter long before the term was coined: a man of multiple interests—scientific, artistic and athletic—with the money to satisfy each whim. When Ladew purchased his Maryland farm in 1929, he was so eager to host a party he invited guests before the renovation was finished. The rough floor nails tore the hems of the ladies' gowns.

No doubt these ladies forgave him, but there may have been others less forgiving at the dinner party he once gave where guests and horses were served at table with silver dishes! Ladew's farm was purchased for a fox-hunting retreat, and the hunt motif is everywhere—on the china, in photographs and paintings, on clocks and wall hangings.

Ladew achieved notoriety when he rode in two hunts—one in America and one in England—within 72 hours. Often a quarry himself, he never was caught by any of the ladies who vied for his attention. He preferred the unencumbered life of bon vivant and world traveler. On a scientific journey in Bolivia he had a mouse named after him, Thomasomy Ladewi. He would rather have had the title, King of the Dudes, that his uncle, E. Berry Wall, gained after making 40 complete costume changes to be dressed appropriately for all his activties during a single day of the 1888 season in Saratoga Springs, New York. Ladew himself came to be known as the best dressed man in America.

He decorated his home with great imagination. A dressing room, frequently used by his sister Elise, has one wall covered by a trompe l'oeil painting partially done by Ladew. Painted on the wall is a chest with lace trimmed undergarments spilling out of open drawers, and chairs on either side cluttered with a black tricorn hat, a negligee and a black lace mask. When you visit his studio you'll see examples of Ladew's paintings.

The library is one of the most beautiful rooms in the house. It was added by Ladew after he returned from England with an oval Chippendale partner's desk too large for any of the existing rooms. Being nothing if not determined, Ladew built an oval library around the desk. Whimsy intrudes even here; he hung a tennis net under a hunt table to hold his empties. He also built an escape door into the bookcase so that he could make a getaway if a party got too dull.

It was while visiting England that Ladew acquired a passion for topiary, the art of sculpturing trees and shrubs. You'll see his favorite figures, a mounted hunter riding behind the hounds after a fox, bounding across the front lawn. The garden boasts a giraffe, camel, goat, reindeer, rabbit, Scottie and even a unicorn. The aviary has swimming swans, nesting hens, a rooster and lyre birds. A striking vista is presented by a corridor of topiary hedges more than a third of a mile long!

With so much emphasis on topiary art, most first-time visitors are pleasantly surprised to discover 15 flowering garden "rooms" also designed by Ladew. Many of these rooms, as he called his garden areas, are color coordinated. The white garden has 35 varieties of flowers all in white. There are also pink, yellow and red gardens. Other motifs include the berry garden, the Victorian garden, the wild garden, the rose garden, the iris garden and the water lily garden. The steps leading to the garden of Eden are carved with a Chinese proverb Ladew evidently took to heart: "If you would be happy for a week, take a wife; if you would be happy for a month, kill your pig; but if you would be happy all your life, plant a garden." Humor abounds inside and out. You'll leave this Maryland estate wishing you could have attended just one of Mr. Ladew's parties.

Ladew Topiary Gardens offers house and garden tours Monday through Friday from 10:00 A.M. to 4:00 P.M., Saturday and Sunday 10:30 A.M. to 5:00 P.M. The Ladew Cafe serves lunch during garden hours. Admission is charged.

Directions: From the Baltimore Beltway (1-695) take Exit 27B and go north on Route 146 (Dulaney Valley Road). Ladew Topiary Gardens is five miles past Jacksonville (or 14 miles from the Beltway on Route 146 on the right hand side of the road.

Susquehanna State Park and Steppingstone Museum

An Earlier Step for Mankind

In woodsy Harford County you'll discover the multiple delights of **Susquehanna State Park**—Steppingstone Museum, the Carter Mansion, the Jersey Toll House and Rock Run Mill—and these are just the historic attractions. There are also nature trails, fishing areas, campgrounds, picnic tables and a boat launching ramp.

Captain John Smith once thought the mighty Susquehanna River, named for the Indians Smith encountered, might be a route to the fabled Northwest Passage, a water route to the Asian continent. He was so enthusiastic about the river he declared, "Heaven and earth seemed never to have agreed better to frame a place for man's commodious and delightful habitation."

The 3,600-acre Susquehanna State Park capitalizes on its riverfront location. This section of the Susquehanna is popular with fishermen in April when the shad run up the river. At other times pike, perch and bass lure the sportsmen. In addition to the river's recreational and scenic appeal, three of the historic points of interest are located at the juncture of Rock Run and the Susquehanna River.

A stone four-story, water-powered grist mill was built here in 1794 by John Stump. This picturesque riverside mill offers grinding demonstrations from 2:00 to 4:00 P.M. on weekends and holidays from May through October. The mill's 12-ton wheel still grinds flour that is sold at the mill.

Just upriver is the **Jersey Toll House**, once the residence of the canal toll-keeper at Rock Run. Inside you will see a diorama of this part of the Susquehanna River in 1850. Rock Run House, also called the **Carter Mansion**, is on a hilltop overlooking the river. This 13-room house, now furnished with antiques, was built in 1804 by John Carter. The stone house has an indoor smokehouse and a wine cellar in the cool basement. The Jersey Toll House and Carter Mansion are open 10:00 A.M. to 6:00 P.M. on weekends Memorial Day through September. There is no fee.

The most interesting attraction in the park is the **Steppingstone Museum**, a short distance from the Rock Run area, off Quaker Bottom Road. This outdoor living history agricultural museum presents a complete picture of rural life around 1900. The modest stone farmhouse with walled rear terrace is furnished comfortably. The parlor has a heavy Victorian sofa and you can imagine the family gathered around the piano for an evening sing-along. There's also another small parlor filled with books, a well-stocked kitchen, and up the narrow, winding staircase, a small bedroom.

In one of the adjacent barns you'll find the **J. Edmund Bull Antique**

Tool Collection. Tools are arranged by their use—layout tools, rough shaping tools, smoothing planes, shaping tools, finishing saws and many others. There is usually a volunteer on hand to demonstrate how they were used.

Volunteers also man the large shed that houses the support industries on which the farmer depended. You'll see a blacksmith practicing his craft, a cooper making barrels or perhaps a woodworker or tinsmith. Another large barn has an **Old Country Store** filled with hand-crafted items, hard candy, plus a wide array of exhibits. The faded family-size Flexible Flyer conjures up Norman Rockwell images. There's a collection of old carriages, unusual kitchen gadgets and looms. Volunteers frequently demonstrate the looms as well as carding, spinning and weaving. You will find a few craftspeople at Steppingstone Museum, but its festivals feature a full range of craft demonstrations (see Calendar of Events). The Steppingstone Museum is open weekends May through the first Sunday in October. Admission is charged.

Susquehanna State Park also offers camping, picnicking and hiking along its 12 miles of trails, some of which are accessible to bikers and horseback riders. The park's Lapidum Landing is a year-round boat launching facility.

Directions: From the Baltimore Beltway (I-695) take 1-95 north for 25 miles to Exit 89, Route 155. Take Route 155 west. After ¼ mile turn right on Earlton Road and follow for ½ mile. Then make a left on Quaker Bottom Road, follow for roughly one mile to Steppingstone Museum entrance on the right. For the Rock Run area stay on Quaker Bottom Road to Rock Run Road and turn right. The Carter Museum will be on your right and the Jersey Toll House and the Rock Run Mill will be along the Susquehanna River.

U.S. Army Ordnance Museum

Anzio Annie Survives

As you wander up and down the museum's rows of tanks, armored cars, howitzers and associated artillery, you're likely to overhear stories recounted by visiting veterans about the days when their lives depended on these weapons. Such stories are more than matched by the legends and lore associated with field pieces in the **U.S. Army Ordnance Museum** collection at the Aberdeen Proving Ground.

Anzio Annie, a major piece in the collection, is the name the Allies on Anzio gave the German Leopold gun that held them pinned to a sandy beachhead. The Allied High Command was mystified by it; they couldn't imagine how a gun large enough to fire a 550-pound shell could escape their bombing and naval attacks. But the Leopold

The U.S. Army Ordnance Museum, the world's most complete weapons collection, houses—outside and indoors—exhibits from the Revolution through the Vietnam War.

survived numerous raids. The puzzle was solved when the Allies broke from their beach position. The Germans retreated, leaving Anzio Annie hidden in a mountain tunnel. The gun was mounted on 24 railroad wheels and was only rolled out to be fired. Annie is the only German railroad gun known to survive World War II.

Another massive weapon is the atomic cannon introduced in the early 1950s. This 166,638-pound weapon fired both conventional and atomic munitions at targets up to 18 miles away. Speaking of large weapons, consider the Nazi V-2 rocket on display. It is scary to learn that if Heinrich Himmler, head of the SS, had not arrested two top V-2 engineers they very likely would have perfected a rocket capable of hitting New York City. And the space age might well have started earlier, for the rocket contained the basic elements of later space vehicles.

These are just some of the more than 250 pieces in the outdoor exhibit which, when combined with the indoor displays, forms the world's most complete weapons collection. The weapons have more than historical value; they are also highly useful for research. They enable engineers to develop and modify existing models, as well as learn how to defend against various weapons.

As you enter the museum you'll see the Civil War-era Gatling gun, which illustrates the research value of this collection. In 1902-1904 experiments were done with the Gatling gun to develop a more rapid firing weapon. At that time the need for speed was not critical so the experiment was discontinued. When aircraft armaments were needed in the 1940s, the Ordnance Museum supplied information from the earlier tests and the Gatling gun principle was used to develop the Vulcan, an aircraft weapon.

The museum's exhibits include the history and development of ammunition and examples of every kind of rifle imaginable. There is case after case of rocket launchers, machine guns and submachine guns.

The U.S. Army Ordnance Museum is open at no charge Monday through Sunday from 10:00 A.M. to 4:45 P.M. It is open on selected National holidays. The museum does open for Armed Forces Day, Memorial Day, Veterans Day and Independence Day.

Directions: From the Baltimore Beltway, I-695, take I-95 north 21 miles to Exit 85 for Route 22. Turn right on Route 22 and proceed to the Aberdeen Proving Ground Military Police Gate. The museum is one mile beyond the gate on the right side.

CECIL COUNTY

Mount Harmon Plantation and C&D Canal Museum

See World's End from Widow's Walk

Maps refer to land the second Lord Baltimore granted Godfrey Harmon in 1651 as **World's End**. Around 1730 William Ward built an elegant five-bay Georgian mansion here, on a knoll surrounded by the creeks and inlets of the Sassafras River. **Mount Harmon Plantation** at World's End, as the manor house was called, was a typical colonial frontier plantation.

In the early 1960s Mrs. Harry Clark Boden IV restored the interior of Mount Harmon to its 18th-century appearance. She filled the rooms with English, Irish and American period furnishings, including some lovely Chippendale and Hepplewhite pieces. It is, however, the portrait of Lady Arabella Stuart that captivates visitors. The painting is done on what looks like an accordion-pleated board, the angled surfaces allowing the painter to capture three different views. When seen from the left it is a traditional portrait of Lady Arabella. If you look straight at the picture, she appears to be behind bars, as indeed she once was. The painting becomes macabre when viewed from the right—all you see is her skeleton. It is a disquieting and unusual work of art.

The entranceway wallpaper, crafted in Hong Kong in a silver tea-box pattern, creates one of the most attractive areas in the house. The Oriental motif continues up the opulent Chinese Chippendale staircase. Each of the 21 railing panels leading to the third floor has a different pattern. Visitors are encouraged to tackle the few extra steps beyond the staircase to the widow's walk, an opportunity permitted in few old homes.

And what a view there is from this height! Looking in one direction you'll see part of the winding two-mile approach lane; in places the road is a veritable tunnel through the dense Osage orange trees. Between the house and the Sassafras River is the boxwood and wisteria garden. The bird's-eye view lets you appreciate the serpentine brick wall that encloses this garden.

You'll also see the out-kitchen, which can be toured after the house, and the tobacco prize house at the river's edge. The entire estate is a wildlife and nature preserve. There are cleared trails winding through the forest along McGill Creek and the Sassafras River. Nature lovers will welcome the chance to see the American lotus, which rarely grows wild in Maryland. This lotus is the largest wild-

Mount Harmon Plantation at World's End was built around 1730 on a knoll overlooking Sassafras River. The view from its widow's walk will take your breath away if the stairway doesn't.

flower found in the United States. The American bald eagle, also rare, nests in this area and is often seen at Mount Harmon.

Mount Harmon is open for tours April through October on Tuesday and Thursday from 10:00 A.M. to 3:00 P.M. and on Sunday 1:00 to

4:00 P.M. from April through October and at other times by appointment; call (410) 275-8819. Admission is charged.

On your way to Mount Harmon, immediately after crossing the Chesapeake City Bridge at Chesapeake City, turn right for the **C&D Canal Museum.** It's well worth a stop. A six minute audio visual program introduces visitors to the C&D Canal. The canal opened on October 17, 1829. Crossing the Delmarva Peninsula to connect the Chesapeake Bay with the Delaware River, it cuts 300 miles of passage between these two bodies of water by eliminating the voyage around Cape Charles. Today the C&D Canal is one of the world's busiest canals, with thousands of vessels a year taking this shortcut. Most museum visitors have the chance to watch huge ships slip beneath the bridge that connects the north and south sides of Chesapeake City.

A working model at the museum demonstrates how the canal's lift lock works. There are also models of vessels that have plied the canal. The most colorful ship represented is James Adams's floating theater, which once brought entertainment to Chesapeake City and other towns along the canal. There is also a model of a canal barge, a pipeline dredge and various Chesapeake Bay sailing craft. Those interested in the mechanical operation of the canal locks will be fascinated by the two steam engines and the cypress-wood lift wheel in the Old Lock Pump House.

The C&D Canal Museum, on Second Street at 815 Bethel Road, is open at no charge Monday through Saturday 8:00 A.M. to 4:00 P.M. Chesapeake City has a number of specialty shops and restaurants. The Bayard House, at Bohemia Avenue and the C&D Canal, is a restored Federal-style tavern and inn with great views of the canal (410-885-3314). The Inn at the Canal is a bed and breakfast with six guest rooms in an old Victorian house (call 410-885-5995). Italian food is featured at The Tap Room, on the corner of Second and Bohemia (410-885-9873). The Canal Creamery, 9 Bohemia Avenue, is an ice cream parlor with freshly baked pies and other tempting desserts including their special hot fudge brownie sundaes.

Just outside Chesapeake City is the 130-acre **Sinking Springs Herb Farm** with an 18th-century log plantation home shaded by a sycamore tree that dates back to 1578. You can enjoy palate tempting herbal luncheons, take a tour of the gardens and grounds or overnight in the garden cottage. The farm is open Monday through Saturday from 10:00 A.M. to 4:00 P.M. It is closed on Sundays. For additional information call (410) 398-5566.

Directions: From Baltimore take 1-95 north and exit on Route 279, which joins Route 213 at Elkton. For Mount Harmon Plantation take Route 213 south to Cecilton and turn right on Route 282. After 2.5 miles take a left on Grove Neck Road. Signs will indicate Mount Harmon entrance on the left. For Sinking Springs Herb Farm take Route 213 out of Chesapeake City and make a left at the light at Locust Point

Road. Travel 1½ miles and turn left onto McKeown Road. Take that for a ½ mile to the stop sign and turn right on Elk Forest Road, continue on that for ½ mile to farm sign and turn right onto the farm entrance lane.

Port Deposit Historic District

Worth Investing In!

You could consider **Port Deposit Historic District** Maryland's Brigadoon, as time seems to have forgotten this tiny community nestled between cliffs of granite and the shores of the Susquehanna River. It was a bustling shipping town in the 1800s when it served as the collection point for lumber floating down river from Pennsylvania. Just before the Civil War, this was the eighth largest city in the state serving as the junction point for lumber, grain, coal, whiskey and tobacco trade. The area was also noted for its granite deposits, which architects prized for their tone and texture. The quarries were north of the town and while shipments were sent to Washington, Philadelphia and Baltimore, many of the local builders also used the granite. The town had one of the strongest stone masonry traditions in the country. Attesting to its economic significance, in 1834 Port Deposit had its first bank. For many years this was the only bank between Wilmington and Baltimore.

In 1927, the completion of the Conowingo Dam ended Port Deposit's river connection to the north. But the river commerce was replaced by the railroads, and Port Deposit continued to prosper. A railroad link to the quarries connected the town with major markets to the north and south. In 1941, the town's private Tome School for Boys, which operated from 1894 to 1940, became a U.S. Navy Training Center. At its peak it housed 35,000 recruits. Before it closed in 1947, the Bainbridge Naval Training Center had trained more than a half million men.

Now a Riverwalk along the east bank of the Susquehanna River links recreation and open space areas along the shore. The entire mid-nineteenth century industrial town is on the National Register of Historic Places. As you stroll past the homes and businesses you will see a wide range of architectural styles: Georgian, Greek Revival, Federal, Victorian, Italianate and other more eclectic designs. You can pick up a walking tour guide that will point out historical and architectural highlights. The walking tour encompasses over 50 points of interest. As you explore be sure to note the charming terraced gardens.

One of the town's most architecturally significant homes is the Gerry House at 16 South Main Street. This late Georgian house with Greek Revival porches was built in 1813. In 1824, when Lafayette toured the country, he was entertained here. Next door is the 1860s **Winchester Hotel**, which now offers fine dining (for reservations call 410-378-3701). Another interesting house at 50 South Main Street is the 1836 Italianate-style Schaeffer House with its five gables, two wings and lovely bay windows.

The **Paw Paw Museum**, at 98 North Main Street, was built in 1821 as the town's first Methodist Church and is named for the two paw paw bushes which flank the entrance. Exhibits include Native American arrowheads, Civil War memorabilia and an extensive collection of photographs that capture Port Deposit over the decades. The museum is open on the second and fourth Sunday from May through October from 1:00 to 5:00 P.M.

On the third Saturday in September the town holds its annual **Port Deposit Heritage Day** with tours of many of the historic homes and buildings, craft demonstrations and sales, children's activities, food and entertainment. In odd years, in mid-December a Candlelight Tour gives you an opportunity to see a number of the town's lovely old homes decorated for the holidays. For details call (410) 378-4480.

There are two popular restaurants just outside the town's historic area. **Union Hotel** is a log-style home built in 1790. If you look carefully you can see the V-notched log construction. Colonially garbed staff serve period food in this rustic setting location on Route 222 (1282 Susquehanna Road, 410-378-3503). At 600 Rowland Road, you can enjoy waterfront dining at **Tome's Landing Restaurant and Yacht Club** (410-378-4005).

Directions: Take I-95 approximately 45 miles north of Baltimore to Exit 93 and follow Route 222 to Port Deposit's Main Street

Upper Bay Museum and Elk Neck State Park

Ducks ... Duck!

On the upper Chesapeake Bay, both commercial and recreational hunters enjoy the bounty of the Susquehanna Flats. Five rivers join the Bay here: the Susquehanna, North East, Elk, Sassafras and Bohemia.

You can practically smell the cordite at the **Upper Bay Museum.** A wide range of hunting paraphernalia has been preserved here, including an extensive collection of duck decoys, sculling oars, gunning lights and old boats. Where else could you learn about sneak-boating, body booting, sinkboxes and all types of decoys?

Both the body booting and the sinkbox were designed to let a hunter take a position within a group of decoys and lure the unsuspecting birds in for the kill. According to volunteers at the Upper Bay Museum, it gets plenty cold standing neck deep in the water even with body booting.

The sinkbox, now outlawed, also provided visual protection and offered a bit more comfort. The sinkbox surrounded a coffin-like boat with a wood-and-canvas-covered deck on which there were 20 to 30 wing decoys, some of cast iron to weigh down the sinkbox. It was outlawed in 1934 because the combination of hunters, pollution and lack of nesting areas had decimated the canvasback population.

Other boats are displayed at the museum. One building has a wide assortment of outboard motors and old bushwhacking boats. In the main museum you'll see a punt-gun skiff with an absolutely enormous gun, two railbird skiffs, a Susquehanna River sportfishing boat and a one-log canoe.

The museum, on the North East Creek and the North East River, used to be a fish packing house. One section has been turned into a replica of a decoy maker's shop. Most of the equipment, furnishings and half-completed decoys were transplanted from Horace Graham's shop in Charlestown. As you peer into the shop, you'll see the gently flowing North East Creek out the far window.

The Upper Bay Museum is open at no charge on Sundays from 10:00 A.M. to 4:00 P.M., Memorial Day to Labor Day. It is also open on occasional Saturdays. Donations are welcomed. The museum is one of 14 points of architectural or historic interest in North East. If you have time, pick up a tour map and stroll along Main Street. While you stroll you can drop in the Five & Dime for penny candy or a double dip ice cream cone. **Woody's Crab House**, 29 South Main Street, has been recognized two years in a row by *Chesapeake Bay Magazine* as having the best crabs and crab cakes in Maryland. It is open March through December; call for more information (410) 287-3541. Another popular dining spot is The Blue Heron Room, 1500 Chesapeake Club Drive, a fine dining establishment overlooking the rolling hills of Chesapeake Bay Golf Club (410-287-0200). You can also stop by the Aft Deck for waterfront dining at the Town Park and Cherry Street.

Continuing down Route 272 past the Upper Bay Museum, you'll reach **Elk Neck State Park.** The park is bounded by the Elk River, North East River and the Chesapeake Bay. The Blue Trail at Turkey Point takes you to land's end. It is one of five blazed trails that together cover more than eight miles.

This land was once traversed by the powerful Susquehannock Indians who impressed Captain John Smith, the first white man to visit the headlands of the Chesapeake Bay. He wrote of the friendly reception they gave him in the record of his 1608 journey.

Like the Indians, current visitors enjoy the bounty of bay and rivers. Fishing and crabbing are popular park activities. Boaters can launch their craft at the dock and boats are available to rent. There is a large swimming beach on the North East River with a bathhouse. The park has 300 camper units for tents and trailers as well as nine cabins. For information on camping and cabins call (410) 287-5333.

An interesting stop in the town of North East is the **Day Basket Factory**, 714 S. Main Street, where, during certain hours, you can watch artisans craft baskets using techniques that span a century. Edward and Samuel Day settled in North East in 1876. Edward had been a basket maker in Massachusetts and had been supplying cotton baskets for the southern market. They moved to North East to reduce their transportation costs and to have an abundant source of white oak from the forests along the Susquehanna River. During World War I their factory produced 2,000 baskets weekly. Day baskets are still made from 100% white oak in a wide range of styles. For more information, you can call (410) 287-6100 or (800) 382-3105.

Directions: From Baltimore take 1-95 north to the exit for the town of North East, also marked Route 272 south. For the Upper Bay Museum turn right on Walnut Street in North East. For Elk Neck State Park continue south on Route 272 to the park.

Eastern Shore
Introduction

M ore than the 4.3-mile Chesapeake Bay Bridge separates the Eastern Shore from Maryland's mainland—there is also a cultural, economic and scenic difference. Here you're worlds away from the bustling, populous counties of the Capital Region, and the passing scenery bears no resemblance to the rugged mountain terrain of the Western region. Here, for centuries, livelihoods have been earned from the Bay, as you will discover at the Chesapeake Bay Maritime Museum and the Richardson Maritime Museum in Cambridge.

It was in Kent, one of the region's eight counties, that English settlers first established an outpost in Maryland. Fort Kent was the site of the first Church of England service in the state, and Stevensville's Christ Church has relics of that earlier church.

The bounty of nature extends beyond the fishing industry, as you'll discover at Eastern Neck and Blackwater National Wildlife Refuges. It is a stirring sight to see as many as 50,000 Canada geese massed at these refuges. Whistling swans, snow and blue geese and more than 20 varieties of ducks are also part of the waterfowl population. Once you discover the beauty of these migratory birds, you will have an even greater appreciation for the artistry displayed at the Ward Museum of Wildfowl Art.

Port towns such as Chestertown and St. Michaels provide reminders of the country's earliest years. The Chestertown Tea Party is a fascinating, albeit infrequently told, story and there is an ingenious saga about St. Michaels, "the town that fooled the British" during the War of 1812.

The region rests between the bountiful waters of the Bay, the continent's largest inland estuary, and the crashing waves of the Atlantic Ocean. Assateague Island is an ideal place to get away from daily pressures. If you prefer a beach with more action—everything from amusement rides to myriad beach eateries—then you can join the more than four million summer visitors at Ocean City. If you want to escape the sun, head for the Ocean City Life Saving Station Museum, where you'll discover how rescue workers challenge the treacherous nature of the Atlantic.

KENT COUNTY

Chestertown

Braver than Boston

Every schoolchild knows the story—the American colonists of Boston were incensed about the high tax England imposed on tea. A tumultuous meeting on December 16, 1773, led to decisive action. Under cover of darkness, 40 to 50 radicals, disguised as Indians, crept aboard three British ships and dumped 342 chests of tea into the Boston harbor.

Few schoolchildren, even in Maryland, realize there was a second tea party, more courageous and closer to home. Like their Boston counterparts, the people of **Chestertown** were angered by the tea tax. On May 23, 1774, in broad daylight, the irate townsfolk rowed out to the brigantine *Geddes* and dumped not just tea but crew members as well into the Chester River. This Maryland "tea party" is re-enacted each year on the Saturday before Memorial Day. It's part of a day-long festival that includes a parade, historical vignettes, music, crafts and escorted walking tours.

The May celebration is an ideal time to get acquainted with Chestertown, but some visitors prefer it when the streets are empty and only the ghosts of the past share the old brick sidewalks. A "Walking Tour of Old Chester Town" brochure, available at the Visitor Center on Cross Street or in most of the shops along High Street, provides information on the historic district and the town's lovely Georgian and Federal houses. Many of these houses were built before the Revolution.

Chestertown, when it was one of Maryland's most prosperous ports, was a major stop between Philadelphia and Virginia. Cargo from around the world passed through the **1746 Customs House**. It is one of the largest surviving custom houses built in the 13 original colonies. It's just one of 28 locations marked on your tour map.

Of the private homes only the **Geddes-Piper House** at 101 Church Street is open regularly to the public (May to October, on weekends from 1:00 to 4:00 P.M.). The 3½-story Philadelphia-style townhouse was the home of William Geddes, the Collector of Customs for the Port of Chester Town. It was his ship that his neighbors boarded and off-loaded so unceremoniously in 1774. Tea not only contributed to Geddes's livelihood but to the decor of his home. His lovely collection of teapots is proudly displayed.

If you find yourself wishing you could see the interior of the town's lovely old houses, plan to return on the third Saturday of September for the annual **Candlelight Walking Tour**. This is the only time some

The Chestertown Tea Party, which followed the Boston Tea Party by five months and bears the distinction of having been brought off in broad daylight, is re-enacted each year in Chestertown.

of these private residences can be toured. One other chance to see a selection of Chestertown's spectacular properties is during the December Historic House Tours. Call (410) 778-0416 for additional information. You can also obtain information on the Internet at www.KentCounty.com.

Try to arrange your day so that you're in Chestertown at tea time (3:00 to 5:00 daily), and you can partake of a delightful colonial experience at the **White Swan Tavern**. This is an establishment that George Washington once patronized. It's now a bed-and-breakfast with five 18th-century rooms. For reservations call (410) 778-2300. One of the guest bedrooms was the one-room dwelling of the first owner of the property, John Lovegrove, the "Shoemaker of Chestertown." The property was enlarged by subsequent owners and served as a tavern between 1803 and 1853.

Reflecting turn-of-the-century style is the newly restored **Imperial Hotel**, which was built on High Street in 1903. Its 12 bedrooms and dining room are furnished in Victorian froufrou. If you are not staying overnight, try at least to have a meal here. The menu features American and French cuisine, and the wine cellar is so extensive that overnight guests may pre-arrange a cellar tour during their stay. For reservations call (410) 778-5000.

Chestertown has fewer shopping options than Annapolis or Ellicott City, but they are worth exploring as you roam along the town's red-brick sidewalks.

Twelve miles south of Chestertown, in Rock Hall, are two museums of interest. The **Rock Hall Waterman's Museum**, next to Haven Harbour Marina, is open daily without charge from 10:00 A.M. to 5:00 P.M. You'll see exhibits on oystering, crabbing and fishing. There is a reproduction of a shanty house, like the "shanties" or "arks" the watermen built on a scow or barge and towed behind their boats to the netting grounds on the Bay. The watermen frequently spent the night in these one-room shanty houses. The museum also has a collection of boats, decoy carvings and historical photographs.

In Rock Hall's Municipal Building you'll find **The Rock Hall Museum** with a collection of arrowheads from the Ozini tribe, an indigenous tribe that once inhabited Kent County. The museum also has boat models and ship artifacts including maps, clocks, lights and compasses. There is a display of china and agateware, as well as paintings and prints. The museum is open 2:00 P.M. to 4:30 P.M.

Directions: From Baltimore take Route 97 or Route 2 south to Route 50. Head east across the Bay Bridge. When Route 301 splits off Route 50, head north on Route 301. Take the Centreville/Chestertown exit and follow Route 213 north for 20 miles through Centreville and Church Hill to Chestertown. To reach Rock Hall from Chestertown take Route 291 south and proceed ¼ mile to Route 20. Turn right and travel 12 miles south on Route 20 to Rock Hall. Haven Harbour Marina is one mile south of the traffic light in Rock Hall, on the right.

Cray House and Stevensville Train Depot

First English Settlement in Maryland

U.S. history books never leave out the story of Jamestown, Plymouth Rock or the Massachusetts Colony, but what they rarely tell is the story about the first English settlement in Maryland. In August 1631, three years before Lord Baltimore's ships landed at St. Clement's Island, William Claiborne landed on the Isle of Kent, met with the Native Americans, gained land for the Crown of England and established the first English settlement in Maryland. The story goes untold because the settlement did not survive and, in fact, after more than

350 years of erosion the land it occupied is most likely under the Eastern Bay.

Claiborne built a fort, church, houses and boats. Farms were established and 2,000 tobacco plants were the start of what would be the lifeblood of Maryland's colonial economy. The first European woman in Maryland, Joane Young, came to this settlement as a maid servant. After Lord Baltimore's ships, the *Ark* and the *Dove,* arrived in 1634, there was a struggle for possession of Kent Island. The first naval battle in the New World was between Lord Baltimore's and Claiborne's ships.

In 1652, Christ Church at Kent Fort, where the first Church of England service conducted on Maryland soil took place, was moved to the developing community of Broad Creek. It remained at that location for 228 years until 1880 when it was taken to Stevensville. (There are still gravestones that can be seen enclosed by a white fence where the church once stood in Broad Creek.) Although for a time some historians believed that Broad Creek was later called Stevensville, there is now general agreement that they were two different settlements.

Stevensville was named for the Charles Stevens family, who sold the land on which the community was developed during the 1850s and 1860s. The entire village of Stevensville was placed on the National Register of Historic Sites in 1986. There are several sites here of historic interest. Stevensville's **Christ Church**, built in 1880, is the oldest surviving church on Kent Island. Within the church you can see the Baskett Bible and a 17th-century communion chalice and paten. Also in this small community is the **Stevensville Bank** built in 1909. It is typical of a country bank, and the vault and original furnishings are still in place.

From May through October, from 1:00 to 4:00 P.M., on the third Saturday of the month, the **Cray House**, another property that is on the National Register, is open for tours. This house on Cockey's Lane stands on "Stevens' Adventure" a tract of land granted to Francis Stevens in 1694. The land was sold several times but the increase in price from $43 in 1809 when John Denny purchased it to $400 in 1817 when he sold it to William Patterson indicates that a building was constructed. Historian-architects believe that the gambrel-roofed, wooden house was built in 1809. Although the one-and-half story house is small, its simplicity is matched by its rare, if not unique, construction of post and planks. Three-inch horizontal planked walls are pegged into slotted posts. An addition was added to the house somewhere between 1840 and 1850. In 1976, the house was given to the Kent Island Heritage Society by the heirs of Nora Cray, who had purchased the house at public auction in 1914. You can arrange to tour at times other than the scheduled Saturday openings by calling (410) 604-2100.

Also on Cockey's Lane you'll find the original **Stevensville Train**

213

Depot, built in 1902. The Kent Island Heritage Society has restored the Queen Anne's Railroad Company station. The line, established in 1898, covered 60 miles from Kent Island to Lewes, Delaware, a distance that took two hours to travel. Thanks to the train, Stevensville residents could get daily newspapers that were printed in Baltimore in the morning and delivered before dark. In 1938, the trains stopped passenger service; freight service continued for a time, but the Stevensville station and others along the line were closed by 1953. When you stop by to see the train depot, you'll also see a vintage Kent Island smoke house that is on the premises.

Directions: From Baltimore take Route 97, or Route 2, south to Route 50. Head east across the Bay Bridge. Immediately on the other side of the bridge, take Route 18 north for Stevensville. It is directly off Route 50 with easy access back to the highway.

Eastern Neck National Wildlife Refuge and Chesapeake Farms

Splendor in the Grass and Sky

A chance to view both public and private wildlife management areas is offered by the geographical proximity of Eastern Neck National Wildlife Refuge and Chesapeake Farms. Both are "no frills" wildlife exposures. There are no visitor centers, no slick exhibits and displays—just the splendor of nature.

The opportunity to see the largest concentration of wintering Canada geese in the world is one you shouldn't miss. At **Eastern Neck National Wildlife Refuge** and the nearby Blackwater National Wildlife Refuge (see selection) you'll see striking Canada geese and other waterfowl in their natural habitat. The best season to visit is winter, or late fall, when the birds have arrived for their seasonal respite from the northern chill. Because the marsh terrain does not change with the seasons (the marsh grasses winter over) you will see approximately the same vista summer and winter. Only the sky may be different; it is more apt to be gray than blue in winter. The time of day to visit is either dawn or dusk, though most day trippers find dusk a more convenient hour. When the sun rises or sets, the thousands of geese can be seen in flight. The sight and sound of these magnificent birds on the wing is truly a wilderness adventure.

It would be worth the drive if the Canada geese were the only attraction, but you'll also see thousands of white tundra swans that migrate here from as far north as Alaska. They use Eastern Neck as a major staging or stopping area before continuing their migration either south in winter or north in the summer. Large rafts of canvasback ducks can once again be seen around the island and up to 32

214

Thousands of white tundra swans migrate to Eastern Neck National Wildlife Refuge from as far north as Alaska. The refuge also boasts the largest concentration of wintering Canada geese in the world.

species of waterfowl have been documented at Eastern Neck.

Eastern Neck is on the east side of the Chesapeake Bay at the mouth of the Chester River. Except for the **Ingleside Recreation Area**, which is closed October through April, this 2,285-acre refuge is open year-round at no charge during daylight hours. There are six miles of roads and self-guided nature trails through the woodland and marsh. A boardwalk (accessible to the disabled) and an observation tower give visitors access to the marsh area. You'll want to bring binoculars so that you can get a close look from the observation tower. The birds start arriving as early as October and leave by April.

On a pleasant winter's day the woodland nature trail may yield unexpected surprises; through the sparse undergrowth of winter you are apt to see a Delmarva fox squirrel, one of an endangered species. This squirrel can be identified by its large size, white belly and feet.

215

You may also see bald eagles that nest on the island, white-tailed deer, raccoon, opossum, muskrat, red fox or woodchuck.

If you visit Eastern Neck during the late spring or summer, you can try your luck at crabbing. If you don't want to go to the trouble of bringing your own boat, try wading out with a net and a bushel basket. Old hands recommend that you balance your basket in an inner tube; this will leave both hands free for netting. Blue crabs are caught as early as May, but July is the best month for crabbing. Fishing off the bridge that accesses the island can be exciting when yellow perch are running and striped bass are feeding.

Less than ten miles away is **Chesapeake Farms,** a privately owned agricultural and wildlife management research, demonstration and educational area that is operated by the Agricultural Products division of E.I. DuPont de Nemours and Co. The self-guided tour of this 3,300-acre farm and wildlife management area is free and open to the public from February through mid-October. The waterfowl rest area is open for viewing from vehicles year round.

This area is managed to demonstrate environmentally sound agricultural practices and also how to have abundant wildlife on farms. The Chesapeake Farms mission is to (1) promote, demonstrate and investigate productive, profitable, environmentally sound and socially acceptable agricultural and wildlife management practices; (2) help farmers be successful through technology and service; and (3) promote the principle that environmental stewardship is an integral component of economic success. Visitors can see parts of a sustainable agriculture research project along with a multitude of wildlife that inhabits the ponds, hedges, woods and fields of Chesapeake Farms. Commonly observed wildlife include Canada geese and other waterfowl (during fall and winter), bald eagle, osprey, great blue heron and white-tailed deer. This property is permanently protected from development by a conservation easement.

Directions: From Baltimore take I-97south to Route 50 and cross the Chesapeake Bay Bridge. When it veers off from Route 50, take Route 301. Follow Route 301 north to the intersection with Route 213. Turn left on Route 213 and take Route 213 into Chestertown. When you intersect with Route 291 turn left and then make a right on Route 20. Travel 8.5 miles on Route 20 and turn left on Ricauds Branch Road. Chesapeake Farms main entrance is on the right about 0.5 miles from Route 20. For Eastern Neck National Wildlife Refuge continue on Route 20 to Rock Hall and then take Route 445 eight miles south to the island refuge.

QUEEN ANNE'S COUNTY

Tuckahoe State Park

Tucked Away

Have you ever been to a "swamp brunch", or on a "Barking Up the Right Tree" guided walk? These are two innovative nature programs offered at **Tuckahoe State Park.** It hosts a swamp brunch on some of its short canoe trips and also schedules all-day canoe trips down Tuckahoe Creek.

Tuckahoe Creek, which runs through the park, is the county line between Queen Anne's and Caroline Counties. Tuckahoe Park's 3,500 acres include a 60-acre lake, wooded swampland and a 500-acre arboretum. The latter, **Adkins Arboretum,** is an ideal place to identify the trees, plants and shrubs of Maryland. You will indeed learn how to "bark up the right tree." Three miles of loop trails lead through examples of the trees and vegetation typical to the Delmarva Coastal Plain.

Many of the trees along the arboretum trails are labeled. Growing in one portion are forests of white pine, hemlock, yellow poplar, spruce and fir. In the central section are shortleaf and Virginia pine, sweet gum, yellow poplar, black gum and basket oak. Plans call for planting loblolly pine, pond pine, Atlantic white cedar and cypress along the third loop. Nature lovers will want to monitor the progress of such a comprehensive arboretum.

Located seven miles west of Denton, the park offers 71 campsites for tent and trailer camping. Campers and day trippers can fish the lake from the shore, rent canoes, or launch their own boats from the shore or a ramp. A tidal fishing license is needed to fish the creek south of the dam, and a non-tidal license is needed for lake fishing.

Although fishing is permitted, there is no swimming in the lake. You may, however, have a picnic beneath the pines overlooking the scenic lake. Trails give hikers a chance to wander along the shoreline. The park has a physical fitness trail, a self-guided nature trail and the Piney Branch Trail. Hunting is permitted in season, roughly mid-October to mid-February, in designated areas.

The park is open daily during daylight hours, although certain sections, such as the campgrounds area, are closed in late fall and winter. A Visitor Center has a calendar of park activities and special events.

Near Tuckahoe in Centreville are two old homes open on summer Fridays. They depend on volunteers, however, and do not always open on schedule. Centreville was Queen Anne's county seat in

1782. A statue of Queen Anne stands in front of the **Court House**, circa 1791, the oldest in the state still in continuous use. The **Taylor House** on S. Commerce Street (Route 213) is considered the oldest original house in Centreville. The lot, the second to be purchased in town, was bought in 1792. The house, now furnished with period pieces, takes visitors on a limited basis on Fridays during the summer from 12:30 to 3:30 P.M. Do call ahead, (301)758-1208. **Wright's Chance** across the street opens to visitors at the same hours (call 301-758-0658 to verify). This old plantation house was moved into town in 1964. Listed as an "old dwelling" in a 1744 survey; its four rooms and nursery are furnished with period pieces.

Directions: From Baltimore take Route 2 south to Route 50. Take Route 50 east across the Bay Bridge. At Wye Mills bear left on Route 404 and then follow Tuckahoe State Park signs. Centreville is located off Route 301 on Route 213.

TALBOT COUNTY

Chesapeake Bay Maritime Museum

All Quiet on the Eastern Shore

The shipbuilding heritage of **St. Michaels** stems from colonial days. There is a marvelous, but perhaps apocryphal, story about how this quaint town managed to survive unscathed the second American-British confrontation. Before dawn on August 10, 1813, the British navy anchored offshore and began firing at St. Michaels. Residents hung lanterns high in the trees, thus tricking the British into over-shooting the town, which thereafter called itself The Town That Fooled the British.

For more St. Michaels, as well as Chesapeake Bay, history visit the multi-dimensional **Chesapeake Bay Maritime Museum.** It's a 16-acre complex that includes an 1879 lighthouse, a small boat exhibit, bell tower, bandstand and several museum outbuildings.

Few can resist heading directly to the stilt-legged **Hooper Strait Lighthouse**. This is one of only three remaining "cottage" lighthouses. Great screw pile supports almost literally screwed these lighthouses into the muddy Bay bottom. The lighthouse's spartan furnishings remind visitors that even these watermen who never fished lived a rugged life tending the warning lights. The light keeper's family were allowed to spend only two weeks a year at the lighthouse, although the keeper did get periodic leave.

From the top of the lighthouse you'll have a sweeping view of the Bay and harbor. Every day, unless weather makes the Bay unnavigable, oysterman, crabbers and fishermen sail in and out. One skipjack that is no longer part of the work fleet is the *Rosie Parks*, now a museum exhibit. In the boat shop craftsmen restore and repair the museum's fleet of historic workboats. St. Michaels' builders are credited with crafting the first Baltimore Clipper and the first racing log canoe. The techniques and tools of boat building are explained, and finished products can be seen at the nearby small boat shed, which has yachts, workboats and hunting skiffs.

You can move from hunters' boats to their guns and decoys on display in the Waterfowling Building. In the autumn the shores around St. Michaels are crowded with the migrating fowl so painstakingly duplicated by decoy carvers. Sportsmen not only hunt, they also fish these waters, and for a look at what they are likely to catch, visit the museum's **Waterman's Wharf**.

The wharf features interactive stations. In them you can roll up your sleeves, get your hands wet and be a waterman for a day. You can help tend the crab tank, pull up an eel pot or hand wind a heavy oyster dredge. If you haven't tried to nipper for large oysters in shallow water, this is your chance. You'll also learn how to set a fishing net. A replica of a waterman's shanty features a tool shed and work room. You'll gain a new empathy for what it is like to earn a living on the unpredictable waters of the Bay.

Docked alongside Waterman's Wharf is the museum's floating fleet. *Martha*, a Hooper Island draketail used primarily for oystering and crabbing, dates from 1934. There is also a Potomac River dory boat with a wide hull designed for harvesting herring and shad as well as oysters. You'll also see the small, easily maneuverable pot pie skiff with a tuck stern used to trotline for crabs.

To put everything you've seen in perspective stop at the museum's Chesapeake Bay Building. It traces life back to the formation of the Bay during the last Ice Age. In the prehistoric period this region was part of the valley of the Susquehanna River, but as the glaciers melted it became a "drowned river." The story continues with the advent of precolonial Indians who fished and traveled the region. The Bay's role in the American Revolution, War of 1812 and Civil War is reviewed, as is the life of the watermen who've worked the Bay for centuries.

The museum has numerous special exhibits, many traveling shows from other maritime history museums as well as paintings by significant artists of the Chesapeake Bay. One permanent exhibit in the steamboat building centers on propulsion and features a collection of antique steam and gas engines. In the boat yard, craftsmen demon-

The 1879 stilt-legged Hooper Strait Lighthouse at the Chesapeake Bay Maritime Museum is one of only three remaining "cottage" light-houses. There is a sweeping view of the Bay from the top.

strate such skills as blacksmithing, sailmaking, trapmaking and operating a steam-powered engine. Children's programs year round include fish painting, beginner's sailing and meteor shower cruises. One of the favorite exhibits for youngsters is the life-size sculpture of a Bay retriever; it can be touched and climbed.

The Chesapeake Bay Maritime Museum is open daily from 9:00 A.M. to 5:00 P.M. Closed Thanksgiving, Christmas and New Year's Day. Admission is charged.

Be sure to save time to stroll the quiet streets of St. Michaels. Along Talbot Street you'll find an assortment of boutiques, antique shops, specialty stores plus a deli and the town saloon. The harbor area boasts three popular restaurants: the Crab Claw, Longfellows and the Town Dock. There are also several bed and breakfast spots in town.

Directions: From Baltimore take Route 2 south to Route 50, cross the Chesapeake Bay Bridge and continue on Route 50 to Easton. From Easton take Route 33 west to St. Michaels. In St. Michaels turn right on Mill Street for the museum located at the end of the street at Navy Point.

CAROLINE COUNTY

Martinak State Park

Roadside R&R

Baltimore and Washington area residents heading for the Atlantic beaches have seen signs for **Martinak State Park** along the way. And many have stopped to discover the charms of this picturesque 107-acre park on the Eastern Shore. It's an ideal spot for a highway pull-off. Picnic tables beneath shady oaks on the banks of the Choptank River make it a cool lunchtime oasis even on a hot, muggy summer day.

Quite a number of those who have stopped to picnic here return for a longer stay in one of the 60 campsites that can be rented on a nightly or weekly basis. Historians know that in 1669 the Choptanks, a subtribe of the Algonquins, had a reservation down river near Secretary. They suspect there was a village on the high ground within this park.

The Indians came for the excellent fishing here, and so do many modern visitors. A fishing license is required in the tidal waters of the Choptank River and Watts Creek. The park has a boat pier and a launching ramp. Don't let the nearby wreckage of an old pungy, a turn-of-the-century sailing vessel, scare you—these waters are quite calm.

Children will enjoy the playground. But this is not the spot to let your pet out for a run; pets are not permitted at Martinak. The park has over three miles of trails, including a fitness trail and a nature trail.

Martinak State Park is open for 24-hour camping from the first weekend in April through the last weekend in October. Daytime use continues year-round. During the summer months canoes can be rented for a daily fee so that visitors can explore Watts Creek.

Directions: From Baltimore take Route 2 south to Route 50. Take Route 50 east across the Bay Bridge, then turn east on Route 404 to Denton. Martinak State Park is two miles south of Denton off Route 404 on Deep Shore Road.

DORCHESTER COUNTY

Blackwater National Wildlife Refuge

Take a Gander

If you enjoy National Geographic television specials, you'll love the experience of being part of the natural world at **Blackwater National Wildlife Refuge.** In fact, camera buffs can bring equipment and shoot their own nature film complete with sound effects—the honking and rustle of wings of thousands of geese arriving or departing. The sound could be mistaken for the boisterous enthusiasm of a crowd at a football game. In late November there may be as many as 50,000 Canada geese at Blackwater. The five-mile scenic Wildlife Drive, which you can hike, bike or drive, will give you a close look at these substantial birds, some of which weigh as much as ten pounds. Bring your binoculars for birdwatching either from the Drive or the refuge's observation tower.

The striking Canada geese mate for life, and only if a partner dies will one occasionally take a new mate. Most of these geese nest during the summer at James Bay in Canada, but some pairs nest at

222

A Great Blue Heron stands guard at the Blackwater National Wildlife Refuge. As many as 50,000 Canada geese winter here. Their sound can be mistaken for a football crowd.

Blackwater. In the spring you may see strings of five to eight goslings being closely supervised by their parents. Canada geese form a close-knit family; they are social birds and fly in large V-formations with older birds alternating the lead.

The waterfowl population at the 23,000 acre-Blackwater refuge also includes whistling swans, snow and blue geese, plus 20 varieties of ducks. This refuge was established in 1932 as a home for migratory ducks, but due to its popularity with geese they now outnumber the ducks. You can spot many different birds on the ⅓-mile Marsh Edge Trail. You'll see biting insects too from mid-April through late September, so be sure to bring insect repellent.

Two endangered species are nurtured at Blackwater. The large, gray Delmarva Peninsula fox squirrel, unique to Maryland's Eastern Shore, lives in the refuge's woodland area. Its numbers have declined with the elimination of local forests. You are most likely to spot one of these foragers on the Woods Trail. The trail also gives you a chance to see varieties of birds different from those spotted elsewhere in the refuge. Here you'll see towhees, woodpeckers, brown-headed nuthatches and other forest birds.

The other endangered species, the bald eagle, nests here. The eagle nesting spots are protected from man's encroachment, but if you see a large pile of sticks and twigs at the top of a tree, you'll likely have spotted an eagle's nest. In spring, if you watch patiently, you may see one of the mature eagles returning with food for the young.

You can explore Blackwater National Wildlife Refuge from dawn to dusk. The Visitor Center is open 8:00 A.M. to 4:00 P.M. Monday through Friday and from Labor Day to Memorial Day on weekends from 9:00 A.M. to 5:00 P.M. If you have time, continue into southern Dorchester County, drive across scenic Narrow Ferry Bridge, which opened in 1980, and on to **Hoopers Island.** Here you'll see picturesque fishing villages such as Honga, Fishing Creek and Hoopersville. A number of seafood packing houses operate in these waterfront towns where fishing, oystering and crabbing are a way of life.

Directions: From Baltimore take Route 2 south to Route 50. Cross the Bay Bridge and continue to the outskirts of Cambridge, where you will come to a traffic signal. Immediately before the light there is a large brown sign on the right directing you to the refuge. At the light you will see the Dorchester Square Shopping Center (which includes a Walmart). Turn left onto Route 16 west. Follow Route 16 until you pass the Dorchester High School. Turn left onto Egypt Road just past the school buildings. Follow Egypt Road for approximately 8 miles until it dead ends at Key Wallace Drive. You will see another brown refuge sign directing you to turn right onto Key Wallace Drive to the Visitor Center, which will be on your left in about ½ mile.

Cambridge Historic District and Brannock Maritime Museum

Historical View of the Bay

James Michener visited **Cambridge** while researching Maryland's Eastern Shore for his novel *Chesapeake*. He was captivated by High Street, as are most visitors who discover the stately mansions along the tree-lined street. In the spring the delicate blossoms of the Bradford pear trees top off the charm.

In almost any Cambridge shop or restaurant you can pick up a walking tour guide. It provides the historic and architectural background of the homes, churches and businesses in the historic district. Most of the district was built in the 19th century, but next door to **Christ Church** is Josiah Bayly's law office, built in 1796. It's the oldest continuously used business office in Maryland. Be sure to take the time to go inside Christ Church. The Rose Window, crafted in London, is a sparkling gem. The church also has some not-to-be-missed Tiffany windows. A church has stood here since 1693, although the present structure was not erected until 1883. Buried in the church cemetery are early settlers, Revolutionary War heroes and several Maryland governors.

At the end of High Street a town park overlooks the yacht basin and busy harbor. Picnic tables and benches make this an ideal spot for a midday break. If you prefer to dine in a restaurant, just off High Street on Commerce is **Snappers**, a waterside eatery with both indoor and outdoor dining. The seafood is fresh daily and Snappers is popular with both natives and visitors.

For an overview of Cambridge's maritime heritage, visit **Brannock Maritime Museum.** You'll learn all about the Maryland Oyster Navy and its commanders. It had no military affiliation; it was simply the colloquial name for the Chesapeake Bay marine police.

Cambridge was home to both ship sailors and ship builders. This was once an important shipbuilding center. Legend has it the ship that pursued Moby Dick was built in Cambridge. The museum displays photographs of the whaling vessels built here, as well as models of other vessels.

The first steamboat in the Bay, the *S.S. Chesapeake*, was built and captained by William Trippe, a Dorchester County native. The museum has photographs of all but one of the steamboats that made Cambridge a port of call.

Early maritime history is recalled through navigational tools dating from the 1700s. The museum showcases the career of Matthew Fontaine Maury, the father of oceanography and other naval heroes. There is also a library for research on maritime history and the Chesapeake Bay. The Brannock Maritime Museum, at 210 Talbot

Street, is open on weekends from 1:00 to 4:00 P.M. and weekdays by appointment.

Boaters and historians will also want to visit the **Richardson Maritime Museum** at 401 High Street. James B. Richardson was a renowned boat builder who incorporated the techniques of generations of Chesapeake boat builders in his work. At Richardson's death in 1991 this collection was immediately begun so that his life's work would be preserved. The museum includes builders' plans and half-models as well as models of bugeyes, pyngy, skipjacks, log canoes, a merchant brig and others. You'll learn about woods used for boats and have a chance to go through a model boat building workshop. Richardson, called the "Admiral of the Chesapeake Bay," is remembered fondly at this museum open April through October on Wednesday, Saturday and Sunday from 1:00 to 4:00 P.M. Appointments can be made to visit at other times by calling (410) 221-1871.

Directions: From Baltimore take Route 2 south to Route 50. Cross the Bay Bridge and go about 45 miles to Cambridge. After you cross the Choptank River Bridge into Cambridge proper, turn right on Maryland Avenue and cross over Cambridge Creek. Bear right for High Street. Park and explore High Street and the historic district on foot. For the museum, take High Street down to the Choptank River and turn left on Water Street and then left again on Talbot Avenue.

Dorchester Heritage Museum and Spocott Windmill

Winner by a Neck

Dorchester County's Neck District is bounded by the Choptank and Little Choptank Rivers, which are all but connected by the finger-like creeks that crisscross the land between them. You're rarely out of sight of water as you drive the quiet back roads, all of which dead-end at water's edge. Scenic appeal is only part of the reason to head east from Cambridge into the Neck District for a self-guided tour. If you arrive on a weekend you can also explore the **Dorchester Heritage Museum.**

The museum is located on what was once the estate of Francis du Pont. He bequeathed the land to the city of Cambridge, and the city then gave it to the University of Maryland to use for Environmental and Estuarine Studies. High school students became involved and enlisted community support for preserving the history of the county. The result of their efforts is the Dorchester County Museum, housed in an old airplane hangar.

Early aviation is one of the major themes here. The hangar sits beside one of the country's best grass-stripped runways. Each May, on the weekend prior to Memorial Day, the museum sponsors an Antique Aircraft Fly-In. This annual festival gives visitors a chance to see vintage aircraft in action, plus talk to the owners who have lovingly restored these classic planes. There are also aviation exhibits inside the museum.

Another focus of the museum is local archeology. One room displays some of the 30,000 artifacts volunteers and museum staffers have excavated from 17th- and 18th-century sites on the museum grounds. The first house on the "Horne" site was built around 1670. It burned to the ground in 1700. The ruins were cleared and a second house built, but it too was destroyed by fire around 1770. The remains of these two tragedies have yielded rich details about upper-middle-class family life during the colonial period.

Other museum exhibits feature tools and household items of the region's watermen and farmers. In Dorchester County the same family names appear generation after generation, and many heirs of these long-time residents have contributed memorabilia. The Dorchester Heritage Museum on Horn Point Road is open 1:00 to 4:30 P.M. on weekends from mid-April through October. There is no charge for admission.

After your visit to the museum, head back down Horn Point Road, then turn right at Lovers Lane, the first road to the right. At the intersection with Route 343 (Hudson Road) turn right; in two miles you'll see the distinctive **Spocott Windmill** on your left. It is open daily from 9:00 A.M. to 5:00 P.M.

This is Maryland's only fully operating English-style post windmill for grinding grain. It was built in 1850 by John Anthony LeCompte Radcliff as part of a self-contained community that included sawmills, blacksmith shops and shipyards. The windmill that you will see was reconstructed in 1971 using millstones and other parts of the original, blown down during the blizzard of 1888.

Nearby on the windmill grounds is the one-and-one-half story **Colonial Tenant House**, built in 1800. From 1880 to 1930, it was the home of Adaline and Columbus Wheatley who worked at Spocott Farm. The house is restored and filled with furnishings from the time.

A one-room schoolhouse, circa 1870, also stands with the windmill on the greensward along the marshy banks of the Little Choptank River. This too is open to the public. A fourth building, the 1935 Country Store, is only open on special occasions. These are among the most picturesque sites along the Neck District Tour. If you continue your drive along the "neck" you will pass several charming community churches. Once you've completed your visit to this Eastern Shore region, simply reverse direction and head back to Cambridge.

Directions: From Baltimore take Route 2 south to Route 50 east. Cross the Chesapeake Bay Bridge and go about 45 miles to Cambridge. After you cross the Choptank River Bridge as you come into Cambridge, turn right on Route 343 for the Neck District.

Meredith House and Neild Museum

Maryland Lore

The 18th-century Georgian-style **Meredith House,** overlooking the Choptank River in Cambridge, is known as the house of chimneys. John Woolford built this Flemish-bond-brick plantation house with three chimneys in 1760. It is now the home of the Dorchester County Historical Society. Docents entertain visitors with stories about the early county residents whose portraits grace the dining room walls. You'll learn about Anne Francis Tilghman, whose smile suggests the Mona Lisa. Her son, Trench Tilghman, was the only aide George Washington retained throughout the Revolutionary War. Another portrait is of Mary Richardson LeCompte, daughter of one of the early Huguenot families in Dorchester County.

Antique buffs won't want to miss the Chippendale, Hepplewhite and Sheraton furniture in the downstairs rooms. Younger visitors usually linger upstairs with the doll collection: baby buggies, high chairs and cradles all holding period dolls. History buffs may learn about Maryland in the Dorchester County Room. Six Maryland governors came from this county: Hicks, Henry, Lloyd, Harrington and both Charles and Philip Lee Goldsboro. A seventh, Thomas King Carroll, though not born in Dorchester, is buried here in Old Trinity Church near Church Creek.

On the third floor of the Meredith House are two country bedrooms decorated with spool beds, rag rugs, lace night shirts and two old quilts. The splendid "Star of Bethlehem" quilt, made in 1762, still is surprisingly vibrant.

Adjacent to the Meredith House is the **Neild Museum,** filled with artifacts from the past. The collection represents early American life along the river, in the home and on the farm. You'll see shipbuilding tools, an old dugout canoe and several ship models. Farm tools include an 1831 McCormick Reaper, an 1820 Fanning mill, which was used with a threshing machine, and a life-size horse model that once stood in front of Philips Hardware Store displaying the latest in harnesses.

One exhibit focuses on Annie Oakley, who, with her husband, Colonel Frank Butler, settled along the Choptank River at 28 Bellevue Street. Oakley chose this location, declaring it was the most beautiful she had discovered on her nationwide travels with Buffalo Bill's Wild West show. After your museum visit, take Cambridge's Scenic Drive past their house. They built a modest place; it's said that Oakley had lived out of trunks so much of her life she forgot to include closets in her house and they had to be added later. When you drive past, notice the sloping roof. Legend has it that the slant was added so that Little Miss Sure Shot, as Oakley was called, could step out her bedroom window and shoot passing wildfowl. Locals tell the story of the time Butler went out in his skiff to retrieve some of her birds. He was smoking, a habit she detested, so she took aim and shot the offending cigarette from his mouth.

The Meredith House and Neild Museum are open on Fridays from 9:30 A.M. to 4:30 P.M. and at other times by appointment. Call (410) 228-7953. On the grounds between these two attractions you'll see an 18th-century smokehouse and colonial herb garden.

Directions: From Baltimore take Route 2 south to Route 50 east. Cross the Bay Bridge and follow Route 50 to Cambridge. Once you cross the Choptank River Bridge into Cambridge turn left on Maryland Avenue (that's at the first traffic light after crossing the bridge). Turn left off Maryland Avenue onto LeGrange Avenue for the Meredith House.

WICOMICO COUNTY

Poplar Hill Mansion and Pemberton Hall

Newtown Is an Old Town

Do you like gingerbread—not the kind you eat, but the architectural type of the Victorian era? If so, then you'll like Newtown, too. Fish-scaled towers, conical turrets, elaborately balustraded porches, bay windows, a gabled pavilion, mullioned transoms and colored leaded windows ornament the houses of Salisbury's **Newtown Historic District**. Isabella Street and William Street, both off Poplar Hill Avenue, have the greatest concentration of houses with these ornate features. A walking tour guide describes the architectural details of 27 homes in this district. To obtain a copy write the Wicomico County Convention and Visitors Bureau at P.O. Box 2333, Salisbury, MD 21802-2333, or call (410) 548-4914.

In 1886 a fire raged through Salisbury, destroying many residential communities. Newtown, like a phoenix, rose from the ashes. It was the first neighborhood to be rebuilt. Within this historic district is **Poplar Hill Mansion,** which survived the fire and is the oldest house in Salisbury.

This 19th-century country transitional Georgian-style mansion was begun around 1799 by Major Levin Handy, who came to the Eastern Shore from Rhode Island. Handy acquired a sizable acreage in

229

Colonel Isaac Handy's 1741 Pemberton Hall, on the Wicomico River, is one of the first gambrel-roofed plantation houses in the Chesapeake region. The estate also had one of the earliest wharves on the Bay dating from 1747.

Maryland, but after his death in financial problems forced his wife Nellie to sell 228½ acres at public auction on March 31, 1804. The land on which Poplar Hill stands was purchased by Peter Dashiell who transferred it to his brother-in-law, Dr. Huston, Salisbury's first prominent physician. The house was completed by Dr. Huston in 1805.

The front door of Poplar Hill is flanked with fluted pilasters and crowned with a broken pediment arch and a fan-shaped window. Splendid bulls-eye windows grace the east and west peak roof lines. The interior has the original heart pine floors, hand carved cornices and chair rails. Tours are given of Poplar Hill Mansion, at 117 Elizabeth Street, Tuesday through Saturday from 9:00 A.M. to 5:00 P.M. (with extended summer closings) and on some Sundays from 1:00 to 4:00 P.M. The house is closed on Mondays and major holidays. At is advisable to call the CVB and verify the hours. A nominal admission is charged except on Sundays.

Another Handy, Colonel Isaac Handy, built **Pemberton Hall** on the Wicomico River near what is now Salisbury (formerly Handy's Landing). This 1741 eastern shore plantation house in one of the first gambrel-roofed plantation houses in the Chesapeake region. Colonel

Handy was a merchant (he owned three ships), a Justice of the Peace, member of the provincial assembly and a colonel in the colonial militia. At his death in 1762 the inventory of his slave holdings and property placed him in the upper five to six percentile of wealth in Somerset County.

Archaeological excavations on the grounds at Pemberton have aided the reconstruction and renovation work. Careful research has insured a faithful reconstruction of the mansion which features three rooms above a raised cellar. A second floor has a wide hallway with four rooms while the upper floor is accessed by a narrow closed corner staircase. The Great Room still has its original fielded paneled walls and fluted pilasters with a mammoth fireplace. The 1740s buffet with arched glass doors has been reconstructed and restored to its original location. All the paint colors are original, though some visitors may be surprised at the bright lively hues with their high gloss glaze.

Five original household inventories beginning with Isaac Handy's 1763 listing have provided details that have proved helpful in the ongoing efforts to furnish the house with appropriate period pieces. Also continuing are the reconstruction of the surrounding plantation buildings, or dependencies, and the snake fences, orchards, gardens and wharf.

Excavations have revealed that Pemberton had one of the earliest wharves on the Chesapeake Bay. From dendrochronology, tree ring dating, it was learned that the massive pine timbers for Pemberton's 200-foot wharf were cut in 1747.

On the grounds the Wicomico Historical Society maintains a museum and gift shop as part of **Pemberton Historical Park**. The museum has artifacts, many uncovered in the six major investigations at Pemberton, and exhibits on the history of the people of Wicomico County. The park also has five miles of nature trails. The last Saturday in September from 10:00 A.M. to 4:00 P.M. the Pemberton Colonial Fair provides first person re-enactors, entertainment, craftsmen and food.

Pemberton Hall and the Wicomico Historical Society are open Wednesday through Saturday from 10:00 A.M. to 4:00 P.M. Admission is charged.

Directions: From Baltimore take Route 2 south to Route 50 east. Follow Route 50 across the Bay Bridge approximately 80 miles to Salisbury. For Pemberton Historical Park turn right on Route 349 west and then make an immediate left onto Pemberton Drive. Continue two miles to Pemberton Historical Park entrance on the left. For Poplar Hill turn left off Route 50 on North Division Street. Continue to W. Isabella streets to Elizabeth Street and turn right at the light. Proceed one block to Poplar Hill Avenue and turn left. The mansion is one block down the street.

Ward Museum of Wildfowl Art
and Salisbury Zoo

Compare the Decoy with the Live Bird

Seeing is not believing, certainly not at first glance, at the Ward Foundation's **Ward Museum of Wildfowl Art** in Salisbury. The woodcarvings exhibited here are so realistic, right down to the wispy delicacy of a single feather, they seem ready to take wing.

The transition from functional decoys to decorative wildfowl carvings was led in the mid-1920s by Crisfield, Maryland, carvers Steve and Lem Ward (see Crisfield selection). The Ward Foundation, formed to preserve and perpetuate the art of the handmade decoy, was named in their honor and memory. Their Sackertown Road decoy shop in Crisfield is re-created at the museum with carving memorabilia including Lem Ward's poetry. It is a moving, personal look at these rugged pioneers.

The best way to explore the Ward Museum of Wildfowl Art is to pick up a self-guiding tour brochure and explore both galleries and the local wildfowl who reside on Schumaker Pond. The decoy story begins with an Indian reed-and-feather decoy found in Lovelock Cave, Nevada, and dating from 1000 A.D. The first European settlers also crafted decoys, but they used wood remnants and driftwood for their working materials. Accompanying the display on early decoys and the next display on pre-Civil War decoys are hunting rifles—a flintlock shotgun and a breech-loading shotgun.

In the late 1800s and early 1900s there was a tremendous demand for wildfowl by restaurants across the country. Market hunting became a big business and special boats were constructed to increase the number of birds bagged. You'll see an example of a sinkbox (also displayed at the Upper Bay Museum, see selection). This boat, resembling a coffin, had wooden and canvas wings on which 20 to 30 decoys were mounted. When in use the sinkbox was surrounded by 200 to 300 floating decoys completely camouflaging the hunter. A similar "icebox" was used in winter. Another camouflaged craft you'll see is a sneakbox, a floating blind that was surrounded by scores of decoys.

Market hunting ended with the passage of the 1918 Migratory Bird Act prohibiting the sale of wildfowl for food. Although this much-needed law saved the birds, it was a blow to hunters, who lost their livelihood. It was at this time that many who, heretofore, had made only working decoys began to carve decorative pieces to help make ends meet.

Personal style became more apparent with decorative decoys, but there had always been regional differences in the hunting decoys. The next section of the museum displays styles originating in 14 geographic regions. Two are from the Maryland area—Crisfield and the Susquehanna Flats—and two are from Virginia—the Back Bay and the Eastern Shore.

It is in the championship gallery that the art of carving is displayed. Since 1971 the Ward Foundation has hosted an annual World Championship Wildfowl Carving Competition. The $90,000 in prize money and the chance to compete against fellow craftsmen attract carvers from all over the world. There are four main categories: Decorative Pairs, Decorative Miniatures, Decorative Lifesize and Interpretative. The World Class winners in these competitions provide the nucleus of the museum's collection. Recently added to the event are painting and fish carving competitions.

One interesting display features three variations of a Canada goose. The Canada by Hans Bolte has fine feather details, the one by William Burns features the wood grain and transparent paint, and Lem Ward's pose and features are highly stylized. Lem's Canada goose is only one of many decoys made by the Ward brothers. Incidentally, they started out earning 50 cents per piece in 1918 but eventually commanded upwards of $2,000 each.

The Ward Museum of Wildfowl Art is open Monday through Saturday 10:00 A.M. to 5:00 P.M. and Sunday NOON to 5:00 P.M. Donations and memberships are encouraged. For tour information or to contact the museum, call (410) 742-4988.

Nearby **Salisbury Zoo** is "one of the finest small zoos in North America," according to Dr. Theodore Reed, Director Emeritus of The National Zoo in Washington, D.C. Here you'll find many of the same wildfowl captured so realistically at the Ward Museum of Wildfowl Art. But you'll also see more exotic species: brilliant blue peacocks, bright yellow sun conjures, and orange-beaked toucans as well as guanacos, capybaras and jaguars. The more than 400 mammals, birds and reptiles share naturalistic enclosures, and many of the birds seem to have the run of the park. This is an inviting and relaxing zoo to explore.

Less than five minutes off Route 50, the Salisbury Zoo and an adjacent picnic area and playground make an ideal stop for beach-bound families. There is no charge to visit the zoo, which is open daily, except Christmas and Thanksgiving, from 8:00 A.M. From Memorial Day to Labor Day the zoo closes at 7:30 P.M.; at other times it closes at 4:30 P.M.

Directions: From Baltimore take Route 2 south to Route 50. Follow Route 50 east across the Bay Bridge 80 miles to Salisbury. From Route 50 turn right on Beaglin Park Drive south and proceed to Schumaker Drive, where you turn left. Follow the goose signs once in Salisbury on Route 50. For the Salisbury Zoo take Route 13 and head north until you reach East Main Street. Turn right on East Main and then right again on Snow Hill Road. Then take the first left onto South Park Avenue. After you pass the picnic and playground area, you'll find the zoo entrance on your left. To reach Salisbury Zoo directly from Route 50, turn right on Civic Avenue and follow the zoo signs.

SOMERSET COUNTY

Crisfield

Islands in the Sun

It is certainly worth taking a day trip that includes for lunch the "best crab cakes in the world." Such noted publications as *The Washington Post*, *The New York Times*, *People Magazine* and *Southern Living* have raved about the crab cakes at Capt's Galley Restaurant on the Tangier Sound waterfront in **Crisfield.**

Just about everything in this picturesque southern Eastern Shore community is on the waterfront. While in town you can visit the **J. Millard Tawes Museum,** which commemorates the two-term governor (1959-67) born in Crisfield on April 8, 1894. The museum displays the papers, pictures and memorabilia of Governor Tawes, whose 45 years of public service spanned a period of enormous growth and change in the United States. Inaugural gowns worn by the governor's wife, the former Helen Avalynne Gibson, are shown, too.

Another Crisfield native, Dr. Sarah Peyton, is also remembered in the Tawes Museum. She was one of the first women physicians at the School of Medicine at Johns Hopkins. Included in this display is her father's 1890s prescription counter.

The museum has exhibits tracing the history of the Lower Shore region back to the Indians who once camped along these shores. The work of the region's current residents, the watermen, is covered too. Many visitors come to the area during the hunting season. Decoy making is a fine art in these parts. The museum has re-created the decoy carving workshop of Lem and Steve Ward (see Wildfowl Art Museum selection). There are splendid examples of this regional craft to see.

The J. Millard Tawes Museum is open year-round on weekdays from 9:00 A.M. to 4:30 P.M. From Memorial Day through October it is also open on weekends from 10:00 A.M. to 3:00 P.M. A nominal admission is charged.

Two walking tours begin at the museum: the Port of Crisfield Escorted Walking Tour and the Ward Brothers Heritage Tour. The first tour will provide a glimpse of the activities of this busy port and take you inside a modern crab and oyster processing facility. This gives you a chance to see how the products of the Chesapeake Bay are prepared for market. On the Ward Brothers tour, you visit the workshop of Lem and Steve Ward and stroll around the picturesque Jenkins Creek area.

At the marina just outside the museum, cruise boats depart daily during the summer months for **Smith Island.** This is the largest inhabited offshore island in the Chesapeake Bay. The boat trip is roughly

Nearly everything in Crisfield happens on the waterfront. Called the "Seafood Capital of the World," Crisfield also lays claim to the world's best crab cakes.

12 miles across Tangier Sound from Crisfield and passes the 5,000-acre Glenn L. Martin Wildlife Sanctuary. The island was mapped by John Smith in 1608 and settled in 1657. English accents still can be heard in the islanders' speech, as well as names of the early settlers— Bradshaw, Evans, Tyler and Marshall.

The island has three villages, Ewell, Tylerton and Rhodes Point. Cruise boats dock at Ewell and you'll have plenty of time to explore the eight-mile long, four-mile wide island. Ewell and Rhodes Point are connected by a bridge and tours are given, on a school bus, covering both these communities (the third village is only accessible by boat and only the *Captain Jason* stops there). One of the pleasures of this tour is the opportunity to eat at one of the island's family-style restaurants. The Harbor Side Restaurant, Bayside Inn and Ruke's Seafood Deck are all popular with visitors. If you prefer you can bring a picnic lunch and dine alfresco.

Cruise boats leave Crisfield at 12:30 and return at about 5:15 to 5:30 P.M. You can call Capt. Alan Tyler at (410) 425-2771; Capt. Larry and Capt.Terry Laird at (410) 425-4471/ (410) 425-5931; or Capt.

Otis Tyler at (410) 968-3200 or (410) 425-2201. You can also book full- and half-day sportfishing trips aboard charter boats from Somers Cove Marina (call (800) 967-FISH).

If you want to enjoy an island adventure but don't have enough time for a voyage to Smith Island, head over to **Janes Island State Park,** just 1½ miles outside Crisfield. The park's Hodson Area, on the mainland, has log cabins and a conference center that can be rented, campgrounds, a small marina and a picnic area. Across Annemessex Sound, reachable only by boat, is the park's island area. During the summer months you can rent boats at the marina or join a pontoon party to cross to the island's trails and beaches. This area is predictably popular with fishermen and hunters.

Directions: From Baltimore take Route 97 south to Route 50. Take Route 50 across the Bay Bridge to Salisbury. At Salisbury take Route 13 south for approximately 15 miles to Route 413. Make a right on Route 413 and head down to Crisfield. The Gov. J. Millard Tawes Historical Museum is located on 9th Street on the grounds of the Somers Cove Marina.

Eastern Shore Early Americana Museum

Imagine the Smithsonian's Attic

Covered wagon jacks, a tattoo machine, a jigsaw puzzle cutter, slot machines, toy trains and cow horn cutters ... a Salisbury hearse, a surrey with the fringe on top, bone-meal grinders, door hinges, old irons; an addressograph ... feather pluckers, pea hullers, stump pullers, corn shelters ... parcel-post fresh egg shippers, cherry seeders, cream separators ... a barber's chair and a shoe-shine chair ... a rickshaw and a pony cart, a bowling ball shiner, a broom-making device ... eel gigs, model airplanes, Christmas decorations, Avon products, political buttons, oyster tonging forks ... an Erector set, ferris wheel and a loom. All this and more, and more, and more fill the **Eastern Shore Early Americana Museum.**

It's impossible to estimate the number of items Lawrence Burgess has collected in his Marion Station museum. When queried, Burgess just chuckles and counters with "What's an item?" There are literally millions of old things that this enthusiastic collector has spent 30 years gathering at farm auctions. He is still buying by the boxfull. He never discards, just groups his items by use. Burgess's collection is displayed in a converted two-story poultry broiler house. Visitors wander bemusedly down the 300-foot-long corridors between displays as Mr. Burgess points out the oddities of his eclectic assortment.

You'll envision bygone days when you spot items that you, or your grandparents, once used. You'll marvel at the specialization of the early 19th-century tools. The museum provides an overview of the progress of technology in the home, on the farm, in fishing and in various trades. Probably the ideal visiting pair at this museum would be a grandparent with grandchild; it's the best place imaginable to talk about the "good old days." But no matter what your age, there is something—or a lot of somethings—to fascinate you.

In addition to the main collection, there's a second building filled with the merchandise from four old country stores. All were once neighborhood gathering spots in their Eastern shore communities. The glass counters are filled with items you're not likely to find today: men's stiff celluloid shirt collars still in their original boxes, "Roll Your Own" Bull Durham tobacco and boxes of slate pencils. And you're not going to find prices any more like those posted in this old store: Coca Cola is advertised at 5 cents, stamps at 3 cents.

The museum is open year-round and there is a nominal admission charge (children are free). To be sure someone is on hand to escort you, it is best to call ahead, (410) 623-8324. The buildings are not heated, so visitors are advised to dress warmly during the winter months.

Directions: From Baltimore take Route 2 south to Route 50 and then go east. At Salisbury take Route 13 south to the intersection with Route 413. Go right on Route 413, then make a left on Old Westover Road to Hudsons Corner and the Eastern Shore Early Americana Museum. If you are going north on Route 13, bypass Pocomoke and travel one mile then make a left on Route 667. The museum is at the end of Route 667.

Teackle Mansion and Princess Anne

Lord Littleton's Palace

Princess Anne's **Teackle Mansion** is one of Maryland's best examples of early Federal architecture. It was built by one of Somerset county's most prominent citizens almost two centuries ago. Littleton Dennis Teackle designed and built this gracious mansion in two stages between 1802 and 1819. Both he and his wife, Elizabeth Gore Upshur Teackle, were born and raised in wealthy families in Accomac County, Virginia. Shortly after their marriage in 1800, they moved to Maryland where he purchased nine acres of land on what was then the outskirts of Princess Anne and began the construction of their home. They called it "Teackletonia", but a young guest in the early 1800s referred to it as "Lord Littleton's Palace."

Following the demands of neoclassical architecture the mansion's temple-front center section is enhanced by a Flemish-bond brick facade and a carved cornice with decorative plaster panels above the front door and first-floor windows. Symmetry was an intricate part of the design both on the outside and for the interior arrangement. False arches and doorways balance actual entryways. The mansion is also noted for its mirrored windows, marble-laid bath and underground cistern.

Littleton Dennis Teackle had a diverse career as a merchant, statesman and entrepreneur. He owned and managed extensive agricultural and timber lands and traded local and imported goods with merchants in England and the Caribbean. In 1813, he helped found and was elected first President of the Bank of Somerset. He also served 12 years in the Maryland House of Delegates where he made a survey of state educational needs. He was appointed first Commissioner of Public Schools in Maryland. He also tried unsuccessfully to establish a state bank. Despite his wide ranging business pursuits, financial stability eluded him. During several long periods only financial aid from family members allowed the Teackles to continue living in their lavish mansion. Eventually the mansion property was deeded to their daughter, Elizabeth Ann Upshur Teackle Quinby who, after her mother's death, sold it in 1839. Several years later, after selling the remainder of his property, Littleton Dennis Teackle moved to Baltimore where he died in the Exchange Hotel in 1848.

The Teackle Mansion is filled with period furnishings. Inside the double door entrance is a traverse hall containing an enclosed stair along the south wall with a classical plaster arch, balanced at the north end by a recessed niche. A small exhibit of Teackle memorabilia includes the family Bible, other books, currency from the Somerset Bank and the Teackle door knocker. In the drawing room the ornate mirror over the fireplace is from the Ogle House in Annapolis. Also present are a desk by the Baltimore cabinetmaker John Needles and an 1807 Broadwood pianoforte. After the drawing room, you'll proceed to the dining room in the south wing where you'll also see a gift shop and the old kitchen with a seven-foot fireplace and beehive oven.

From the drawing room you'll go on to the south wing of the mansion where there is a small sitting room, or retiring room as it was called, a dining room and the old kitchen. The kitchen's restoration was enhanced in 1974 when workers exploring behind one of the walls uncovered the seven-foot fireplace and beehive oven that had been walled up for over a century.

The second floor also has museum rooms. The bedroom contains a 19th-century bed, coverings and accessories. The children's room displays toys and clothing while the study has local artifacts and both English and Maryland law books.

The Somerset County Historical Society owns the north wing which is open at the same time as the central and south wings of the mansion. In the north wing you see the marble laid bath containing its own cistern, quite advanced for its era. On either side of the bathroom are dressing rooms. The other rooms in this wing showcase a collection of furniture, paintings, books and artifacts donated by the local community.

The Teackle Mansion can be toured April through mid-December on Wednesday, Saturday and Sunday from 1:00 to 3:00 P.M. The remainder of the year it is open Sunday afternoons only. Admission is charged.

After touring Teackle Mansion you may want to stroll around **Princess Anne.** You can pick up a self-guided walking tour brochure at the mansion which includes 37 points of architectural and historical interest (as well as some antique shops and a pottery shop). Littleton Dennis Teackle and his wife are buried in the St. Andrew's Episcopal Churchyard on Church Street. On Somerset Avenue you can stop for lunch or dinner (or even stay overnight) at the **Washington Hotel**, built in 1744. The hotel retains anachronistic touches like the separate ladies and gentlemen staircases. Like so many early American towns, Princess Anne was ravaged by fire; but some lovely colonial and Federal homes have survived. Each year during Olde Princess Anne Days, the second weekend in October, a number of these private homes, both in town and in the surrounding countryside, are open to the public.

Directions: From Baltimore take Route 97 south to Route 50. Continue on Route 50 to Salisbury, then take Route 13 south to Princess Anne. Turn left at the third Princess Anne exit, Deal Island Road, Route 363. Proceed one block. Turn right at the stop sign onto Mansion Street. The Teackle Mansion is located on the right at number 11736 and there is parking in front of the property.

WORCESTER COUNTY AND OCEAN CITY

Assateague Island

Not Far from the Madding Crowd

Even longtime beach buffs get confused when questioned about **Assateague Island**. Is it in Maryland or Virginia? Is it a national or state park? Where is it in relation to Chincoteague Island?

Here are some answers: Assateague is a 37-mile-long barrier island that has its northern two-thirds in Maryland and its southern third in Virginia; no road connects the two sections. In fact, much of the island is accessible only by boat or on foot. Assateague shelters the smaller Chincoteague Island located west of the Virginia portion in the Chincoteague Bay. As you cross the bridge from the Maryland mainland, you'll immediately see the state park. Most of the island,

Assateague Island, the 37-mile-long barrier island that has its northern two-thirds in Maryland and its southern third in Virginia, is home to the wild, free-roaming ponies.

however, is part of the Assateague Island National Seashore. A National Wildlife Refuge is located at the Virginia end of the island.

The barren, unsettled island is constantly shifting. The fragile dunes, anchored by equally fragile grasses, protect the low-lying bay side portion of the island. Those who despair at the body-to-body throng around Ocean City delight in the endless stretches of relatively empty sand approximately 15 miles to the south. Because the human population is so carefully controlled by limited roadway access, the animal population is plentiful. The best-known four-legged inhabitants are the wild ponies. Reputedly descended from survivors of a wrecked Spanish galleon, they more likely come from stock grazed by settlers. You're also likely to see a variety of birds in the small, marshy island meadows.

For many it is the denizens of the sea, not the land, that provide the inducement. Fisherman flock to the island. Surf casting, clamming and crabbing are all popular.

The two-mile Maryland state park on Assateague has bathhouses and campsites open from April through October. Food service and protected beaches are available in summer only. Just to the south is a National Park Service beach, which is open for day use. Near the place where you start across the Sinepuxent Bridge onto the island there is a Visitor Center. You can see an aquarium here and a natural history film that will familiarize you with happenings on Assateague. There are also maps and brochures to be had showing the various park areas on the island. Visitor Center hours are 8:30 A.M. to 5:00 P.M.

Directions: From Baltimore take Route 2 south to Route 50. Follow Route 50 to the outskirts of Ocean City. Turn right on Route 611 to the Visitor Center and the Sinepuxent Bridge over to Assateague.

Furnace Town

Pig Iron

The south had plantations worked by slave labor, while the north had industrial villages worked by laborers who were virtual serfs on feudal-like estates. Just a few miles from Snow Hill, you can visit a re-created 19th-century industrial town that was run in this manner. The Nassawango Iron Furnace operated from 1832 to 1847. Step back in time at this remarkably intact historical site.

Bog ore was discovered along the Nassawango Creek as early as 1789. But 40 years passed before the Maryland General Assembly, in 1829, granted a charter to the Maryland Iron Company, after which the company acquired 5,000 acres of forest and swamp land around the creek. Originally it built a cold blast furnace but switched between 1834 and 1837 to the hot blast technique developed in Scotland. It is this hot blast furnace you'll see today and that calls up mental pictures of the miners, sawyers, colliers, molders, firemen, carters, draymen and bargemen who lived and worked in **Furnace Town** in its heyday.

Originally the ore was thought to be a higher grade than it actually was; thus the furnace was never as profitable as had been anticipated. The bog ore was obtained beneath the creek waters by miners using picks, shovels and rakes. Ore was then carried to the shore in flat-bottom boats. It was smelted day and night in the 35-foot-high furnace.

The furnace is recognized by historical experts as one of the finest examples of its kind in the country. It offers insights into how the smelting process worked. Because the trough, in which the molten ore was cooled after it had passed through the casting hearth, looked to some people like a sow with piglets, this cast iron came to be called pig iron. The entire iron-making process is explained at the Furnace Town museum. Be sure to stop there before you see the furnace; it will give you an appreciation and understanding of what you'll be seeing. Other buildings at Furnace Town include a country store selling local handicrafts, a blacksmith shop, smokehouse, broom house, 19th-century print shop and the Old Nazareth Church, circa 1874.

A fictional account of the decline of the Nassawango Iron Furnace is included in George Alfred Townsend's novel, *The Entailed Hat* (see Gathland State Park). The book, published in 1884, is out of print but can be obtained through the Maryland public library system.

The **Nassawango Creek and Swamp** come under the jurisdiction of the Nature Conservancy. If you have the time, take the nature trail that begins at the furnace site. The trail is particularly enjoyable in the spring when the wildflowers bloom. It is always a mecca for bird lovers.

Furnace Town hosts many festivals throughout the spring, summer and fall. Living history is an integral part of these special events (see Calendar). Furnace Town is open daily from 11:00 A.M. to 5:00 P.M. Admission is charged.

Directions: From Baltimore take Route 2 south to Route 50. Take Route 50 east about 90 miles to Salisbury, then take Route 12 south about 16 miles to Old Furnace Road. Turn right at the highway sign for Furnace Town.

Julia A. Purnell Museum and Snow Hill

An Old Town that Loved an Old Woman

The story of the founding of Snow Hill's **Julia A. Purnell Museum** is guaranteed to warm a mother's heart. William Z. Purnell was justly proud of the needlework his mother, Julia Lecompte Purnell, created. He felt it was all the more remarkable since she didn't take up fine stitching until she was 85. She started her new hobby after a fall confined her to a wheelchair. Miss Julia lived to be 100; she was born in 1843 and died in 1943. During the last 15 years of her life she produced nearly 3,000 needlework pieces. A fraction of these are framed and displayed at the museum.

William Purnell and the town residents were not the only ones to recognize Miss Julia's accomplishments. After ten years of needle-working, she sent her work to the Philadelphia Hobby Show and won both a First Prize and the Grand Prize. Two years later, when she was just shy of 100, she was inducted into the Hobby Hall of Fame of America.

Miss Julia's creations, however, are only a small part of the museum's collection. The museum also covers the history of **Snow Hill** and this part of Maryland from the days of the Indians through the Victorian era. The story of the Pocomoke River region unfolds chronologically beginning with the Nanticoke Indian arrowheads and other artifacts. Next come the hand-hewn utensils and tools from the colonial period. You'll see such oddities as a Johnny cake board, handmade wooden pitchers, a foot warmer with a built-in lamp, a mangle and a mustard dipper. Handmades soon gave way to trade goods, for by 1690 Snow Hill was a Royal Port with a lively trade linking it to other parts of the world.

Like the rest of the country, Snow Hill was divided by the Civil War. In fact, dissidents sought refuge in the tangled forest along the banks of the Pocomoke River. Runaway slaves also found sanctuary here. The museum has reminders of the slave trade, such as the 1852 slave allowance list. You'll see that slaves were given white bread on Sundays. They were fed meagerly and their size was measured by a slave stick, like the one displayed, before they were auctioned at the Snow Hill Courthouse.

One of the major Snow Hill events of the late 1800s was the Great Fire of 1893 (an earlier fire in 1834 had consumed 40 homes, 8 stores and 2 hotels). Newspaper stories tell of the town's difficulties in 1893. Fire buckets and grenade bottles are reminders of citizen involvement in fire fighting. Other exhibits deal with agriculture and trade tools. There are carpenters' tools, tanners' fleshing knives, weights and measures to check store scales, and both a Snow Hill dentist and doctor tools.

A selection of lighting devices ranges from pitch pipes to electricity. There are lighter knots (torches made from pine knots and used at outdoor meetings), sperm oil lamps, a baker's lamps and even a courting lamp. The latter enabled the girl's father to measure out the oil in keeping with the desirability of the suitor. If the gentleman did not seem promising, a modest amount of oil would insure an early end to the evening.

The Victorian era is brought to life with a re-creation of Miss Julia's sewing room. There is also a collection of old gowns and accessories—lace mitts, hair combs and a courting mirror. Everything in the museum was donated by friends and relatives of the Purnells and by Snow Hill residents.

Be sure to pick up a Snow Hill Walking Tour map and stroll the tree-lined streets. There are some 100 buildings in Snow Hill that were built before 1877. The tour map gives brief descriptions of 50 of these old structures—homes, churches, government buildings and also a one-room schoolhouse.

While you're exploring, take time out to enjoy lunch, dinner or an overnight stay at the **Snow Hill Inn**, built circa 1790. This inn has four bedrooms furnished with period pieces. The restaurant offers regional cuisine. Call (301)632-2102 for accommodations or reservations. If you plan a weekend visit, you should make lunch or dinner reservations ahead; this is a popular spot.

Directions: From Baltimore take Route 2 south to Route 50. Go east 90 miles on Route 50 to Salisbury, then take Route 12 south to Snow Hill. Turn right on Market Street. The museum is four blocks west on the right.

Ocean City and the Ocean City
Life-Saving Station Museum

The Place to Go Overboard

One of the most popular year-round resorts on the East Coast is **Ocean City**. The ten miles of white sandy beach and three-mile boardwalk have metamorphized from a row of cottages and boarding houses to multi-story condominiums and hotels. Sun worshippers now have plenty to do in the evening from the arcade games and amusements along the boardwalk to fancy eateries and nightclubs. There are eight golf courses and plenty of miniature golf layouts that are popular with young visitors.

There are even plenty of things to do when it rains. You can wile away a cloudy afternoon at the **Ocean City Life-Saving Station Museum** opposite the Inlet Village specialty shops at the south end of the boardwalk.

This museum explores both the history of the U.S. Life Saving Service and Ocean City's boardwalk attractions. Most visitors have never heard of the U.S. Life Saving Service, forerunner of today's Coast Guard. The Service was formed in 1848, but it wasn't until December 25, 1878, that the first Ocean City Life Saving Station opened. It was one of a series of stations along the country's 10,000-mile coastline. The picturesque building in which the museum is located was built in 1891 to replace the small original station.

The museum's boat room contains apparatus used by lifesavers to rescue shipwrecked seamen along the perilous coast line. The largest piece is the fully restored surf rescue boat from Caffey's Inlet Station in North Carolina. Visitors are fascinated by the surfcar, or life car. Into this small, 11- by 4-foot claustrophobic contraption four people could be squeezed, if necessary. Speed was essential in saving passengers from wrecked vessels. The breeches buoy, which you will see in old photographs, could handle only one survivor at a time. Surfcars were necessary because ships laden with immigrants frequently ran aground along the Atlantic coast off Ocean City. To appreciate the rescue service in action, there is a short film about the rescue of the crew of the *Olaf Bergh*, a Norwegian freighter that was hugging the shore in fear of German submarines and foundered off Ocean City (around 94th Street). A faded photograph shows the Norwegian consul watching as a survivor is brought to shore in the breeches buoy.

The collection of life-saving equipment is reputed to be the largest in the country. It includes old uniforms, photographs, boats and other equipment. The museum exhibits shift from sea rescue to sea salvage with a collection of articles recovered from shipwrecks. The assorted bottles and rusted artifacts are not likely to inspire you to don a wet

The Ocean City Life-Saving Station Museum is at the southern, or inlet, end of the Ocean City boardwalk. The museum houses the largest array of life-saving equipment in the country.

suit and start searching for treasure.

The swimsuits collected here date from the turn of the century and include rental suits. Beach trips were so infrequent that families simply rented swimwear for the day. These vintage outfits were hardly figure-flattering. Take, for example, the 80-year-old suit made from ten yards of heavy wool. The exhibits progress gradually from bloomers to bikinis. If you are tempted to chuckle at these far-from-fetching suits, you can chime in with Laughing Sal, a mannequin remnant of **Jester's Funhouse**. Sal, a busty, oversize lady whose laugh once echoed down the boardwalk, bows and waves her arms while cackling uproariously. Hers is no fleeting fame: she was immortalized in John Barth's "Lost in the Funhouse" stories. He wrote of her laugh, "You couldn't hear it without laughing yourself." Push her button and see if you agree.

Laughing Sal is not the only exhibit that brings back the good old days. There is a model collection of 12 formerly well-known boardwalk hotels, some of which still stand. The models, which include a

245

miniature grocery store, pharmacy and even the museum, are exact to the smallest detail. You can see Lilliputian people strolling along the boardwalk (none wear slogan-covered T-shirts).

The Ocean City Life Saving Station Museum is open June through September from 11:00 A.M. to 10:00 P.M. daily. In May and October the museum is open daily from 11:00 A.M. to 4:00 P.M., and November through April it is open on weekends only from NOON to 4:00 P.M. A nominal admission is charged.

Directions: Take Route 2 south to Route 50 and go east to Ocean City (about 120 miles). The museum is located at the south end of the boardwalk.

Pocomoke River State Forest and Park

Two-Firs

Both sides of the Pocomoke River are included within the 14,745-acre **Pocomoke River State Forest and Park**. On one bank you'll find the **Milburn Landing Area** (370 acres) and four miles north, on the opposite side, the **Shad Landing Area** (545 acres).

The Pocomoke River winds through the cypress swamps and primitive forests of Maryland's lower Eastern shore. The river has both scenic and historical appeal. Captain John Smith explored the Pocomoke River around 1608. Although the swamp proved an impenetrable barrier to colonial settlement, the river did carry trade vessels to and from Snow Hill. Years later, Civil War deserters and escaping slaves sought haven along the Pocomoke River and its tributaries.

These days the Pocomoke belongs to wildlife; you'll hear the splash of jumping bass, the amazingly diverse bird calls and the croaking of the ubiquitous frogs. The Pocomoke River area supports more bird species than almost any other in the Atlantic inland area. Rare prothonotary warblers and elusive pileated woodpeckers can be sighted in this birdwatcher's paradise. Each park area has a nature trail to bring visitors into close proximity with the park's birds.

At Milburn Landing the one-mile, self-guided Bald Cypress Nature Trail winds through three different forest areas. In a once cultivated area, loblolly pines grow where corn was harvested. Gradually the pines will be replaced with the second type of growth, the hardwood forest. Hardwoods include red maple, American hornbeam, dogwood, oak and sweetgum. The third area is the bald cypress swamp.

Across the river at Shad Landing you can explore the ¾-mile Trail of Change. This 45-minute hike gives you a chance to observe the changes taking place in the Pocomoke Forest. Over the years both nature and man's use of this area have changed. The trail was once a

246

road used by shad fisherman, who brought their catch in at the river landing. Along the trail there were scattered home sites, now reclaimed by the forest. Man's impact can also be observed in the non-indigenous vegetation such as prickly pear cactus, black walnut and Norway maple—all added by long-ago residents.

The bald cypress swamp, primordial in its appearance, is a natural world like that found in the Dismal and Okefenokee swamps. This is the northernmost limit of the bald cypress (see Battle Creek Cypress Swamp sanctuary selection). To learn more about the wetlands, visit the Nature Center at Shad Landing. You'll see hands-on exhibits focusing on the flora and fauna of the park. The park is open year round for camping and day use. Guided canoe trips are organized during the summer. Call ahead (410) 632-2566 to register for these trips.

Boat docks and launching ramps are at both park areas. Shad Landing also has a marina where you can rent canoes. If you have your own boat, you can rent one of the 23 marina slips; all have water and electrical hookups.

Both areas offer picnicking and fishing. Shad Landing also has a Camp Store, a swimming pool, athletic fields and camping. Pets are only allowed in the Milburn Landing Area camping area.

While you're down near the southernmost tip of the state, why not head just a bit farther down Route 113 to Pocomoke City? The Victorian Italianiate, home of the city's first mayor, is on the National Register of Historical Sites. The 1870 **Costen House**, 206 Market Street, can be toured from April through October three days a week, call (410) 957-1297 for specific times. The house was built just after the Civil War and occupied by the family for more than a century. Costen had been a Confederate blockade runner carrying food and supplies across the lower Chesapeake Bay to the Hampton Roads area. His reputation was enhanced by his work with victims of typhoid fever. He was elected mayor of Pocomoke City in 1888. Just around the corner from the Costen House is the **Hall-Walton Memorial Garden**. Ernest and Julia Hall Walton were enthusiastic supporters of the restoration of Costen House. In fact, Julia was a cousin of the Costens. Only the lush crepe myrtles remain from the once lovely Walton family garden; but new trees, shrubs and plants have been added, as have decorative Charleston Battery benches and a Victorian gazebo.

Directions: From Baltimore take Route 97 south to Route 50. Take Route 50 east about 90 miles to Salisbury. Then take Route 12 south 20 miles to Snow Hill. At Snow Hill turn right on Route 394 and right again on Route 113; this will lead to Shad Landing. For Milburn Landing from Route 12, proceed seven miles south on Route 354.

Southern Maryland
Introduction

Southern Maryland's three counties date back to the 1600s, the earliest days of European settlement in America. St Mary's County was established in 1637, Calvert in 1654 and Charles in 1658. The past comes alive in Historic St. Mary's City, a living museum, that recreates the early days of Maryland's oldest permanent settlement. Excavators have uncovered remnants of this settlement in a search that has covered over 800 acres.

You can board a replica of the *Maryland Dove*, experiencing first hand the cramped quarters of the intrepid band of settlers who sailed to Lord Baltimore's colony. Historic St. Mary's also recreates a 17th century tobacco farm where authentically garbed interpreters take time from chores to talk about their daily life. The political side of the Maryland colony is revealed at the Reconstructed State House of 1676.

Another site that acquaints visitors with St. Mary's early inhabitants is St. Clement's Island-Potomac River Museum. Both St. Mary's and St. Clement's devote time to the indigenous population, but to find real reminders of the region's earliest days you must head to Calvert Cliffs where you are apt to see fossilized remains of giant sharks and other sea life that inhabited the water that covered this area over 15 million years ago. Battle Creek Cypress Swamp Sanctuary's bald cypress trees also evoke the past; they have been growing in the Chesapeake Bay region for more than 120,000 years.

Three historic houses provide stories that also illuminate our past. The Thomas Stone National Historic Site commemorates a signer of the Declaration of Independence. Sotterley Plantation recalls the days when pirates preyed on river front plantations. Dr. Samuel A. Mudd House Museum is linked to one of the most heinous crimes in the country's history, the assassination of President Lincoln.

CHARLES COUNTY

Dr. Samuel A. Mudd House Museum

A Clean Slate

For many of Dr. Samuel Mudd's descendants, clearing the family name has been a crusade. None has worked more tirelessly than Mudd's youngest granddaughter, Louise Mudd Arehart. She is president of the Dr. Samuel A. Mudd Society; through her efforts Dr. Mudd's plantation farmhouse has been successfully restored. The building looks today as it did on April 15, 1865, when history rode to the door and forever changed the lives of Dr. Mudd and his family.

The drama began at Ford's Theatre the preceding night when John Wilkes Booth shot President Lincoln. Booth fractured his leg when he leapt onstage to make his escape. The injured Booth and his accomplice, David Herold, rode out of the capital and made their way into Southern Maryland. The two men stopped at Mary Surratt's Tavern (see selection). Booth's leg was causing problems, so they decided to get medical help and set out for Dr. Mudd's farm, farther south. Booth had traveled through this part of Maryland before, ostensibly to buy land and horses (and indeed one of the horses the two were riding as they made their escape was purchased by Booth from Dr. Mudd's neighbor). However, his agenda had also included efforts to enlist support from the region's Southern sympathizers for various plots and plans. On one of Booth's visits, he had met and dined with Dr. Mudd; their paths had crossed again in Washington. Booth and Herold arrived at Mudd's door at 4:00 A.M. Easter Saturday morning.

Herold dismounted and roused the Mudd household. Dr. Mudd had been out late with a patient, but Mrs. Mudd awakened him rather than answer the knock. She was afraid it might be floaters, or free blacks, who were often found in this state that bordered the Confederacy. Herold gave Dr. Mudd false names (Tyler and Tyson) as the doctor helped the wounded Booth into the house. According to some reports Booth, an actor, had disguised himself with a false beard. Herold and Dr. Mudd helped Booth to the red velvet couch in the parlor (this historic piece of furniture has just recently been returned to the house by a Mudd descendant) so that the doctor could examine his leg. Dr. Mudd then moved Booth to an upstairs bedroom, cut off the boot and set the leg. The boot was tossed under the bed and forgotten. It would later be used as evidence.

Later Saturday morning Dr. Mudd and Herold set out to find a carriage for the two travelers to use on the rest of their journey. When none could be found Herold and Booth set off on horseback between

250

2:00 and 4:00 P.M. As they left, Mrs. Mudd got a look at Booth's face which, heretofore, he had kept hidden. She remarked to the doctor that he appeared to be wearing a disguise. This is how the Mudds later explained to authorities why they did not recognize a man who had been a guest in their home.

Dr. Mudd, who claimed not to have known of the President's assassination when he ministered to Booth, was nonetheless convicted by a military court of aiding and harboring an escaping fugitive. He was found innocent of charges that he was involved in the conspiracy to assassinate Lincoln. Mudd was sent to Fort Jefferson Prison in the Dry Tortugas off Key West, Florida.

Dr. Mudd served part of his sentence in chains after an escape attempt. But when a yellow fever epidemic decimated the prison population and the prison doctor died, Mudd was unshackled and began treating his fellow prisoners. Shortly after the end of the epidemic he was pardoned by President Andrew Johnson for his humanitarian work. Dr. Mudd returned to his Maryland farm, and then toured the country lecturing on yellow fever. (He had contracted and survived the disease while at Fort Jefferson Prison.) Dr. Mudd died of pneumonia 13 years after his release from prison.

The **Dr. Samuel A. Mudd House Museum** is filled with furniture and mementos, each piece prompting the costumed docents to tell another story about Dr. Mudd's experiences and the family's travail when Federal troops camped around the house. History comes to life at this out-of-the-way farmhouse, where the clock seems to have stopped in 1865.

The Dr. Samuel A. Mudd House Museum is open Saturday and Sunday afternoons from NOON to 4:00 P.M. from April to late November. Admission is charged.

Directions: From the Washington Beltway (I-495/95) Exit 7, take Route 5 south to Waldorf. Turn left on Route 205. Continue to Poplar Hill Road and make a right. Drive for approximately four miles. Turn right on Dr. Samuel Mudd Road and go .4 of a mile to the house. There is a sign at the entrance.

Port Tobacco

The Town Time (Almost) Forgot

Upon entering the reconstructed Charles County Courthouse, circa 1819, you'll see a copy of the map John Smith drew when he sailed up the Potomac River in 1608. Smith marked the Indian village of Potopaco on the area that subsequently became the town of **Port Tobacco,** the first county seat of Charles County.

The English had started settling this area as early as 1634, which makes the town one of the oldest continuous settlements in the U.S. Four years later, Father Andrew White arrived to convert the Potopaco Indians. He Christianized the Indian village and wrote religious catechisms in the Indian dialect. White also wrote a grammar and dictionary that was printed on one of the first presses in America. This early text was discovered years later in an archive in Rome, Italy.

The **Charles County Museum,** located on the second floor of the Port Tobacco Courthouse, has exhibits detailing the history of the Charles County area. This is not the first courthouse built on this site. In 1727, at the direction of the Maryland Assembly, a courthouse was built at Port Tobacco, then officially known as Chandlers Town. The assembly changed the name to Charles Town, but inhabitants continued to call the village Port Tobacco, or versions of that, like Portafacco, Potobac, Potobag and Porttobattoo. The more popular unofficial name was impossible to dislodge because the town was indeed a port from which tobacco was sent from the colonies to England. Until the Revolutionary War, Port Tobacco was the second largest river port in Maryland, after St. Mary's.

The courthouse, which was built between 1727 and 1729 at a cost of 2,000 pounds of tobacco, was destroyed by a severe windstorm in 1808. In 1819, a brick courthouse was built, but an 1892 fire destroyed it, resulting in the relocation of the county seat from Port Tobacco to La Plata. Because of its historical significance to the county, the Charles County Courthouse was reconstructed between 1965 and 1973.

At the time of the fire the area around the courthouse was bustling. The town had 20 shops, approximately 70 homes, two newspapers, three hotels and numerous businesses. One of the hotels, the Brawner Hotel, was the Federal field headquarters for the manhunt launched to find Lincoln's assassin, John Wilkes Booth. The Federal investigator, Detective William Williams, offered Southern sympathizer Thomas Jones a staggering $100,000 for information leading to Booth's capture. Jones, who did indeed know the assassin's whereabouts, would not betray Booth.

"The Story of Port Tobacco," a 30-minute slide presentation highlighting Port Tobacco's long history, is shown at the courthouse. It illustrates the significance of the restored homes on Courthouse Square, such as the 1765 Chimney House and the 1732 Stag Hall.

Directions: From the Washington Beltway (1-495/95) Exit 7 take Route 5 south to Waldorf, then take U.S. 301 south to La Plata. Turn right on Route 6 in La Plata. Continue three miles on Route 6 to the junction with Chapel Point Road and bear left. You'll see Murphy's Store at this junction. Take Chapel Point Road for one-half mile to Commerce Street and the Port Tobacco restored area.

Smallwood's Retreat

Home of Washington's Friend and Look-Alike

William Smallwood entered the Continental Army as a Colonel in January 1776. By October of that year he was a Brigadier General and by 1780 he was a Major General, the highest ranking Marylander in George Washington's command.

We know little about the private life of this busy public man. He was a bachelor who lived on a 5,000-acre plantation, part of his parents' holdings. He called his tidewater home Mattawoman Plantation; today it is known as **Smallwood's Retreat**.

Despite the peaceful sound of its names, the plantation served as an active meeting spot for political and military leaders. Smallwood and his neighbors across the river, George Mason of Gunston Hall and George Washington of Mount Vernon, would meet at their respective homes to talk of independence from England.

Smallwood was involved in the Revolutionary struggle from the earliest days. When Washington had to retreat after the Battle of Long Island, Smallwood's troops, the Maryland Line, protected his flanks and saved them all from annihilation. Smallwood was wounded at the Battle of White Plains but did not relinquish his command. It was this brave action that led to his promotion to Brigadier General. After keeping the southern wing of the Continental Army from disintegration following the bitterly fought Battle of Camden (South Carolina), Smallwood was formally commended for his bravery and promoted to Major General.

Smallwood's friendship with Washington did not end when the war ended. Both were members of the Masonic Lodge of Alexandria. Smallwood was also active in the newly formed Protestant Episcopal Church. When Washington came to Southern Maryland, he and Smallwood often attended Old Durham Parish Church, built in 1732. Markers at this church indicate their attendance. The church is off Route 425 and open to visitors.

After the Revolution, Smallwood helped form the Society of the Cincinnati for Former Continental Army officers. Smallwood also resumed a political career interrupted by the war. He had represented Charles County in the Colonial Assembly during the 1760s and 1770s. In 1785, he was elected Governor of Maryland and served three one-year terms.

This distinguished Marylander is buried on the front lawn of his plantation. When he died there was no will and the property was divided and sold. The house continued to be occupied for approximately 100 years after Smallwood's death. It fell on hard times, though, and its last known use was as a storage barn for grain and hay. Only remnants of three walls and the foundation remained when the Smallwood Foundation was established to restore the general's retreat.

William Smallwood, friend and look-alike of George Washington's, was the highest ranking Marylander in Washington's command. Smallwood's Retreat has been completely rebuilt.

The fully rebuilt house is open for free tours, conducted by docents in colonial garb, on weekends and holidays from Memorial Day to Labor Day, NOON to 5:00 P.M. Seven rooms have been furnished with 18th-century pieces similar to those Smallwood might have owned. Only three chairs in the dining room were owned by the family; they were made in Annapolis by John Shaw. In the Great Room there is a copy of a portrait of William Smallwood in his military uniform. It is surprising to see how much he resembles George Washington.

One curious feature of the house's design is the warming room, built off the dining room. The servants had to bring all the food through the dining room to the warming room before they started serving the meal. Then, because there was no exit door, they had to stay in the warming room until the meal was finished.

The layout of the downstairs rooms was determined by the debris patterns in the foundation. No such clues were available for the upstairs, so it was designed by conjecture. There is a guest bedroom, a gentleman's large bed chamber and a dressing room. The tour ends in the restored out-kitchen. After your tour be sure to see the herb and vegetable gardens. Throughout the year Smallwood's Retreat hosts special events such as garden parties, candlelight tours, military encampments and craft demonstrations (see Calendar of Events).

Located on Mattawoman Creek, a tributary of the Potomac River, **General Smallwood State Park** also has delightfully situated water-side picnic tables. There are boats for rent and guided nature walks, plus canoe trips for which reservations are needed. For information on guided walks, special events and canoe reservations call (301) 743-7613.

Directions: From Baltimore take I-97 south to Route 301. Continue south on Route 301 to La Plata (eight miles south of Waldorf) and turn right on Route 225. Continue west to the "T" intersection with Route 224 and turn left. Proceed down Route 224 for about six miles to park entrance on the right at Sweden Point Road.

Thomas Stone National Historic Site

Signer of the Declaration of Independence

The United States has no aristocracy, having always favored a meritocracy. But if there were a roster of American nobility, it might well include the brave men who signed the Declaration of Independence at great risk to their personal safety and property. Had England won the Revolution, they would have been judged traitors. As it was, many lost their liberty and their belongings during the war.

Thomas Stone, a well-respected lawyer and prominent political figure, was a signer for Maryland. Stone not only served in the Second Continental Congress, he was also a State Senator. He was selected as a representative to the Constitutional Convention in 1787, but his wife's ill health and his busy law practice forced him to refuse the honor. She died in June 1787, and he soon became ill and died on October 5th of the same year.

They are buried at **Haberdeventure**, the Charles County plantation Stone purchased in 1770. The following year he began constructing his two-story brick country home; it was finished in 1773. After the National Park Service acquired the estate in 1981, restoration work began on the fire-gutted central block of the house. It is being restored to its 18th-century appearance.

Originally Stone's plantation consisted of 442 acres, but by the time of this death the estate was 1,077 acres. Although he increased the plantation's size, Stone never seemed to regard Haberdeventure as a source of income. Only half of the original acreage was suitable for cultivation. The main crops were corn and wheat. He also concentrated on livestock production. Approximately 25 to 35 people are thought to have lived at Haberdeventure including the extended Stone family and slaves.

The **Thomas Stone National Historic Site** visitor center has exhibits on the house and Stone's career. The site is open September through May, Wednesday through Sunday from 9:00 A.M. to 5:00 P.M. and daily during those hours in June, July and August. It is closed on Christmas and New Year's Day. Park personnel provide guided tours of the site or you can take a self-guided walking tour.

There are ten points of interest on the walking tour, including five barns—two horse barns, a hog barn, tobacco barn and a gabled roof barn. There is also a tenant house and the cemetery where Thomas Stone and his wife, Margaret, are buried. Visitors exploring the grounds should be aware that the park is a work in progress.

Directions: From Baltimore take the Baltimore-Washington Parkway, I-295, south to the Washington Beltway, I-495/95 south to Exit 3, Indian Head Highway, Route 210. Take Route 210 south to Potomac Heights and turn left on Route 225 east. Then make a right on Rose Hill Road which will take you to the Thomas Stone National Historic Site.

CALVERT COUNTY

Battle Creek Cypress Swamp Sanctuary

Trees Knees and Bees

Urban adventurers seeking unfamiliar terrain should head for Calvert County's **Battle Creek Cypress Swamp Sanctuary**. Although this unusual 100-acre preserve was established by the Nature Conservancy more than 30 years ago, many day trippers still have not discovered it.

The winding platform trail leads into one of the northernmost stands of bald cypress in North America. Bald cypress trees were found in the Chesapeake Bay region some 120,000 years ago, but the current descendants of these primordial giants could not have been growing for more than 5,000 to 10,000 years due to unfavorable climatic conditions. Walking beneath these trees, some as tall as 100 feet or more, you might easily get the feeling that you've walked back in time. Though the trees are of impressive size, the animals you'll see today—deer, muskrat and opossum—are smaller than the mammoths, prehistoric camels and scaly crocodiles that once roamed this land.

The trees are called bald cypress because they shed their needles each fall. Their most fascinating feature, however, is the root-like protuberance at their base. These "knees" puzzle scientists. One explanation is that the knees stabilize the tree in muddy terrain. Another theory is that the knees provide oxygen to the tree.

Spring is the best time to visit, when the swamp is bordered by a profusion of delicate wildflowers, and migratory warblers flit among the tree tops. If you are not equipped with field guides, the nature center staff is on hand to identify the flowers and birds for you. Visitors will enjoy the recently renovated exhibits featuring interactive displays on the history and wildlife of the area. Some highlights include an observation honey bee hive, a stuffed black bear and bobcat which represent animals once found in this area and a 20-foot replica of a bald cypress tree. Throughout the year the center offers guided walks, lectures and field trips; you can call (410) 535-5327 for information on upcoming programs.

Battle Creek Cypress Swamp Sanctuary is open at no charge April through September, Tuesday through Saturday 10:00 A.M. to 5:00 P.M. and Sunday 1:00 to 5:00 P.M. From October through March the sanctuary closes at 4:00 P.M. It is closed on Mondays, Thanksgiving, Christmas and New Year's Day.

Directions: From Baltimore take I-97 south to Route 3/301 south to Route 4 in Upper Marlboro. Take Route 4 for approximately 23 miles to Prince Frederick. Make a right on Sixes Road and watch for Battle Creek Cypress Swamp Sanctuary signs. Turn left on Gray's Road. The sanctuary is .1 mile down Gray's Road on the right.

Calvert Marine Museum and Calvert Cliffs

Maritime Memories

If you want to capture a unique Maryland memory, head down to Calvert County. All the way down, you'll arrive in Solomons Island, a quaint fishing town built around one of the world's deepest natural harbors. **Calvert Marine Museum** will acquaint you with local maritime history, the paleontology of Calvert Cliffs and the estuarine life of the tidal Patuxent River and adjacent Chesapeake Bay.

Maritime Patuxent: A River and Its People, the museum's first permanent exhibit, tells the story of human activity along the Patuxent River from the 17th-century colonial period to the present. It explores river transportation, trade, shipping, boat building, commercial fishing, military engagements, community life and recreation. Over 500 artifacts and photographs tell the story, including a 28-foot three-log canoe, a tobacco prize used to pack tobacco for shipment, a steam engine, an underwater mine and torpedo from World War II–era testing in the river and a 1956 Cruis-Along power boat built at the M.M. Davis & Sons Shipyard in Solomons.

The next exhibit, *Estuary Patuxent: A River and Its Life*, features a series of 15 aquariums, ranging in size from 50 to 3,500 gallons. Within the aquariums are aquatic plants and animals that exist between the salty waters of the Chesapeake Bay and the fresh water of the upper Patuxent River. Through these aquariums and supporting displays, visitors experience aquatic life of the bay, tidal and freshwater marshes, oyster bars, Patuxent River and its tributaries, and a "hands-on" touch tank with live animals. An outdoor exhibit features two live, and lively, female river otters who entertain everyone from the very young to the young-at-heart.

The newest exhibit, *Treasure from the Cliffs: Exploring Marine Fossils*, takes visitors through recreated settings depicting Southern Maryland's ancient marine and coastal environments. Fossil sharks, fishes, sea turtles, crocodiles, giant sea birds, whales, dolphins, seals, sea cows, a wide variety of fossil shellfish and remains of rare fossil land animals are on display. The exhibit's centerpiece is a full-sized skeletal reconstruction of the giant fossil "megatooth" white shark. A replicated section of the famous Calvert Cliffs explains local geology. A working lab area shows how fossils are prepared after discovery and allows visitors to identify any fossils they have found.

Visitors are encouraged to explore the three themes of the museum by touching and doing. Children and adults alike won't want to miss the hands-on Discovery Room. Before leaving, be sure to explore the exhibits on the museum grounds. A small craft shed displays a gig, skiff, canoe and several work boats. The most picturesque and interesting outdoor exhibit is the 1883 **Drum Point Lighthouse** that once signaled the entrance to the Patuxent River. You can explore it on a 20-minute tour. This is one of only three remaining screwpile cottage-type lighthouses; at the turn of the century 45 of them protected ships that plied the bay waters.

Docked at the museum wharf is the *Wm. B. Tennison*, an oyster bugeye built in 1899. This is the oldest certified passenger-carrying vessel on the Chesapeake Bay. A ride on this boat is an ideal way to end your visit. Call (301) 326-2042 to get additional information about the hour-long cruise.

The Calvert Marine Museum is open daily from 10:00 A.M. to 5:00 P.M. except New Year's Day, Thanksgiving and Christmas. Admission is charged.

Located just .6 mile south of the main museum is the **J.C. Lore & Sons Oyster House**. This 1934 seafood packing house, listed on the National Register of Historic Places, houses exhibits on Patuxent watermen and boat building in Southern Maryland. While in the area there is another significant lighthouse you can see, the Cove Point Lighthouse. Although visitors are no longer permitted on the grounds

Drum Point Lighthouse was a lookout for 80 years at the confluence of Patuxent River and western Chesapeake Bay. The lighthouse is now part of the Calvert Marine Museum.

or in the lighthouse, you can drive by to see the oldest tower lighthouse on the bay.

You can also visit **Calvert Cliffs State Park**. There is a trail down to the cliffs and a picnic and playground area. Watch out for ticks during the summer. You can't dig for fossils but you can scavenge on the beach for exposed fossils and shells. Nearby is the **Calvert Cliffs Nuclear Power Plant Visitors Center**, open daily from 9:00 A.M. to 5:00 P.M. except on major holidays. A converted tobacco barn has dioramas and audio-visual exhibits describing the fossils and the nuclear power plant that you see from an overlook.

Directions: From Baltimore take I-97 south to Route 3/301. Continue south to Route 4 which becomes Route 4/2 and go south to Solomons, about 44 miles. Make a left turn for the Calvert Marine Museum, 200 yards before the Thomas Johnson Memorial Bridge at Solomons. For Cove Point Lighthouse, turn off Route 4/2 at Route 497; signs on Route 4/2 will indicate the power plant.

Chesapeake Beach Railway Museum

Rail, Rod 'n' Reel

Things are pretty quiet around Chesapeake Beach these days, but in the early 1900s this was a popular resort with its own independent short line railroad. Crowds flocked to the beach town by boat and train. Steamboats traveled from Baltimore and trains brought Washingtonians who boarded at Seat Pleasant for the 32-mile trip. Visitors stayed at the elegant Belvedere Hotel while enjoying the mile-long boardwalk, the ballroom, the carousel and the roller coaster that extended out over the bay.

The bayside beach's early years are recalled at the **Chesapeake Beach Railway Museum**, housed in the original railroad station. The station was built between 1897 and 1898. The first train pulled into the Chesapeake Beach Station on June 9, 1900. The museum has photographs of both the early trains and the stations along the line: Seat Pleasant, Upper Marlboro, Owings and Chesapeake Beach. The railroad operated from March 21, 1899, to April 15, 1935. The trains heralded their own demise when they began transporting automobiles to destinations along their line.

Old railroad lanterns, steam engine bells, schedules, tickets, hand-made rail spikes and other memorabilia are part of the museum's still-growing collection. Also displayed is a 1914 Model T Ford Depot Hack. The sight of a carousel kangaroo will cause former patrons to reminisce about old days filled with amusement park rides as well as picnicking and swimming in the saltwater pool. The amusement park closed in 1971. Behind the station, volunteers are restoring half of the Dolores, the line's only surviving passenger car.

The Chesapeake Beach Railway Museum is open Saturday and Sunday from 1:00 to 4:00 P.M. in October and April. It is open daily 1:00 to 4:00 P.M. from May through September. Individual and group visits can be scheduled throughout the year by calling (410) 257-3892.

Across the parking lot from the museum is the **Rod 'n' Reel Restaurant**. Large picture windows in the restaurant give you a ringside seat on the bay action. Boats slowly make their way to the adjacent pier, and ducks and geese are always in evidence. The restaurant also operates an alfresco Boardwalk Cafe that extends out to the water's edge.

There is a small public beach at Chesapeake Beach where you can hunt for shark teeth and enjoy the water. Children can safely wade out for quite a distance. Families also enjoy the **Chesapeake Beach Water Park** at Route 261 and Gordon Stinnett Avenue. There are eight slides (one is even wheelchair accessible). There is a pool for youngsters still in diapers and an activity pool for older children. You can play water volleyball, swim laps, enjoy floating on the "river" or just relax and watch the action. Call (410) 257-2230 for admission prices and up-to-date schedule information.

If you'd just like to stroll along the shore, park at North Beach and enjoy their long boardwalk. Another popular eatery in the area is **Lagoon's Island Grill**, 8416 Bayside Road, with an outside deck overlooking the bay. Here you can enjoy live music on Friday and Saturday evenings.

Directions: From Baltimore take I-97 south to Route 3/301. Continue south to Route 4 in Upper Marlboro. Head east on Route 4 to Route 260. Turn left and take Route 260 to the beach. At the first stoplight turn right on Route 261, and then make a left at the next stoplight into the Rod 'n' Reel parking lot for the Chesapeake Beach Railway Museum. From the Washington Beltway, I-495/95, take Exit 11, Route 4 east and follow above directions.

ST. MARY'S COUNTY

Historic St. Mary's City

The Visitor Center

Historic St. Mary's City is a National Historic Landmark, a site of incredible archaeological and historical richness. As the area faded into obscurity, the original 17th-century city was saved by its remote location to be rediscovered by future generations. Other 17th-century

At the Godiah Spray Tobacco Plantation, living history actors portray the Spray family. Here women are at work in the kitchen garden.

settlements have been destroyed by the tides of time and development. Neglect has been kinder to St. Mary's City. Today you can explore Maryland's early history at a number of exhibits and archaeological sites. Most outdoor exhibits are open daily from the Maryland Day celebration in late March through the last weekend in November. The visitor center, housed in 20th-century barns, is open year-round.

The colonization of Maryland dates to November 22, 1633. It was then that two ships, the *Ark* and the *Dove*, sailed from Cowes on the Isle of Wight. On board were Leonard and George Calvert, representing their brother, Cecilius Calvert, the second Lord Baltimore. Eighteen British gentlemen and about 140 indentured servants were also on the ships.

The 40-ton *Dove* was a pinnace owned in share by the Calverts and others and purchased for the Maryland expedition. The 300-ton *Ark* was a sailing ship rented specifically for this voyage. The ships arrived in Port Comfort, Virginia on February 26, 1634. In early March, Leonard Calvert, Governor of the new colony, sailed up the Potomac to Piscataway to meet with the Indian tayac (emperor) Wannas. During his journey he met a fur trader named Captain Henry Fleete (also spelled Fleet) who served as Calvert's intermediary and interpreter. When Wannas perceived that the colonists were not a threat to his people, he allowed Calvert to make the decision about where to settle. After celebrating Mass on March 25, 1634 (the date celebrated as Maryland Day), Calvert, his men and Fleete sailed down the Potomac to a site that Fleete recommended near the mouth of the river. There they found a Yaocomaco settlement, which consisted of two hamlets on either side of St. Mary's River (which Calvert originally named the St. George's River). Calvert negotiated for the site with the peaceful farming and hunting tribe, giving them a supply of hatchets, hoes and cloth. The bargain called for one hamlet to be turned over immediately and the remaining part of the land over the coming year. Calvert named the settlement Saint Maries.

Soon the *Ark* sailed back to England. The *Dove* remained and was used for local trade, since its small size meant it could easily negotiate narrow inland rivers. In August 1635 the *Dove* was loaded with beaver pelts and timber and set sail for England. She never arrived. According to some accounts, she was "much worme eaten". She may have encountered a violent storm.

The **Maryland Dove** you'll see anchored at St. Mary's is not an exact reproduction of the original because no plans survived. It is, however, a reproduction of a typical 1634 pinnace like the vessel that brought the first settlers to Maryland.

The *Dove* had a crew of seven who lived in crowded quarters. They had to find sleeping space on spare sails or even atop coils of rope. If they were lucky they had a hammock to rig from the beams. The master's "great cabin" wasn't all that great. He had a berth and a table that was used for the passengers' dining table as well as the navigation chart and general work area. It was spartan and a small craft on which to brave the Atlantic.

On the hilltop above the pier where the *Maryland Dove* is anchored is the **Reconstructed State House of 1676**. St. Mary's City was the capital of the Maryland colony for 60 years, but for the first 41 years the colonial legislative body met in taverns and private homes. By 1674 the need for permanent headquarters was apparent, and Maryland's first State House was finished in 1676. Eighteen years later the capital was moved to Annapolis. The State House was converted to a parish church. It was torn down in 1829.

In the visitor venter, you can see a slide presentation and tour the orientation exhibit. This is also the spot to purchase your admission ticket that includes all the exhibits. Nearby, there is a recreated **Woodland Indian Hamlet** with longhouses of the type constructed by the Indians along the Chesapeake Bay.

Governor's Field Exhibits

The Governor's Field is the 17th-century name for the area that included the Town Center of the old capital. Here you will find a large number of exhibits and archaeological sites with a wide range of time periods. Along this promontory overlooking the St. Mary's River, archaeologists have found evidence of over 10,000 years of Native American settlement. In the 17th century, the Governor's Field was the colony's center of social, political and economic life.

Farthing's Ordinary represents an inn of the period. As the capital of a growing colony, St. Mary's became a village of taverns and lawyers' offices after 1670. William Farthing's customers were people who came to the capital from near and far to attend court and Assembly sessions and to conduct business. In places like Farthing's, gossip and news were dispensed along with food, drink and lodging. Today, visitors can purchase carry-out meals. **The Brome-Howard Inn**, which was moved to the historic townlands, offers dining and lodging. This 19th-century plantation house with its outbuildings formerly stood on the site of the 17th century capital's Town Center.

On the townlands is the site of Van Sweringen's Council Chamber Inn, a real colonial victualing and lodging house of the 1680s. It has been partially reconstructed and you can view portions on the 17th-century brick floor of the kitchen where members of the Governor's Council and other visitors enjoyed some of the best cider in the colony.

At the Town Center, archaeologists have uncovered and identified the remains of the home of Governor Leonard Calvert (The Country's House ca. 1635), Smith's Ordinary and Cordea's Hope. Pope's Fort dates to 1645 and Maryland's "Times of Troubles" when the colony was almost lost to a hostile and Protestant Virginia. The discovery of these sites and associated fence lines and roadbeds has helped provide the missing map "St. Maries." In addition, excavations in the

264

Town Center have uncovered evidence of thousands of years of Indian occupation. There are reconstructions of some of the important buildings, connecting roadways, fences and historic gardens. These create a sense of this important 17th-century "city."

St. Mary's City takes its name from the Virgin Mary, while the colony is named after Queen Henrietta Maria. The history of this settlement is known because of several authentic colonials who lived in this area between 1650 and 1660. One settler, Robert Cole, unknowingly made an enormous contribution to the unfolding of St. Mary's story. Cole had a plantation 20 miles from St. Mary's between 1650 and 1662 and his ten-year account book was recovered. It provided invaluable assistance to the St. Mary's living history project.

Cole's detailed day-to-day record showed that although tobacco was a cash crop, a limited amount of corn was grown. Corn was primarily used on the plantation, but some farmers did sell their excess. The yearly production of tobacco per man was three or four hogsheads (large barrels) or 1,300-1,500 pounds. To compute the value of this yield, it helps to know that you could purchase a horse for roughly 500 pounds of tobacco, whereas a slave cost 5,000 pounds. The farmhouse where George Washington was born cost his father 5,000 pounds of tobacco.

The Cole records were used to make St. Mary's City's **Godiah Spray Tobacco Plantation** typical of plantations of the period. It has a kitchen garden close to the house. A picket fence encloses the vegetables and herbs to protect them from foraging livestock. According to Cole's records his farm had 33 cows, 29 hogs, several horses and dunghill fowl, the old name for chickens.

The daily labor on a colonial farm was backbreaking. Hoeing a roughly cleared forest land was a grueling chore, as you will see when you visit. If the men had to endure hours in the hot sun, the women had to endure equally long hours at the fireplace—baking, boiling, roasting and frying meals.

This plantation house is far removed from such gracious 18th-century plantations as Sotterley and Montpelier (see selections). This is the house of a "prosperous" Chesapeake planter, meaning that he worked hard enough and lived long enough to be able to afford a few civilizing touches for his home. The house is of English design and has wood floors instead of dirt, windows with glass and lead panes and plastered walls. There is an old barn, also of English construction. It is heavily framed and elaborately jointed. A second barn and a tenant's house reveal architectural innovations from the old world to the new.

Archaeology Sites

Archaeological exploration continues to help 20th-century scholars and visitors understand 17th-century life. Excavations at the first capital have yielded millions of artifacts and amplified what is known

265

from the historical record.

Work on the Chapel Field uncovered the remains of a wooden Catholic chapel, which constitutes the founding site of the American Catholic Church in the English colonies. Already discovered are the cross-shaped remains of the Great Brick Chapel of the 1660s. Reproduction of this chapel proceeds with the use of old brickmaking methods.

Other Points of Interest

The 17th-century townlands of St. Mary's City hold many more interesting sites. The present Old Trinity Church dates to the 1840s, but the parish traces its history to the 17th century. The graveyard contains the Leonard Calvert Monument, erected on the site of the mulberry tree that once shaded legislators in the original State House yard. Legend has it that here is where the colonists bargained with the Native Americans for the land on which the town is built. The original site of the 1676 State House and the grave of Sir Lionel Copely, Maryland's first Royal Governor are found in the graveyard.

Visible on Route 5 near the Post Office is the **Freedom of Conscience Monument**, a large limestone sculpture by Hans Schuler. The monument was a gift from the counties of Maryland to the State in 1934. It honors the experiment in religious and civil freedom begun by the passage of the 1649 Act Concerning Religion. At the corner of Route 5 and Father Andrew White Road is a monument to the Jesuit missionary who came to Maryland in 1634 and stayed to work among the Native Americans. (If you continue on Father Andrew White Road you will come to a scenic overlook.)

Directions: From Baltimore take I-97 south to Route 3/301. Continue south to the intersection with Route 4 in Upper Marlboro. Go south on Route 4. At Solomons, cross Governor Thomas Johnson Bridge (Patuxent River) into St. Mary's County. Turn left onto Route 235 south and continue until you see the sign for Historic St. Mary's City; make a right onto Mattapany Road and follow signs to the visitor center. From I-495/95, the Washington Beltway, take Exit 7, Route 5 south to St. Mary's City.

Old Jail Museum and Tudor Hall

Sturdy Security

Although justices were appointed to hear cases in St. Mary's Court in 1644, there was no jail to house the accused or convicted. The settlement's sheriff was responsible for securing his own prisoners. In 1662, a private home was purchased by the colonial legislature for a courthouse and prison. On several occasions the Assembly authorized the construction of a log prison, but the records do not indicate that one was built until 1676. In 1708, the county seat was moved from St. Mary's to what is now Leonardtown, named in honor of Leonard Calvert. A courthouse was built there, although there is no mention of a prison there until 1856 when money was appropriated to erect a suitable county jail. Additional funds were allocated two years later; evidently the construction was not speedy.

The **Old Jail Museum** is in the sturdy one-story granite block building that still stands on the Leonardtown Courthouse lawn. Originally consisting of two cells and a hallway, it soon became apparent that the jailor had to have his own quarters, and a second story was added. The first floor was remodeled for the jailor, and there were three cells upstairs: a cell for white men, another for African-American men and the last for women. The massive wooden doors of the cells had small openings through which food could be passed.

In the last years of the jail's operation, its use increased significantly due to the resistance of local residents to the Volstead Act. Some of St. Mary's most respected citizens were bootleggers, and revenue officers frequently boarded those sentenced to 30 days in the old jail. Prisoners checked in at the jail in the morning, then spent the day's early hours playing cards at a nearby hotel, the afternoons fishing in Breton Bay and evenings with their families. Local lore claims these "prisoners" considered their time in the Leonardtown jail as among their finest vacations. The jail was replaced in 1941, after the population of the county increased due to the Navy's Patuxent River Naval Air Station (see selection).

After serving for a time as a county office building, it was eventually leased to the St. Mary's County Historical Society and now serves as their headquarters and museum. Artifacts include a hinge and hasp from the feeding door of one of the jails that predate this one as well as other county memorabilia. Visitors can see the cell reserved for the "ladies". There are reference books, genealogical records, grave registrations, wills, films of the St. Mary's Beacon from 1843 and census records from 1790. The museum also exhibits the office furnishings and equipment used by Dr. Philip Bean from 1914 to 1980. The museum is open from Tuesday through Saturday, 10:00 A.M. to 4:00 P.M. You can also pick up literature about St. Mary's County attractions as this museum serves as a tourist information center.

Tudor Hall is within sight of the old jail on Tudor Way. This Georgian mansion, built in 1756, was owned by the family of Francis Scott Key, author of our national anthem. Although the property previously belonged to Abraham Barnes, a significant colonial political figure, it did not look as it does today until after 1817, when Philip Key obtained clear title to the house and presented it to his son Henry Sotheron Key as a wedding present. It is the latter's home that was the basis for the restoration. In 1950, three floors of the house were converted to use as a library.

Directions: From Baltimore take I-97 south to Route 3/301. Continue south to Waldorf, make a left in Waldorf and continue on Route 5 to Leonardtown. Turn left on Courthouse Drive, and follow the signs to #41625 for the Old Jail Museum.

Patuxent River Naval Air Museum

A-Ok

Youngsters with a military bent won't have to be dragooned into taking a family outing when the destination is the **Patuxent River Naval Air Museum** in Lexington Park. It is the country's only museum devoted to research, development, testing and evaluating naval aviation.

Outside the museum are 15 planes, a sidewinder missile and an MK-82 Snakeye bomb. The Salty Dog 100, the first "J" model F4 Phantom to arrive at the Naval Air Test Center, has been returned here after logging nearly 4,300 flight hours. Another hard-working plane on display is the Grumman S-2 Tracker. These trackers are among the safest planes in the Navy, and have collectively logged more than seven million hours and made over 800,000 carrier landings with an accident rate a fraction of the overall Navy rate.

The first thing you'll see when you enter the museum is a model of the aircraft carrier escort U.S.S. *Commencement Bay*. You'll also see examples of Flight Test Instrumentation: a modular pulse code measurer, a frequency modulation system, an angle of attack indicator and a shielded total pressure instrument. Some of the larger pieces include an Askania Cine-Theodolite camera used during the 1940s to measure the motion and position of rapidly moving objects. With this tool the velocity of an aircraft could be measured and its behavior in dives and curved flights judged.

One of the roles of the Naval Air Test Center was to evaluate the feasibility of innovative and unusual aircraft. Among these experimental crafts on display are a portable helicopter and the Goodyear "rubber" Inflatoplane. A film details the testing of the helicopter and the Inflatoplane.

This free museum is open year-round. From Tuesday through Sunday hours are 10:00 A.M. to 5:00 P.M. If you visit on the first Sunday of the month, you might also want to drive through another St. Mary's County site, the **Seafarer's International Union/Harry Lundeberg School of Seamanship.** It is named for the founder and first president of the trade union for American seamen. At this training base is a small display of sailing vessels and the extensive fleet used for the U.S. Merchant Marine trainees. Visitors are welcome on the first Sunday of the month from 8:00 A.M. to 5:00 P.M.

Just down the road from Lexington Park is Great Mills, where you will find Cecil's Old Mill Arts & Crafts and the Christmas Country Store in **Cecil's General Store.** Both feature a wide variety of hand made items. You can buy homemade honey, baked goods, Christmas decorations, drawings, paintings and novelty items. Artisans display their one-of-a-kind creations, and there is often at least one working artist on hand. You can visit Friday, Saturday and Sunday from 10:00 A.M. to 5:00 P.M. from mid-March to December 24. In October, November and December the shops also open on Thursdays.

Directions: From Baltimore take I-97 south to Route 3/301. Continue south to Route 5 at Waldorf. Turn left on Route 5 and go about 40 miles to Great Mills. For the Great Mill's craft shops turn left on Route 471 and head up the road for just a short way. The stores will be across the street from each other. For the Patuxent River Naval Air Museum return to Route 5 and go south to the next intersection, Route 246, and turn left. Take Route 246 to Route 237 and turn left. Route 237 will take you to Route 235, where you will turn right. Just before the navy base (at the light with the Mister Donut) turn left on Shangri-la Drive, which will take you into the museum parking lot. You do not want to go through the base gate because the museum is enclosed by a fence and cannot be reached once you are on the base. For the Harry Lundeberg School of Seamanship turn right off Route 5 at Callaway (just north of Great Mills) onto Route 249. The entrance to the school is on the left in Piney Point.

Point Lookout State Park

Fort Lincoln and Fiddler Crabs

From a summer resort to a Civil War prison camp and then back to a recreational retreat—that is the story of **Point Lookout.**

In the early 1860s, on the southernmost tip of Maryland's western shore, there was a beach hotel, roughly 100 cottages, a large wharf and a lighthouse. The onset of the Civil War signaled the end of an era for the Point Lookout resort. The U.S. government leased it for use as an army hospital, and the first Union army patients arrived on August 17, 1862. During the winter of 1863 some Confederate prisoners were sent here, primarily southern Marylanders accused of helping the rebel cause.

After the Battle of Gettysburg, in July 1863, a prison camp was built at Point Lookout to hold 10,000 Confederate prisoners of war. By the following summer double that many were crowded into this camp. A year later, in June 1865, the last prisoners left. With a total of 52,264 Confederates imprisoned here, this was the largest prison camp of the Civil War. For a time, Point Lookout had more rebel soldiers than

General Lee had in his army.

The overcrowded conditions took their toll. Filth bred disease and the men alternately froze and baked. More than 3,500 prisoners died. One survivor wrote, "If it were not for hope how could we live in a place like this?"

One of the ironies for these Confederate prisoners was that many of their guards were former slaves. There were even masters who found their own slaves now in a position of authority over them. As one prisoner remarked, "The bottom rail's on top now."

The Union soldiers and guards who worked at the prison were stationed at Fort Lincoln, built on the banks of the Potomac River between 1864 and 1865. The fort's earthworks were reinforced by a wooden wall, and there was a guardhouse, enlisted men's barracks and two officers' quarters. Today if you walk up from the park's swimming beach along the historic trail, you can see the remains of Fort Lincoln. The earthworks are original, and part of the wooden walk and the walled entrance walk have been rebuilt. The guardhouse has been rebuilt and furnished and is open daily. The officers' quarters and the enlisted men's barracks have been rebuilt and are open daily. From the fort's southeast corner you can see a section of the prison stockade fence just 150 yards away. It too has been rebuilt, although not from chestnut trees, which were used for the original, but are no longer abundant in this area.

To get a better idea of how Fort Lincoln looked during the Civil War, stop at the Visitor Center Museum, where a complete model is displayed and audio-visual exhibits highlight prison camp life. An additional presentation points out the recreational options available at Point Lookout State Park.

The visitor center also has live specimens of animal life at the park: Eastern box turtles, black rat snakes and fiddler crabs. Check with the park naturalist or park historians about guided hikes, canoe trips, seafood cooking demonstrations, Civil War weapons demonstrations, nature craft, junior Ranger programs and special events (call 301-872-5688).

From the visitor center you can take **Periwinkle Point Nature Trail**, which winds through marshy terrain. This wet ground means that there are mosquitoes, so bring bug repellent.

Many visitors come to Point Lookout not for history but for the excellent fishing along the park's three miles of sandy beaches, where the Potomac River empties into the Chesapeake Bay. Anglers also fish from the causeway. They sit beside their cars with their poles in the bay waters. This part of St. Mary's County is considered one of the ten best fishing areas in the United States. Croakers, blues, flounder and Norfolk spot are all found here, as are crabs, oysters and soft shell clams. Boats can be rented at the park marina or you can try your luck from the shore. Many fishermen enjoy camping at the park. One hundred and forty-three campsites are available; of these, 26 sites have full hookups and an additional 29 have electric hookups.

Point Lookout State Park is open 8:00 A.M. to sunset and the visitor center is open daily from 10:00 A.M. to 6:00 P.M. from Memorial Day to Labor Day and on weekends in April, May, September and October. It is closed the rest of the year.

Directions: From I-495/95 take Route 5 south. Point Lookout is located 60 miles south of Waldorf at the southern end of Route 5.

St. Clement's Island–
Potomac River Museum

Landfall

The **St. Clement's Island-Potomac River Museum** tells the story of the settlers who came to St. Clement's Island. You will discover who the settlers were and why they left England. Mannequins and historical background will acquaint you with members of the Calvert family: Mathia DeSousa, prominent early Black Marylander; Rose Gilbert, who was widowed and left in the Maryland wilderness with her two young daughters; Father Andrew White, the Jesuit priest who established the first missions in the colony; Margaret Brent, the first woman to fight for the right to vote in the New World and Kittamaguund, the Emperor of the Piscataways. There are models of the *Ark* and the *Dove* on which Father White and the settlers sailed to the New World.

At St. Clements, Father White celebrated the first Roman Catholic Mass in the English speaking colonies. The museum explores the subject of religious toleration as opposed to religious freedom and the concept of separation of church and state. Both of these principles are part of the St. Clement's story.

The museum does not overlook the earlier inhabitants. You will learn what has happened along the Potomac since prehistoric man traversed these shores. The story of the Maryland watermen who worked and lived along the river is another story. The Potomac River Room has a scaled replica of the Island Lighthouse and Bell Tower which stood watch over the river for more than a century.

The **Little Red Schoolhouse**, part of Charlotte Hall School in 1820, has been relocated to the museum grounds. Plans are underway to make this a children's museum. There is also a country store and a gift shop.

The museum is open from late March through September on weekdays from 9:00 A.M. to 5:00 P.M. and on weekends from NOON to 5:00 P.M. From October until late March it is open Wednesday through Sunday from NOON until 4:00 P.M. An admission fee is charged; children 12 and under get in free.

The museum includes a second site, the **Piney Point Lighthouse Museum and Park**. This classic brick tower design lighthouse 14 miles upstream from the mouth of the Chesapeake Bay was built in 1836 by John Donahoo of Havre de Grace. The fixed white beacon of this lighthouse was visible for over 11 miles and was in use until 1964. The light in the tower is still active although not officially. This is one of only four surviving lighthouses on the Potomac.

When the lighthouse was built, a one-story lighthouse keeper's dwelling was constructed. Over the years the building has changed. In the 1950s a chief petty officer's cottage and garage were built. The latter now serves as the park's museum.

Museum exhibits detail the construction and operation of the lighthouse, which is known as the *Lighthouse of Presidents*, because many presidents, beginning with James Madison, spent part of their summers at Piney Point. There is also an exhibit with photographs and models on one of the "Wonder Weapons" of World War II, the German U-1105, Black Panther submarine. This was the first stealth weapon as it was coated with rubber that rendered it "invisible" to the sonar of the day. When the U.S. Navy captured it at the end of the war, they deliberately sank it off Piney Point. The submarine has been designated as Maryland's first Historic Shipwreck Diving Preserve. Experienced divers can inquire about recreational diving on the submarine, but need to keep in mind the submarine is protected by federal law.

The grounds of the six- acre park are open daily from sunrise to sunset. The museum and gift shop are open May through October on weekends from NOON to 5:00 P.M.

St. Clement's Island-Potomac River Museum hopes to resume boat service to St. Clement's Island where a large cross commemorates the Mass of thanksgiving offered by Father Andrew White. The ships had lost sight of one another during a violent storm and the settlers were thankful for their safe arrival after their rough four-month crossing. While the settlers were still on St. Clement's Island, Leonard Calvert, son of the Proprietor George Calvert, issued a proclamation formally taking possession of "Terre Mariae." Historic markers explain the events on this island during Maryland's earliest days. The island has picnic tables, barbecue grills, restrooms and two piers. Call (301) 769-2222 to get an update on the museum's plans for again providing access to the island.

Directions: From Baltimore take I-97 south Route 3/301. Continue south to Waldorf, make a left in Waldorf and continue on Route 5 through Mechanicsville (where Route 5 will turn right) to Morganza. At Morganza turn right on Route 242 and follow this to Colton's Point. Turn left onto Bayview Road and follow museum signs. For the Piney Point Lighthouse, stay on Route 5 through Leonardtown to Callaway, where you will turn right on Route 249. Take Route 249 for nine miles, then turn right on Lighthouse Road and follow that to the end.

Sotterley Plantation

Old World Feud Recalled in Spectacular Setting

A 500-year-old rivalry and a reckless roll of dice are both part of the story behind **Sotterley**, an 18th-century working plantation in Hollywood, Maryland.

The families Plater and Satterlee were English political rivals in 1471, when King Edward IV confiscated the original Sotterley Hall estate from the Satterlees and gave it to the Platers. In 1717, when later Platers established this American colonial plantation, they named it for the home their ancestors had been given. Alas, in 1822 George Plater V gambled the whole property away in a dice game. The Satterlees gained some measure of revenge for the king's theft when a descendant, Herbert Satterlee, purchased the plantation in 1910. Herbert Satterlee was the son-in-law of J.P. Morgan.

The brilliant red parlor where the notorious dice game occurred offers visitors still more drama. A narrow, hidden staircase leads from the parlor to an upstairs bedroom, otherwise accessible only by the bedroom next to it. It is easy to weave that staircase into a romantic scenario. The parlor also contains a secret compartment that was used to hide messages carried by a network of Confederate sympathizers. Although Maryland was a Union state, many southern Marylanders supported the South. During the Civil War the Briscoe family lived at Sotterley, and three of their sons served in the Confederate army.

The secret staircase may not have served romance. During the Plater residency, when plantations along the water were frequent victims of marauding pirates, the staircase may have been used for hiding. A story is told about one time when pirates did stop. The pirates chose early morning thinking the men would be at work in the fields. Unluckily for them a hunt breakfast was in progress, and the gentlemen riders routed the pirates, leaving two attackers fatally wounded. It is said the slain pirates were buried in the field at Sotterley between the house and the river.

The large drawing room has the elegance we expect from the best of the southern plantations. Indeed, it is included in Helen Comstock's "100 Most Beautiful Rooms in America." The Great Hall, as it is called, was exquisitely carved by Richard Boulton, an indentured carpenter. Architectural experts consider the shell alcoves he carved on each side of the ornate fireplace to be some of the finest work ever done for an 18th-century house.

Boulton also carved the delicate tracery of the mahogany Chinese Chippendale staircase. It is said that his indenture expired when he had only a small bit of moulding on the stairs left to be carved. To this day it is still not finished.

In the library you'll see a rare jail Agra rug. Queen Victoria ordered

Muslim prisoners—jailed because they wouldn't handle cartridges they believed to be greased with pig fat—to weave these rugs. The rugs are highly prized for their singular origin and limited number. Another rare find is the painting of George Washington floating on a cloud. His head is encircled with a halo, and the angels that surround him all bear Washington's visage.

The dining room, copied from Brighton pavilion, enchants all visitors; antique buffs especially rhapsodize over the partners' desk. Those who enjoy an actual taste of the past may want to purchase a smoked ham from Sotterley's smokehouse. Garden fanciers should stroll through the restored 18th-century garden; it is particularly attractive in the spring when the lilacs bloom.

Sotterley still has a number of dependencies, including a gate house now furnished to represent an old-fashioned schoolhouse and one remaining cabin from a row of slave cabins along the rolling road leading to Sotterley's dock. This plantation was a port of entry into the colony, and tobacco from Sotterley and nearby plantations was loaded at the wharf.

Sotterley's grounds are open year round from 10:00 A.M. to 4:00 P.M. The estate is closed on Monday. Tours of Sotterley are given daily at 11:00 A.M. and 2:00 P.M. Groups can arrange separate tours as well as breakfast or lunch on the portico. For additional information you can call (301) 373-2280 or (800) 681-0850.

Directions: From Baltimore take I-97 south to Route 3/301. Continue south to Route 5. Turn left on Route 5 at Waldorf and go 20 miles to the fork of Route 5 and Route 235. Follow Route 235 about 10 miles to Hollywood and make a left turn onto Route 245. Take Route 245 three miles to Sotterley.

Calendar of Events

JANUARY

Mid:

Baltimore on Ice Winterfest, Multiple Downtown Locations, (410) 837-4635, (800) 282-6632

Winter/Spring Display, Brookside Gardens Conservatory, (301) 949-8230

Late:

Civil War Living History, Historic Frederick, National Museum of Civil War Medicine, (301) 695-1864

Chesapeake Bay Boat Show, Baltimore Convention Center, (212) 984-7018

FEBRUARY

Early:

Civil War Living History, Historic Frederick, National Museum of Civil War Medicine, (301) 695-1864

Antique Valentine Display, Surratt House Museum, (301) 868-1121

Mid:

Cabin Fever Weekend, Grantsville, Spruce Forest Artisan Village, (301) 895-3332

Seaside Boat Show, Ocean City Convention Center, (410) 641-6301

Late:

Maryland Recreational Vehicle Show, Timonium, Maryland State Fairgrounds, (410) 687-7200

The Outdoorsman Fishing & Hunting Show, Westminster, Carroll County Agricultural Center, (410) 922-5549, (410) 655-8469

Cabin Fever Day, Wheaton, National Capital Trolley Museum, (301) 384-6088

MARCH

Early:

Maryland Home and Flower Show, Timonium, Maryland State Fairgrounds, (410) 863-1180

Civil War Living History, Historic Frederick, National Museum of Civil War Medicine, (301) 695-1864

Spring Bear and Doll Show & Sale, Savage, (301) 498-6871

Mid:

St. Patrick's Day Bash with the 1844 Committee of the Maryland
Historical Society, Baltimore, (410) 685-3750
Elkton Salutes St. Patrick, Elkton, (410) 398-1528
St. Patrick's Day Parade and Festival, Ocean City, (410) 289-6156,
(410) 289-2800
Baltimore Saint Patrick's Parade, Washington Monument-Market Place,
(410) 837-0685
Maple Syrup—From Sap to Syrup, Oakland, Swallow Falls State Park,
(301) 334-9180
Maple Syrup Demonstration and Mountain Heritage Festival, Thurmont,
Cunningham Falls State Park, William Houck area, (301) 271-7574
Turning Sap to Syrup and All-You-Can-Eat Pancake Breakfast, Oakland,
Herrington Manor State Park, (301) 334-9180

Late:

Artists of the Chesapeake, Centreville, (410) 758-2520
Civil War Living History, Historic Frederick, National Museum of Civil
War Medicine, (301) 695-1864
Maryland Department of Agriculture Open House, Annapolis, (410) 841-5882
Maryland Days, Historic St. Mary's City, (800) 762-1634, (301) 862-0990

APRIL

Early:

Maryland Archeology Month, Statewide, (410) 514-7661
Sugarloaf's Annual Spring Gaithersburg Crafts Festival, Montgomery
County Fairgrounds, (301) 990-1400, (800) 210-9900
Carroll County Easter Farmers Market, Westminster, Agriculture Center,
(410) 848-7748
Bay Country Annual Boat Show, Hollywood, (301) 373-5468
Carroll Carvers Annual Festival of Carving, Westminster, Carroll County
Agriculture Center, (301) 854-0067
Children's Museum Opening Weekend, Frederick, Rose Hill Manor
Children's Museum, (301) 694-1650
Fruhlings Fest, Frederick, Schifferstadt Architectural Museum, (301) 663-3885
Hearthside Sampler, Frederick's Museums, (301) 663-8687
Savage Mill Woodworking Show, Savage, (301) 490-0187
Hayride in Bunnyland, Germantown, Butler's Orchard, (301) 972-3299

Mid:

Easter Egg Hunt, Marbury, Smallwood State Park, (301) 888-1410,
(800) 784-5380
Easter Egg Hunt, North East, Elk Neck State Park, (410) 287-5333
Easter Egg Hunt, Oakland, Herrington Manor State Park, (301) 334-9180
Prehistoric Egg Hunt, Lusby, Calvert Cliffs State Park, (301) 872-5688
Tuckahoe Easter Egg Hunt, Ridgely, Tuckahoe State Park, (410) 820-1668
My Lady's Manor Steeplechase Races and Champagne Reception,
Monkton, Ladew Topiary Gardens, (410) 557-9466
John Wilkes Booth Escape Route Tour, Clinton, Surratt House Museum,
(301) 868-1121

Sunrise Service, Scotland, Point Lookout State Park, (301) 872-5688
Welcome the Skipjacks Bull & Oyster Roast, Havre de Grace, Hutchins Park, (800) 406-0766
Estuarine Research Center Earth Day Family Open House, St. Leonard, The Academy of Natural Sciences, (410) 586-9700, (410) 586-9722
Spring Walk on 18th-Century Farm, Elkton, Sinking Springs Herb Farm, (410) 398-5566
Upper Chesapeake Bay Skipjack Invitational Races & Earth Day Festival, Havre de Grace, Concord Point Lighthouse, (800) 406-0766
Gardenfest, Solomons, Annmarie Garden, (410) 326-4640
Marching Through Time, Glenn Dale, Marietta House Museum Grounds, (301) 464-5291
Museum Open House, Clinton, Surratt House Museum, (301) 868-1121
Solomons Spring Launch, Island-wide, (410) 326-2020
Calvacade of Street Cars, Wheaton, National Capital Trolley Museum, (301) 384-6088
Muzzleloader Shoot, Big Pool, Fort Frederick State Park, (301) 841-2155

Late:
Towson Gardens Day, Courthouse Fountain Plaza, (410) 825-2211
18th-Century Market Fair and Rifle Frolic, Big Pool, Fort Frederick State Park, (301) 842-2155
Maryland International Kite Festival, Ocean City Beach, (410) 289-7855, (410) 289-2800
Sugarloaf's Annual Spring Timonium Crafts Festival, Timonium, Maryland State Fairgrounds, (301) 990-1400
Ward World Championship Wildfowl Carving Competition, Ocean City, Convention Center, (410) 742-4988, x106, (410) 289-2800
Springtime at the Mill, Ellicott City, (410) 795-2021
Celtic Festival of Southern Maryland, St. Leonard, Jefferson Patterson Park and Museum, (410) 257-9003, (410) 267-9394
Nanticoke River Canoe and Kayak Race, Nanticoke River, (410) 543-1244
Nanticoke River Shad Festival, Vienna, Town Square, (410) 873-2102
Oxford Day, Town-wide, (410) 226-5730
Delmarva Birding Weekend, Eastern Shore Locations, (800) 852-0335
Farm and Family Festival, Frederick, Rose Hill Manor Park, (301) 694-1650, (301) 694-1648
Queen Anne's Historic Sites, County-wide, (410) 827-4810
Martinak Spring Fest, Denton, Martinak State Park, (410) 820-1668
Old Bowie Antique & Craft Spring Fling, Bowie, (301) 262-3743

MAY

Early:
May Flower Mart, Chestertown, Fountain Park, (410) 778-0453
Baltimore Museum Antiques Show, Baltimore Museum of Art, (410) 396-6314
Decoy, Wildlife Art & Sportsman Festival, Havre de Grace, Decoy Museum, (410) 939-3739
Landon Azalea Garden Festival, Bethesda, Landon School Grounds, (301) 320-3200 x1066

Salisbury Dogwood Festival, Riverwalk Park, (410) 749-0144

Spring Upper Marlboro Antiques Show, Marlboro Tobacco Market, (301) 888-9123, (301) 888-9429

Herb Market Thyme on Historic Farm, Elkton, Sinking Springs Herb Farm, (410) 398-5566

Patuxent Family Discovery Day, Solomons, Calvert Marine Museum, (410) 326-2042

Spocott Windmill Day, Lloyds, Spocott Windmill, (410) 228-7090

Spring Festival, Brandywine, Cedarville State Forest, (301) 888-1410, (800) 784-5380

Flower and Plant Market, Union Mills, Union Mills Homestead, (410) 848-2288

Janes Island State Park Native American Indian Festival and Pow Wow, Crisfield, Janes Island State Park, (410) 623-2660

Smallwood's Relief—Marylanders in the Revolution, Marbury, Smallwood State Park, (301) 888-1410

Whitbread Chesapeake Celebration, Annapolis, Sandy Point State Park, (410) 260-8710

Summer Display, Wheaton, Brookside Gardens Conservatory, (301) 949-8230

Bridge Walk Rendevous, Stevensville, Chesapeake Bay Business Park, (410) 643-8530

Civil War Encampment at Steppingstone Museum, Havre de Grace, Susquehanna State Park, (410) 939-2299

Great Chefs and Champagne, Hydes, Boordy Vineyards, (410) 592-5015

May Fair at Woodend, Chevy Chase, Woodend, (301) 652-9188

Montpelier Spring Festival, Laurel, Montpelier Mansion Grounds, (301) 776-2805

Springfest Boat Show, Ocean City, Shantytown Village, (410) 213-1121, (410) 289-2800

Preakness Celebration, Baltimore Area, (410) 837-3030

Art Blooms in Maryland, Annapolis, Government House, (410) 974-3531

Cylburn Market Day, Baltimore, Cylburn Arboretum, (410) 367-2217

Herb Festival, Sykesville, Piney Run Park Grounds, (410) 795-3274

Ladew Plant Sale, Monkton, Ladew Topiary Gardens, (410) 557-9466

Laurel Main Street Festival, Laurel, (301) 483-0838

Marlboro Day Festival, Upper Marlboro Main Streets, (301) 627-2828

Mid:

William Paca Gardens Spring Plant Sale, Annapolis, William Paca Gardens, (410) 267-6656

Preakness Crab Derby, Baltimore, Lexington Market, (410) 685-6169

Mid-Atlantic Maritime Festival, St. Michaels, Chesapeake Bay Maritime Museum, (410) 820-8606, (410) 745-2916

Colonial Highland Gathering and Scottish Games, Elkton, Fair Hill Race Track, (302) 453-8998

Kent Island Days, Stevensville, Historic Cray House, (410) 827-4810, (410) 643-5969

Spring Festival, Derwood, Agricultural History Farm Park, (301) 924-4141

C&C Canal Fest, Cumberland, Canal Place, (301) 724-3655

Cambridge Watersports Show, Cambridge, Sailwinds, (410) 228-3092

Days in May Festival, Ocean Pines, White Horse Park, (410) 641-5306

Department of Defense Joint Services Open House, Camp Springs, Andrews Air Force Base, (301) 568-5995

Rose Hill Days Festival, Frederick, Rose Hill Manor Children's Museum, (301) 694-1648, (301) 694-1650

Wine in the Woods, Columbia, Merriweather Post at Symphony Woods, (410) 313-7275

Antique Vehicle Run, Chesapeake Beach, Cheasapeake Beach Railway Museum (410) 257-3892, (301) 855-6472

Bowie Heritage Day, Bowie, Belair Mansion/Stables & Huntington Railroad Museum, (301) 805-5029

International Museum Day, Solomons, Calvert Marine Museum, (410) 326-2042

Living American Flag Program, Baltimore, Fort McHenry National Monument, (410) 563-3524

Late:

African-American Community Day, St. Leonard, Jefferson Patterson Park and Museum, (410) 535-2730

Baltimore Herb Festival, Leakin Park, (410) 448-0406

Sharpsburg's Memorial Day Parade, Town Square, (301) 432-8410

Civil War Living History, Historic Frederick, National Museum of Civil War Medicine, (301) 695-1864

Waterside Music Series, Solomons, Calvert Marine Museum (410) 326-2042

Beyond the Garden Gates, Frederick Gardens, (800) 999-3613, (301) 694-2489

Chestertown Tea Party Festival, Chestertown Historic District, (410) 778-0416

French and Indian War Rendevous, Big Pool, Fort Frederick State Park, (301) 842-2155

Strawberry Wine Festival, New Market, (410) 795-6432, (301) 831-5889

The Planting Season, Historic St. Mary's City, (800) 762-1634, (301) 862-0990

Memorial Day Weekend, Berlin, (410) 641-4775

Southern Maryland Quilt and Needlework Show, Hollywood, Historic Sotterley Plantation, (301) 373-2280, (800) 681-0850

Memorial Day Street Fest, Elkton, (410) 398-4999

Harborplace & The Gallery Summer Series, Baltimore, Harborplace Amphitheatre, (800) HARBOR-1

Bob Litzenberg Hunting Decoy Show, North East, Upper Bay Museum, (410) 287-2675

JUNE

Early:

Country Heritage Festival, Leonardstown, St. Mary's County Fairgrounds, (301) 884-3024

Fine Wine Time, Hunt Valley, Oregon Ridge Park, (410) 296-2272, x5221

Frederick Festival of the Arts, Frederick, Carroll Creek Linear Park, (301) 694-9632

Strawberry Festival, Thurmont, Cozy Village, (301) 271-7373, (301) 271-4301

Children's Day on the Farm, St. Leonard, Jefferson Patterson Park and Museum, (410) 586-8501

Civil War Living History, Historic Frederick, National Museum of Civil
War Medicine, (301) 695-1864
Queen Anne's County Waterman's Festival, Grasonville, Kent Narrows,
(410) 827-4810, (410) 643-5536
Scottish Festival, Havre de Grace, Susquehanna State Park Museum,
(410) 939-2299

Mid:
St. Nicholas Greek Folk Festival, Baltimore, St. Nicholas Church on
Ponca Street, (410) 633-7700, (410) 633-5020
Confederate POW Commemoration, Scotland, Point Lookout State Park,
(757) 427-5065
USNA Flag Day, Annapolis, U.S. Naval Academy, (410) 263-6933
Heritage Days Festival, Cumberland, (301) 777-2787
National Pause for the Pledge of Allegiance, Baltimore, Fort McHenry
National Monument, (410) 563-3524
North Bay Deer Creek Fiddlers' Convention, Westminster, Carroll County
Farm Museum, (410) 876-2667
Cypress Festival, Pocomoke City, Cypress Park, (410) 957-1919

Late:
Maryland Arts Festival, Towson, Towson University Fine Arts Center,
(410) 830-ARTS
Blue and Gray Days, Scotland, Point Lookout State Park, (301) 872-5688
Civil War Encampment/Lifestyles, Westminster, Carroll County Farm
Museum, (410) 876-2667
Maritime Festival of the Harvre de Grace Maritime Museum, Havre de
Grace, (410) 939-4800, (410) 734-6357
Midsummer Village Faire at St. Mary's City, Historic St. Mary's City, (800)
762-1634, (301) 862-0990
Susquehanna Wine Festival, Havre de Grace, Susquehanna State Park
Museum, (410) 939-2299
Cylburn Solstice Celebration, Baltimore, Cylburn Arboretum, (410) 367-2217
Grantsville Days, Grantsville Park, (301) 334-1948
Mid-Atlantic Wine Festival, Crownsville, Anne Arundel County
Fairgrounds, (410) 280-3306
Rose Hill Manor Quilt Show, Frederick, Rose Hill Manor Park, (301)
694-1650
Montpelier Summer Concert Series, Laurel, Montpelier Mansion
Grounds, (301) 776-2805
Civil War Living History, Historic Frederick, National Museum of Civil
War Medicine, (301) 695-1864
Tilghman Island Seafood Festival, Tilghman Island, (410) 886-2677
American Indian Inter-Tribal Cultural Organization PowWow, Frederick
County Fairgrounds, (301) 869-9381

JULY

Early:
Havre de Grace Independence Celebration, Havre de Grace, Tydings
Park, (410) 939-4362

Bay Country Festival, Cambridge, Sailwinds Park, (410) 228-7762
Harborplace Birthday Celebration, Baltimore, Harborplace
  Amphitheatre, (800) HARBOR-1
Rock Hall Fireworks and 4th of July Celebration, Rock Hall Harbor, (410)
  778-0146
Family Day on the Day, Chesapeake Beach, Rod 'N' Reel Restaurant,
  (301) 855-8351 (410) 257-2735
Accident's Fourth of July Homecoming, Accident, (301) 746-6346
Baltimore's Fourth of July Celebration, Baltimore, Inner Harbor
  Amphitheatre, (410) 837-4636, (800) 282-6632
Bowie 4th of July Celebration, Bowie, Allan Pond Park, (301) 262-6200,
  x3068
Chestertown Fireworks, Chest River Waterfront, (410) 778-0500
Fourth of July Fireworks Jubilee, Ocean City Beach/Boardwalk, (410) 250-0125
Old-Fashioned July 4th, Westminster, Carroll County Farm Museum,
  (410) 876-2667
Sassafras Boat Parade, Galena, Sasafras River, (410) 648-5510,
  (410) 778-0416
Solomons July 4th Celebration, Solomons Island-wide, (410) 326-4251
The World's Greatest Crab Feast, Music Festival & Fireworks, Baltimore,
  Scarlet Place-Inner Harbor, (410) 484-5600

Mid:
Ice Cream Festival, Baltimore, Lexington Market, (410) 685-6169
Summerfest and Quilt Show, Grantsville, Spruce Forest Artisan Village,
  (301) 895-3332
Tuckahoe Steam and Gas Show, Easton, Tuckahoe Showgrounds,
  (410) 822-9868
*John Paul Jones Da*y, Annapolis, U.S. Naval Academy, (410) 263-6933
Children's Games Day, Havre de Grace, Susquehanna State Park
  Museum, (410) 939-2299
Fiddler's and Banjo Contest, Friendship, Town Park (301) 746-8194
Calvert County Farm Tour & Produce Sale, County-wide, (800) 331-9771

Late:
Allegany County Fair and Agricultural Expo, Cumberland, Allegany
  County Fairgrounds, (301) 777-0911
Greek Festival, Ocean City, Convention Center, (410) 524-0990,
  (410) 289-2800
Military Field Days, Big Pool, Fort Frederick State Park, (301) 842-2155
Tidewater Archaeology Dig, Historic St. Mary's City, (800) 762-1634,
  (301) 862-0990

AUGUST

Early:
Old-Fashioned Corn Roast Festival, Union Mills, Union Mills
  Homestead, (410) 848-2288
Pine'eer Arts and Craft Festival, Berlin, White Horse Park in Ocean
  Pines, (410) 208-6833
Crab Days, St. Michaels, Chesapeake Bay Maritime Museum, (410) 745-2916

Jonathan Hager Frontier Craft Days, Hagerstown, Jonathan Hager House & Museum, (301) 739-8383

Thunder on the Narrows, Kent Narrows, Kent Island Yacht Club, (410) 827-8210

Wings of Fancy-Butterfly Show, Wheaton, Brookside Gardens South Conservatory, (301) 949-8230

Hunting and Fishing Show, Frederick, Frederick County Fairgrounds, (301) 865-3019

Worcester County Fair, Snow Hill, Furnace Town Historic Site, (410) 632-1972

Carroll County Farmers Market Peach Festival, Westminster, Agriculture Center, (410) 848-7748

Dorchester Chamber Seafood Feast-i-val, Cambridge, Sailwinds Park, (410) 228-3575

Maritime Maryland, Annapolis, U.S. Naval Academy, (410) 263-6933

Butler's Orchard Peach Festival, Germantown, Butler's Orchard, (301) 972-3299

Kunta Kinte Heritage Festival, Annapolis, St. John's College, (410) 349-0338

Peach Festival, Thurmont, Cozy Village, (301) 371-7373, (301) 271-4301

Howard County Fair, West Friendship, Howard County Fairgrounds, (410) 442-1022

Garrett County Agriculture Fair, McHenry, Garrett County Fairgrounds, (301) 334-4715, x321, (301) 245-4224

Mid:

Bay Breeze Summer Concert, Chesapeake Beach, Chesapeake Beach Railway Museum (410) 257-3892

Augustoberfest, Hagerstown, Downtown, (301) 739-8577, x116

Caroline Summerfest, Denton, Courthouse area, (410) 479-3721

Crab Fest & Seafood Festival Parade, Port Deposit, Marina Park, (410) 378-5786

Havre de Grace Art Show, Tydings Memorial Park, (410) 939-9342

Antique Car Show & Summer Social, Frederick, Rose Hill Manor Park, (301) 694-1648, (301) 694-1650

Late:

Balloon Fest, Frederick, Husky Park & Frederick Municipal Airport, (301) 694-1100

Montgomery County Agricultural Fair, Gaithersburg, Montgomery County Fairgrounds, (301) 926-3100

Celebrate Taneytown Festival, Taneytown, Memorial Park, (410) 751-1100

Country Fest and Auction, McHenry, Garrett County Fairgrounds, (301) 746-8429, (301) 895-3268

North Beach Bayfest, North Beach Waterfront, (301) 855-6681, (410) 257-9618

National Hard Crab Derby and Fair, Crisfield, Somers Cove Marina, (410) 968-2500

Calvert County Jousting Tournament, Port Republic, Christ Church, (410) 535-1710

Maryland State Fair, Timonium, State Fairgrounds, (410) 252-0200, x226

Maryland Renaissance Festival, Annapolis, Crownsville Road, (410) 266-7304, (410) 573-1508

SEPTEMBER

Early:

Maryland Coast Day, Berlin, Assateague State Park, (410) 629-1538
Labor Day Weekend, Chesapeake Beach, Rod "n" Reel Restaurant, (410) 257-2735
Apple Butter Boil, Oakland, Herrington Manor & Swallow Falls State Parks, (301) 334-9180
Solomons Arts & Crafts Festival, Solomons, Calvert Marine Museum Park, (410) 326-3848, (410) 326-3166
Working Hands, Historic St. Mary's City, (800) 762-1634, (310) 862-0990
Grand Parade, Frederick, Market Street, (301) 694-1100

Mid:

Steam Show Days, Westminster, Carroll County Farm Museum, (410) 876-2667
Tuckahoe Championship Rodeo, Easton, Tuckahoe Showgrounds, (410) 822-9868
Art in the Park, Chestertown, Fountain Park, (410) 778-5789, (410) 348-2280
City of Bowie ARTS EXPO, Bowie, Allen Pond Park, (301) 262-6200, x-3068
Exotic and Native Plant Sale, Baltimore, Cylburn Arboretum, (410) 367-2217
Smallwood Festival, Westminster, Reese Carnival Grounds, (410) 848-8254
Traditional Boat Festival, St. Michaels, Chesapeake Bay Maritime Museum, (410) 745-2916
Boonesborough Days, Boonsboro, Shafer Park, (301) 432-5889
Canal Apple Festival, Hancock, Widmeyer Park, (301) 678-5325, (301) 678-6555
Duck Fair, Havre de Grace, Decoy Museum, (410) 939-3739
Fells Point Art and Craft Show, Baltimore, Living Classrooms Maritime Institute, (410) 239-9467
Milburn's Craft Show, Elkton, Milburn Orchards, (410) 398-1349
Travel Back in Time (A Civil War Camp Out), Scotland, Point Lookout State Park, (301) 872-5688
Tuckahoe Outlaw Days, Denton, Tuckahoe Equestrian Center, State Park, (410) 479-1183
William Paca Garden Fall Plant Sale, Annapolis, William Pace House & Garden, (410) 267-6656
John Wilkes Booth Escape Route Tour, Clinton, Surratt House Museum, (301) 868-1121
Shaker Forest Festival, Gaithersburg, Seneca Creek State Park, (412) 643-6626, (412) 847-4303
African-American Heritage Festival, Berlin, Stephen Decatur Park, (410) 641-3255
Children's Day at Ladew Topiary Gardens, Monkton, (410) 557-9466
Honey Harvest Festival, Westminster, Hashawha Environmental Center, (410) 848-9040
Septemberfest, Havre de Grace, Downtown, (410) 939-3303
Anne Arundel County Fair, Crownsville, County Fairgrounds, (410) 923-3400
Charles County Fair, LaPlata, Fairgrounds, (301) 932-1234, (301) 932-1300
Sharpsburg Heritage Festival, Sharpsburg, Antietam National Battlefield, (800) 228-STAY

The Maryland Steam Show, Arcadia, Carnival Grounds, (410) 239-6949, (410) 239-7447
Chestertown Jazz Festival, Wilmer Park, (410) 348-5528
Candlelight Walking Tour of Chestertown, Historic District, (410) 778-3499
Fall Festival, Historic Elkton, (410) 392-2743
Fall Harvest Day, Marriottsville, Patapsco Valley State Park, (410) 922-3044
Lake Elkhorn Festival, Columbia, Lake Elkhorn Park, (410) 381-0202
Port Deposit Heritage Day, Main Street, (410) 378-2121

Late:
A Taste of Fall Fest, Cumberland, Allegany County Fairgrounds, (301) 729-3321, (301) 729-1522
Maryland State Surfing Championship, Ocean City Beach, (410) 213-0515, (410) 289-2800
Maryland Wine Festival, Westminster, Carroll County Farm Museum, (410) 876-2667
The Chesapeake Airshow, Middle River, Martin State Airport, (410) 686-2233
The Navy Way Days, Annapolis, U.S. Naval Academy, (410) 263-6933
Herb Harvest Swreath and Swag Workshop, Elkton, Sinking Springs Herb Farm, (410) 398-5566
Sunfest Kite Festival, Ocean City, Kite Loft, (410) 289-7855, (410) 289-2800
Westminster Fallfest, City Park, (410) 848-9000
Burtonsville Days Celebration, Columbia Park, (301) 421-4888
Eastern Shore Hunting & Fishing Expo, Ocean City, Convention Center, (410) 798-6304, (410) 289-2800
Children's Day, Wheaton, McCrillis Gardens and Gallery, Brookside Gardens, (301) 949-8230
The Season of Antietam, Frederick, Historic Downtown District, (301) 695-1864
Fall Harvest Festival and Craft Show, Havre de Grace, Susquehanna State Park Museum (410) 939-2299
Governor's Invitational Firelock Match, Big Pool, Fort Frederick State Park, (301) 842-2155
Johnny Appleseed Festival, Elkton, Milburn Orchards, (410) 398-1349
Eastern Shore Fall Festival Championship Jousting Tournament, Ridgely, Tuckahoe State Park, (410) 482-2176
Old Bowie Antique & Craft Fall Fling Street Fest, Old Bowie, (301) 262-2430, (301) 262-3743
Calvert County Fair, Prince Frederick, Fairgrounds, (410) 535-0026

OCTOBER

Early:
Maryland Railfest, Cumberland, Western Maryland Station, (800) TRAIN-50
Hallowscream at Adventure World, Largo, (301) 249-1500
Art Show, Wheaton, Brookside Gardens Conservatory, (301) 949-8230
Chesapeake Celtic Festival, Snow Hill, Furnace Town Historic Site, (410) 632-2032
Mid-Atlantic Small Craft Festival, St. Michaels, Chesapeake Bay Maritime Museum, (410) 745-2916

Blessing of the Fleet, Colton's Point, St. Clement's Island-Potomac River Museum (301) 769-2222, (301) 872-5688

Brunswick Railroad Days, Brunswick, Brunswick Railroad Museum, (301) 834-7100

Fall Color Hayrides, Oakland, Herrington Manor State Park, (301) 334-9180

Fall Craft Show, Crownsville, Anne Arundel County Fairgrounds, (410) 255-5632

Fall Festival, Frederick, Rose Hill Manor Park, (301) 694-1648

Fall Harvest Days, Westminster, Carroll County Farm Museum, (410) 876-2667, (800) 654-4645

Fell's Point Fun Festival, Baltimore, Fell's Point Waterfront, (410) 675-6756

Milburn's Craft Show, Elkton, Milburn Orchards, (410) 398-1349

Mt. Airy Fall Festival, Mount Airy, Main Street, (301) 829-2112

Woodland Indian Culture Days, Historic St. Mary's City, (800) 762-1634, (301) 862-0990

Butler's Orchard Pumpkin Festival, Germantown, Butler's Orchard, (301) 972-3299

Berlin Fall Festival, Stephen Decatur Park, (410) 641-1064, (410) 641-0862

Autumn Glory Festival, Oakland, Townwide, (301) 334-1948

Mid:

Sugarloaf's Fall Timonium Crafts Festival, Timonium, Maryland State Fairgrounds, (301) 990-1400, (800) 210-9900

Cylburn Festifall, Baltimore, Cylburn Arboretum, (410) 367-2217

Germantown Oktoberfest, Germantown, (301) 217-6798

Greeting of the Geese, Upper Marlboro, Merkle Wildlife Sanctuary, (301) 888-1410, (800) 784-5380

Riverfest, Laurel, Riverfront Park, (301) 483-0838

All American Soap Box Derby Rally Race, Leonardtown, Derby Hill, (301) 475-9791

Blacksmith Days, Westminster, Carroll County Farm Museum, (410) 876-2667

Catoctin Colorfest, Thurmont, Community Park, (301) 271-4432

Charles County Wine Festival, LaPlata, Fairgrounds, (301) 645-0558, (800) 766-3386

Columbus Center Celebrates the Spirit of Exploration, Baltimore, (410) 576-5700

German Fest, Thurmont, Cozy Village, (301) 271-7373, (301) 271-4301

Grand Militia Muster, Historic St. Mary's City, (800) 762-1634, (301) 862-0990

Hastings Fair, Glenn Dale, Marietta House Museum Grounds, (301) 464-5291

Olde Princess Anne Days, Princess Anne, Teackle Mansion & Area, (800) 521-9189

Patuxent River Appreciation Days Festival, Solomons, Calvert Marine Museum Grounds, (410) 326-2042

Victorian Mums Show-Fall Display, Wheaton, Brookside Gardens, (301) 949-8230

Family Toon Day, North Bethesda, Strathmore Hall Arts Center, (301) 530-0540

Chocolate Festival, Baltimore, Lexington Market, (410) 685-6169

Fall Maryland Home & Garden Show and Maryland Holiday Craft Show, Timonium, State Fairgrounds, (410) 863-1180

Blessing of Baltimore's Work Boats, Harborplace Amphitheatre, (800) HARBOR-1

Martinak Fall Fest, Denton, Martinak State Park, (410) 820-1668
Tilghman Island Day, Tilghman Island, (410) 886-2677
Oktoberfest at Schifferstadt, Frederick, (301) 663-3885
St. Mary's County Oyster Festival, Leonardtown, Fairgrounds, (301) 863-5015
Trolley Museum Fall Open House, Wheaton, National Capital Trolley
    Museum, (301) 384-6088

Late:
Chestertown Wildlife Exhibition and Sale, Chestertown Historic Area,
    (410) 778-0416
Haunted House, North East, Elk Neck State Park, (410) 287-5333
Point Lookout Ghost Walk, Scotland, Point Lookout State Park,
    (301) 872-5688
Fall Into St. Michaels, Townwide, (410) 745-2200, (800) 660-9471
The Ship of Ghouls, Baltimore, Harborplace Amphitheatre, (800) HARBOR-1
Autumn Walk at Leaf Thyme, Elkton, Sinking Springs Herb Farm,
    (410) 398-5566
Gunpowder Falls State Park Harvest Hoedown, Chase, Hammerman
    Area, (410) 592-2897
Haunts of Smallwood, Marbury, Smallwood State Park, (301) 888-1410,
    (800) 784-5380
Ghost Walk, Big Pool, Fort Frederick State Park, (301) 842-2155
Alsatia Mummers' Parade, Hagerstown, (301) 733-0033, (301) 739-2944
Halloween Hayrides, Oakland, Herrington Manor State Park, (301) 334-9180

NOVEMBER

Early:
Christmas at the Mill, Ellicott City, (410) 795-2021
Annapolis by Candlelight, Historic District, (410) 267-7619
Christmas Wonderland, West Friendship, Howard County Fairgrounds,
    (301) 791-2346
Lighthouse Open House, Scotland, Point Lookout State Park, (301) 972-5688
OysterFest, St. Michaels, Chesapeake Bay Maritime Museum (410) 745-2916
Art Festival, Annapolis, Quiet Waters Park, (410) 268-0474
Muzzleloader Shoot, Big Pool, Fort Frederick State Park, (301) 842-2155

Mid:
Winterfest of Lights, Ocean City, Townwide, (410) 250-0125, (410) 289-2800
Savage Mill Holiday Open House Weekend, Savage, (800) 788-MILL
Waterfowl Festival, Easton, Townwide, (410) 822-4567
Museum Open House, Clinton, Surratt House Museum (301) 868-1121
Potters Guild of Baltimore's Holiday Show, Baltimore, Meadow Mill,
    (410) 235-4884
Sugarloaf's Fall Gaithersburg Crafts Festival, Montgomery County
    Fairgrounds, (301) 990-1400, (800) 210-9900

Late:
Fantasy of Lights, Fort Howard Park, (410) 887-3873
Lights on the Bay, Annapolis, Sandy Point State Park, (410) 260-3161

Symphony of Lights, Columbia, Merriweather Post Pavilion, (410) 740-7666, (410) 740-7645

Giving Thanks, Hearth and Home in Early Maryland, Historic St. Mary's City, (800) 762-1634, (301) 862-0990

Day Basket Factory Open House, North East, (410) 287-6100, (800) 382-3105

Kristkindelsmarkt (A Holiday Festival), Frederick, Schifferstadt Architectural Museum (301) 663-3885

Maryland Christmas Show, Frederick, County Fairgrounds, (301) 898-5466

A Solomons Christmas, Calvert, Solomons Island, (800) 953-3300, (410) 326-6027

Garden of Lights, Wheaton, Brookside Gardens Conservatory, (301) 949-8230

Victorian Christmas at History House, Cumberland, (301) 777-8678

Victorian Christmas, Historic Berlin, (410) 641-4775

Brightest Beacon on the Bay-Lighting Ceremony, Chesapeake Beach, Town Hall, (410) 257-2230

DECEMBER

Early:

Winter Lights, Gaithersburg, Seneca Creek State Park, (301) 258-6310

Madrigals and Carols, Historic St. Mary's City, (800) 762-1634, (301) 862-0990

Symphony Homes for the Holidays, Baltimore, (410) 783-8023

Festival of Lights, Kensington, Washington Temple Visitor's Center, (301) 587-0144

Lighted Boat Parade, Baltimore, Harborplace Amphitheatre, (800) HARBOR-1

Candlelight Tour of Belair Mansion, Bowie, (301) 805-5029

Christmas in the Village, Grantsville, Spruce Forest Artisan Village, (301) 895-3332

State House by Candlelight, Annapolis, Maryland State House, (410) 974-3400

18th-Century Country Christmas, Elkton, Sinking Springs Herb Farm, (410) 398-5566

Holiday House & Yacht Tour, Annapolis & Eastport, (410) 280-0445

Holiday Magic, Frederick, Rose Hill Manor Park, (301) 694-1650

Antietam National Battlefield Memorial Illumination, Sharpsburg, (301) 733-7373

Westminister Holiday House Tour, (410) 848-7967

Wild X-Mas at Merkel, Upper Marlboro, Merkle Wildlife Sanctuary, (301) 888-1410, (800) 784-5380

Candlelight House Tour, Frederick, (800) 999-3613, (301) 694-2489

Dickens' Christmas Weekend, North East, Main Street, (410) 287-2658

Olde Fashioned Christmas Celebration, Hollywood, Historic Sotterley Plantation, (301) 373-2280, (800) 681-0850

Holiday Tour, Westminster, Carroll County Farm Museum, (410) 876-2667, (800) 654-4645

Drum Point Lighthouse Seasonal Tours, Solomons, Calvert Marine Museum, (410) 326-2042

Holly Trolleyfest, Wheaton, National Capital Trolley Museum, (301) 384-6088

Plantation Christmas, Historic St. Mary's City, (800) 762-1634, (301) 862-0990

Candlelight Pub Crawl, Annapolis, Governor Calvert House, (410) 263-5401

Waverly Candlelight Tour, Marriotsville, Waverly Mansion, (410) 313-5400, (301) 596-6542

Holiday Display, Wheaton, Brookside Conservatory, (301) 949-8230

Mid:

Christmas at Ladew, Monkton, Ladew Topiary Gardens, (410) 557-9466

Solomons Christmas Walk, Solomons Island, (410) 394-3029, (410) 326-2042

Sugarloaf Winter Gaithersburg Crafts Festival, Montgomery County Fairgrounds, (301) 990-1400, (800) 210-9900

Garden in Lights, Solomons, Annmarie Garden, (410) 326-4640

Eastport Yacht Club's Lights Parade, Annapolis Waterfront, (410) 263-0415

Holiday Happening, Frederick, Rose Hill Manor Park, (301) 694-1650

Museums by Candlelight, Frederick's Museums, (301) 663-8687

Christmas in St. Michaels, Town-wide, (410) 820-4865

Poinsettia and Greens Sale and Open House, Union Mills, Union Mills Homestead, (410) 848-2288

Santa's Magic Workshop, Denton, Martinak State Park Nature Center, (410) 820-1668

Victorian Yuletide by Candlelight, Clinton, Surratt House Museum, (301) 868-1121

Colonial Christmas at Smallwood, Marbury, Smallwood State Park, (301) 888-1410, (800) 784-5380

The Governor's Holiday Open House, Annapolis, State Circle, (410) 974-3531

Late:

Candlelight Tour of Historic Houses of Worship, Frederick, (301) 663-8687, (800) 999-1613

William Paca House Holiday Event, Annapolis, (410) 263-5553

Baltimore's New Year's Eve Extravaganza, Baltimore Convention Center & Harborplace Amphitheatre, (410) 837-4636

First Night Annapolis, Historic District, (410) 280-0700

Index

About the Author

Jane Ockershausen, born in Richmond, bred in Maryland and now living in Pittsburgh, has been writing about the Eastern seaboard states for more than two decades. She recently revisited Maryland's myriad attractions in order to update this book, one of ten in her best-selling series of One-Day Trip Books for the Mid-Atlantic region.

Always focused on the ever-popular weekend travel market, she has been a correspondent for *The National Geographic Traveler*, and her byline has appeared in *The Washington Post, The Chicago Tribune, Mid-Atlantic Weekends Magazine* and elsewhere. She has addressed numerous statewide conferences on travel and journalism and lectured at the Smithsonian Institution in Washington.

Jane is a member of the Board of Directors of the Society of American Travel Writers and is the Society's president in 1999. She is also a member of the American Society of Journalists and Authors.